BUDDHISM AND MODERN SOCIETY

BUDDHISM AND MODERN SOCIETY

Edited by

PROF. Y. SUDERSHAN RAO
DR. G. BHADRU NAIK

DEEP & DEEP PUBLICATIONS PVT. LTD.
F-159, Rajouri Garden, New Delhi - 110027

BUDDHISM AND MODERN SOCIETY

ISBN 978-81-8450-059-2

Typeset by SHRI GANESH COMPOSERS, R-3/120, Balaji Chowk, Mohan Garden, New Delhi.

Printed in India at NEW ELEGANT PRINTERS, A-49/1, Phase I, Mayapuri, New Delhi-110064.

Published by DEEP & DEEP PUBLICATIONS PVT. LTD.,
F-159, Rajouri Garden, New Delhi-110027. Phones: 25435369, 25440916.
E-mail: ddpbooks@yahoo.co.in • ddpubs@gmail.com
Sales Showroom: 2/13, Ansari Road, Daryaganj, New Delhi-110002
Phone/Fax: 23245122

Contents

PREFACE

Buddhism is understood, interpreted and practised in different ways by its practitioners, preachers, scholars and thinkers ever since the Mahaparinirvana of the Lord Buddha and it continues to inspire the present and future generations of scholars to study it further to discover its relevance to their respective times. Siddhartha Gautama, who lived and interacted with the great scholars, *yogic* practitioners and the lay people alike some two thousand and five hundred years ago, is still revered and adored as a Great Master. Satisfying the modern parameters of history writing, Siddhartha stands as one of the earliest historically known spiritual personalities and the most illustrious path finders from among many great saints and masters who traversed the land of Bharat, i.e. India, and beyond from times immemorial.

The Buddha showed to the world an alternate path to Salvation with his own pursuance and realization. He set aside the reigning notion that an intense study of the Vedas followed by severe practices and elaborate rituals were essential prerequisites to attain Liberation, the ultimate goal of human life. Further, he did not appreciate the mediation of a god or a *guru* on the path of Liberation, i.e. freedom from sorrow. He maintained that one could rely on oneself to get enlightened. He declined to comment on the concepts like soul, Supreme Soul, as he found the discussion irrelevant for a real seeker of Truth. He maintained that the consciousness of 'being' wholly rests on one's desires and the efforts for their fulfillment. The state of desirelessness amounts to the cessation of that conscious existence, i.e., Mahaparinirvana, an unqualified state in the Upanishadic sense.

Fulfillment of desire is inbuilt in the nature of this Universe. Therefore, one has to live or take another birth if warranted for the realisation of his *sankalpa* or fulfilment of his desire. Paradoxically, even the state of desirelessness can be achieved only by having a strong and unswerving desire for it. For that matter any thing can be achieved including an honorable acquittal from this world, whatever name one might give it: enlightenment or final deliverance, *nirvana* or *moksha* by having a strong desire for it. Our ancient knowledge identified three major factors for the fulfillment of one's desires, namely, a strong will or desire for it, technical know-how to go about it and action-oriented pursuance. The Buddha gave a rational explanation to the very existence of this Phenomenon applying the principle of causation.

He found the world full of sorrow, for even the apparent joy and happiness of an individual is temporary soon paving way for disillusionment and sorrow. Painstaking efforts and a long wait laden with anxiety and worries precede the fulfillment of a desire. Even the course of enjoyment is wrought with the fear of losing it at any time. Of course the end of this phase leads one to sorrow. Thus, it becomes clear that desire causes sorrow, to end which one should practice restraint through dharmic living. Leading an honest and simple life, practising truth and non-violence in thought, word and deed, and with *uno animo* approach, one can attain the Enlightenment, which is the final goal of human life. The right knowledge of *Dharma* develops in one the right attitude to life i.e. *'jnana'* as described by the ancient scriptures.

True to his name, Siddhartha was already a contented man in his worldly life. He did not leave his princely life to add something more to it, nor did he have any complaint against it. He set out on the great mission of inquiry to find the root cause of sorrow that engulfed all the living beings. Immortality is attained only through such sacrifice. Siddhartha renounced his worldly life for a universal cause, as if to prove the Vedic dictum that it is neither the sacrifice of one's family nor wealth nor ritualistic practices that would ensure one immortality but it is sacrifice alone. After that he never looked back. That was Mahabhinishkramana. Such disentanglement with the world i.e.,*vairagya* is identified as the penultimate stage on the path of *Jnana* by our ancients. To pursue a strong desire, *kama,* to fruition with great perseverance needs enough courage known as *kshatram.* Siddhartha was a noble *kshatriya* by quality. By then he had already achieved the *dharma, artha* and *kama*, the three *purusharthas* prescribed for attaining *moksha*, the finale, as described in the general parlance of the tradition. But, Siddhartha, instead of seeking *moksha* for himself, had laid a path for others to tread with ease. His path was a via media between the severe austerities and living in ease and comfort following a ritualistic religion. No formal education or training was necessary for taking his path. The only qualification needed was to have a strong resolve to take refuge in the Teachings of the Buddha, in the Order of the Monks, the *Sangha* and follow the prescribed Code of Conduct, the *Dhamma*. Thus the aspirants of *jnana* were freed from the burden of scriptural studies, ritualistic practices such as *yajna* and severe austerities, which marginalized the common man. The Buddha had once again brought both the piety and the laity under his umbrella, the *chatra.* His path was, thus, inclusive of all classes of people. It was not marked by any exclusivity. His personality was such that he was loved by all and despised by none interested in spiritual progress and the general well being of the society.

The Buddha addressed all sections of population irrespective of class, creed, gender, occupation or age. He welcomed all of them to his fold irrespective of their socio-economic, intellectual, ethical and moral background. His main contention was that everyone whether born high or low, rich or poor has a birthright to attain Enlightenment and so, the real seeker should not be prevented on any plea. Those who follow his Eight-fold Path in their normal worldly life would gradually develop the right attitude to the world and eventually renounce the world and attain *nirvana.* Those who could renounce the world straight away joined the *Sangha* and dedicated their remaining life to the service of the fellow beings. The principles of life He taught are pragmatic, neither rigid nor flexible. He struck a balance between the two extremes. Therefore, He was acceptable to all.

The principles like non-violence and truth; qualities like compassion, honesty, charity and humility and attitudes like selflessness, non-attachment and courage have been the part and parcel of the Indian philosophy since our remotest past, which have been reiterated time and again by great sages and men. The Buddha added His flavor to them and demonstrated them through His personal life. The most venerable Buddhist spiritual leader Dalailama rightly says: "The Hindus and the Buddhists, we are two sons of the same mother."

The very sight of the Buddha's noble personality disarmed even His fiercest opponents and critics in no time. The kings, the queens, the rich, the mendicants, great scholars, and the serious practitioners of *Brahmincal* rituals, cruel robbers, women of easy virtue—all fell at His feet and sought His Grace. He did not preach any religion. 'He taught us how to live and to leave in simple words', says Sathguru Sivananda Murty to whom I owe my understanding of the Buddha—his life and teachings. He opines, if there is any philosophy that could be acceptable to all the existing religions in the world without any grudge or prejudice, it is the Buddha Dhamma.

The sixth century before Christ was intellectually a vibrant period through out the civilized world. Confucius and Lao Tse in China, Socrates in Greece, and the Mahavira and the Buddha in India led radical social movements. Buddhist and Jain philosophies had not only addressed social issues but also suggested paths to reach the Ultimate. Of these two, Buddha's liberal approach had a greater appeal to all sections of people cutting across all political and geographical barriers. That is why the Dhamma could spread far and wide across the civilized world much before Christ was born. The Dhamma depicting the finer human values also appealed to the rational mind. Therefore, the Dhamma has universal applicability and relevance to all times and more so, the modern times of stress, strain and strife due to degradation of human element in man.

The original teachings of any great Master are always simple and straight. But with succeeding generations, many developments took place by way of commentaries through intellectual discourses and exercises. A plant grows into a tree spreading across its branches. This does not mean that the branches are different from the original plant. They are the extensions of the same tree. This out look would promote democratic spirit and tolerance to pursue the goal unconcerned with the diversity in their approaches.

The present volume contains select articles presented in the U.G.C. National Seminar on 'Buddhism—Its relevance to the Modern Society' conducted by the Department of History and Tourism Management, Kakatiya University, Warangal. The papers covering various aspects of Buddhism and its place in the modern civic society give us a panoramic view of the present status of the religion and the relevance of its philosophy to the present times. The contributors include great scholars, academics, Buddhist practitioners and social activists. I believe that this book will be welcomed by those who are committed to social justice, religious tolerance, and peaceful coexistence of communities and nations and in other words the general welfare of all creatures. I compliment Dr. G. Bhadru Naik, the then Head of the Department and the Director of the Seminar for having organized such a well attended conference.

Warangal

Y. SUDERSHAN RAO
Formerly Dean, Faculty of Social Sciences
and Professor of History, Kakatiya University, Warangal, A.P.
Former Member, Indian Council of Historical Research, New Delhi (2000-02).
UGC National Fellow (1992-94)

Acknowledgements

Buddha's teachings are more relevant in the contemporary scenario of moral degradation, religious terrorism, chaos, mutual distrust, skyrocketing, consumerism, growing arrogance and engulfing ignorance. Realizing the importance of Buddhism, the Department of History and Tourism Management, Kakatiya University, Warangal, (A.P.) organized a National seminar on **"Buddhism and Modern Society: Relevance, Problems and Perspectives"**, on 1st and 2nd Feb. 2004. Most of the papers appear in this volume were presented during the seminar.

We deeply appreciate the contribution of those who participated and presented papers in the seminar. We also express our thanks to Prof. C.K. Kokate, the then Vice-Chancellor and our colleagues at the Department, for their assistance and valuable suggestions in the organization of the seminar. We would also like to place on record our acknowledgements to Indian Council of Historical Research, New Delhi for their financial support for the seminar. We are grateful to Prof. V. Gopal Reddy, Vice-Chancellor, Kakatiya University, Warangal and Prof. N. Linga Murthy, Co-ordinating Officer, UGC Unit, Kakatiya University, Warangal for their financial Assistants for Publication of this book. We are also thankful to Sri. C. Anjaneya Reddy, IPS, the then Chairman and Managing Director, A.P. Tourism Development Corporation, Govt. of Andhra Pradesh, Hyderabad for inaugurating the National Seminar. We also thank Venerable

Sangha Rakshtha Mahathero, Chairman, Ananda Buddha Vihar, Hyderabad for attending the Seminar as a guest of honour.

We express our sincere thanks to all the contributors to this volume.

DR. G. BHADRU NAIK
Director of the Seminar

INTRODUCTION

On behalf of the Department of History and Tourism Management and on my personal behalf, it gives me immense pleasure to extend you all a hearty welcome to this National Seminar on 'Buddhism and Modern Society' (Relevance, Problems and Perspectives). This seminar is organised by us with the major financial support of the Indian Council of Historical Research, Government of India, the UGC Unit of Kakatiya University and the Dept. of Culture, Government of Andhra Pradesh.

The dynamics of Indian culture and civilization based on the seemingly opposite principles of 'continuity and change' drew the attention of the modern scholars both foreign and native to undertake serious research on many of its aspects since the past two centuries. The pre-independence scholars were classified as imperial and nationalistic, whereas the post-independence scholars subscribing to many sectional interests are divided into numerous groups. Different interpretations from the perspectives of Marxist, Subaltern, Dalit, Gender etc., have come to light on the already established facts making the issues more complicated and controversial than before. Indian culture has accommodated the rise of many religions since ancient past from time to time. Of all these ancient religions of India, Jainism and Buddhism took the shape of formal religions by the beginning of the first millennium A.D. conforming to the principles of modern religion. Buddhism became more popular soon because of many favourable factors.

The foremost of these factors could be obviously ascribed to the nature of the path shown by the Buddha which is known as the Middle Path i.e., a path which was easily understood and followed by one and all without any exclusive rights or privileges for any community or individual based on his/her birth. Buddhism was not only prevalent in neighbouring countries but spread to the countries of South-east Asia, Central Asia etc.

Buddhism had influenced every aspect of human life like art, literature, and architecture in these countries besides their respective religions. Buddhism which stood steadfastly for Dhamma has a universal appeal and its strict moral codes are relevant to all times. But Buddhism lost its vigour and vitality by seventh and eight centuries A.D. on account of many historical reasons. As a natural process, the Buddhism also was disintegrated by branching off into Hinayaana, Mahayaana, Vajrayaana and the like. In India, it is finally absorbed by the dominant Hindu religion. However, Buddhism continue to live in the essence of later Indian religions which came up in India in medieval times such as Saivism, Vaishnavism and various Bhakti strands. The spread of Islam in other parts of Asia has wiped out Buddhism which preached Non-Violence and Peaceful Co-existence for attaining Nirvaana. Buddhism could not withstand militant Islam in those regions. The spread of Christianity supported by imperialist powers in the modern times also became a major threat for the existence of Buddhism which is basically a simple atheistic religion.

The modern times are witnessing unforeseen challenges to the peaceful co-existence of various communities besides the individual freedom to pursue one's own path of salvation. Materialism and Consumerism have reached an all time high mark with its negative countenance blowing away all the niceties of our so far well guarded cultural, moral and religious values. It is time that the intellectuals professing various schools of Philosophy to interact with one another and address the issues relating to the values like tolerance, mutual respect, love, spirit of sacrifice and understanding to promote human dignity, righteousness and justice.

Though most of the modern governments are adopting the democratic system, the governance is far from being satisfactory due to inherent weakness of the system against the strong offender. Nepotism, partisan attitudes, corruption at every level, ignorant political leadership, selfishness etc. are cutting deep into the system. Even in the highest echelons of administration, the persons holding such positions have questionable character. All wings of government suffer from the inadequacies and inefficiency. Many of the modern day problems of government could safely be attributed to the eroded character of the citizen. To combat the contemporary milieu, it is imperative on the part of the social scientists and historians to make in depth analyses of the present situations and find out workable solutions to correct the maladies. Religions play a vital role in shaping the psyche of the common man and the elite alike.

The present scholastic exercise is intended to identify the contemporary issues challenging the very existence of the civilized community and to discover the factors, which are leading to this lamentable situation, and to suggest any remedial measures. The distinguished scholars from various places would examine if Buddhist Thought, which is universal in nature and congenial for all time applicability, could be of any help to the present society in the existing social, economic and cultural scenario.

It is quite gratifying that the senior and distinguished scholars from various parts of our country and our neighboring country, Sri Lanka have shown interest in this area of study and agreed to take part in the two-day seminar. We have received about 38 full texts of scholarly research papers from far and near which are presented and discussed in six technical sessions highlighting the philosophical foundations of the Buddhist Philosophy and Dhamma and its relevance to the modern society and polity.

DR. G. BHADRU NAIK
Director of the Seminar

List of Contributors

Dr. Shiv Bahadur Singh, Head, Dept. of Ancient Indian and Asian Studies, Nava Nalanda, Mahavihara, Nalanda.

Prof. Angane Lal, Former Vice-Chancellor, Dr. R.M.L. Awadh University, Faizabad (U.P.).

Dr. V.V.S. Saibaba, Associate Professor, Dept. of Philosophy and Religious Studies, Andhra University, Visakhapatnam.

M. Rajagopal Rao, H.No. 5-54-118, 6/18, Brodipet, Guntur.

Dr. N. Kanakarathnam, Associate Professor, Dept. of History, Archaeology and Culture, Dravidian University, Kuppam (A.P.).

Sri. C. Anjaneeya Reddy, Chairman and Managing Director, A.P. Tourism Development Corporation, Hyderabad.

Gali Vinod Kumar, Asst. Prof., University College of Law, Osmania University, Hyderabad.

Dr. Lella Karunyakara, Coordinator, Department of History, School for Ambedkar Studies, Babasaheb Bhimrao Ambedkar (Central) University, Lucknow, U.P.

G. Laxmaiah, Junior Lecturer in History, Yellareddy, Nizamabad Dist.

P. Ramakrishna, Research Scholar, Dept. of History, K.U. Warangal.

Dr. Manjual B. Chincholi, Reader and Chairperson, Dept. of Studies in History, Gulbarga University, Gulbarga.

B. Kumara Swamy, Lecturer in History, S.S.R. Jyothi Arts and Science College, Khammam, Andhra Pradesh.

P. Swaroopa Rani, Health Educator, M.P.P.H. (male) Training School, Khammam.

K. Yesudasu, Research Scholar, Department of Public Administration & HRM, Kakatiya University, Warangal, (A.P.).

S. Venkataiah, Research Scholar, Department of Political Science, Kakatiya University, Warangal.

P. Abbai, President, Buddhist Society of India, Hyderabad.

Dr. U.S. Vyas, Former Director, N.N.M. Nalanda (Bihar).

Dr. S. Penchalaiah, Asst. Professor of Philosophy, Dravidian University, Kuppam (A.P.).

Dr. N. Susheela, Asst. Professor in Kannada, Dept. of Comparative Dravidian, Literature and Philosophy, Dravidian University, Kuppam (A.P.)

Ven M. Ratanjothy Thero, (Ph.D. Research Scholar), Thero-Maha Bodhi Society, Chennai.

Dr. M.V. Ramankumar Ratnam, Deptt. of Mahayana Buddhist Centre, Nagarjuna University, Guntur.

L.Udaya Kumar, Research Scholar, Nagarjuna University, Guntar.

Dr. (Smt.) Nanda Parekar, Deptt. of History, Shivaji University.

Dr. E. Sivanagi Reddy-Sithapati, 1-5-67/3/1, Road No. 3, New Marutinagar, Hyderabad, A.P.

Dr. P. Chenna Reddy, Associate Professor, School of History and Archaeology, P.S. Telugu University, Srisailam Campus.

Koppula Saidi Reddy, Research Scholars in the Department of History, Kakatiya University Warangal.

Mohammed Osman Pasha, Research Scholar in the Department of History, Kakatiya University Warangal.

Dr. R.T. Ingalalli, Professor and Chairman, Department of Philosophy, Karnatak University, Dharwad.

Dr. Rahul Raj, Lucknow (U.P.).

Y. Ramayya, (Retd.) Dy. Collector, President, Visakha Upasaka Sabha, Visakhapatnam (A.P.).

Dr. P. Vijayaraghav Reddy, (Retd.) Professor, Central Institute of Hindi, Hyderabad.

J. Krishna Kumari, Lecturer in History and TTM, SRR & CVR Govt. Degree College, Vijayawada.

Dr. G. Chandra Reddy, Reader in History, S.S.R.J. Arts & Science College, Khammam, A.P.

B. Padmalatha, Teacher, P.S., Mallakpally, Mdl: Dharmasagar, Dist: Warangal, A.P.

Dommeti Satyanarayana Bodhi, Chairman, Buddhist Mission Library, Buddha Vihara Trust, Mehar Nagar, Kakinada.

Dr. K. Vijaya Babu, Head, Dept. of History, Kakatiya University Warangal, A.P.

Smt. S. Chandra Kala, Uni. Arts & Sci. College, Warangal.

Annapareddy Venkateswara Reddy, Editor MISIMI, 10-20-14, Mahaabodhi, Indiranagar, TENALI- 522 202.

J. Amar Jyothi, Dept. of Archaeology & Museum, Govt. of A.P., Hyderabad.

Professor Angraj Chaudhary, Vipasana Research Institute, Nasik, Maharashtra.

Dr. Aravind Kumar, Assistant Professor, Dept. of History, Archaeology and Culture, Dravidian University, Kuppam.

B. Devendar, Divisional Engineer, AP GENCO, Q.No. E- 7, B-Colony, Ramagundam, Dist. Karimnagar.

Dr. B.V.S. Bhanusree, Asst. Professor, Department of Philosophy, Andhra University, Visakhapatnam.

Dr. G. Jawaharlal, Former Dy. Director (Epigraphy), Rajahmundry.

Dr. L. Vidyasagar Reddy, Professor, Dept. of History, Kakatiya University, Warangal.

Dr. T. Dayakar Rao, Deptt. of History, Kakatiya University, Warangal.

Dr. P. Sadanandam, Deptt. of History, Kakatiya University, Warangal.

1

BUDDHISM AND SOCIAL HARMONY

DR. SHIV BAHADUR SINGH

The word harmony means concord, unity, peace, amity, friendship, consistency, consonance, conformity etc. The concept of social harmony in Buddhist thought incorporates two aspects of human life, personal life and social life. The ethical standard and moral values of the individuals practiced in their personal life lead to social harmony in their social interactions and social activities. The interpersonal relationship, compassion, religions, toleration and mutual understanding among various social units and religious group are the prime factors of social harmony. We find several literary and archaeological evidences, which reveal great emphasis on social harmony.

Buddhism and social harmony has a great value and an importance in the modern context of national and International level. Today, the whole humanity is fraught with conflicts generated by political, economic, social, religious and racial consideration. There is not a single corner of the world today which is free from conflicts and turmoil. Disharmony and discontentment are ground of war and tension.

Buddhism has given a serious thought to the problem of social harmony and has made, in the past, a sincere effort to promote it through its numerous missionaries, monks, nuns and laymen. Buddhism covers not only about the whole humanity but also about all living beings. We may quote here the following gathas as example:

"Sabbe satta sukhi hontu,
Sabbe hontu cha khemino,
Sabbe bhadrani pussantu,
Ma kanchi dukha magama"

"Let all beings be happy,
Let all beings live without fear,
Let all beings enjoy peace and happiness,
And be free from all sorrows and troubles."

It is rightly believed that the Buddha was a great social reformer, a believer in the equality of all human beings, concerned for the welfare of the whole humanity irrespective of caste, creed and sex. He had tried to solve the social problems as a king of physicians (Anupam Vaidya Raja). The Master preached the gospel of non-violence, social justice, observance of code of ethics, selfless service and friendship among peoples for maintaining proper order and discipline. The Holy orders always stood for fraternity, harmony and for inculcating the spirit of selfless service to the humanity, compassion and tolerance which are based on spiritual wisdom. This doctrine throws perfect light on the relevance of Buddhism in modern Society.

In the present paper I have tried to focus on Some salient characteristics of Buddhism, which can play a historical role in creating a new social order by harmonizing man with society. They are:

1. Emancipation from Craving (tanha)

Buddhism analysed the problem of social conflicts and found

that craving or tanha is the nature of human beings, are the principle factors of social disharmony. Lobha (greed), Dosa (illusion) and Moha (ignorance) is the main factors of craving or tanha. Opposite to these three factors the Anguttara Nikayai enlists five factors of mind which bring forth balance and harmony in the life of an individuals as well as society to which he belongs. And these are (i) absence from greed (Alobha), (ii) absence from malevolence (Adosa), (iii) absence from delusion and to have, (iv) a thorough attention to the cause (Yonisomanasikara), and (v) well directed mind (Sammahita-citta). In this connection we may also quote the Aditta pariyaya Sutta (The five sermon). Thus culturing the mind is more essential for the social harmony.

2. Code of Morals

Buddhist doctrine is based on human ethical values and excellent code of morals which are universal in nature and encourage to cultivate the social harmony. These moral codes of Buddhism are as follows:

(a) **Panca-Sila** or Five precepts of not to kill, not to steal, not to commit adultery, not to lie and not to take intoxicating liquor. Pancasila or five precepts are the guiding principles in attaining moral perfection.

(b) **Brahma-Vihara or Four Sublime States:** the four Brahma viharas or Sublime states namely Metta (loving kindness), Karuna (compassion), Mudita (appreciative joy) and Uppekha (equanimity) occupy an important place in the social harmony.

I. *Metta:* Metta is universal love. One powerful destructive vice in man in anger. The sweet virtue that subdues this evil force and sublime man is loving kindness (Metta). Where there is Metta there can not be nay room for ill-will and kindred state. The spirit of Metta is given in the 'Metta Sutta', where Buddha says that just a mother would protect her only son even at the cost of her life. So should one practice loving kindness towards all living beings.[1]

II. *Karuna:* Karuna is compassion. Cruelty (himsa) is another vice that is responsible for many horrous and atrocities prevalent in the world. Compassion is its antidote. Compassion or Karuna is to feel for the help those who are in trouble. Where there is compassion there can not be indifference towards the suffering of others.

III. *Mudita*: Mudita is sympathetic joy. Jealousy (issa) is another vice that poisons one's system and leads to unhealthy rivalries and dangerous competitions. The most effective remedy for this poisonous drug is appreciative joy (Mudita). It is to feel joy at the happiness of others. Where there is Mudita there can not be any room for jealousy and kindred unhealthy states.

IV. *Upekkha:* Upekkha is equanimity. There are two universal characteristic that upset the mental equipoise of man. They are—attachment to the pleasurable and aversion to the non-pleasurable. These two opposite forces can be eliminated by developing equanimity (upekkha). Thus equanimity means to maintain balance when faced with vicissitudes of life.

These four sublime states are also known as appamannaya or *illimatables* as they lead one beyond all barriers which divide one man from another man, one community is the from another community and one nations from another nation. They are the pillars, so to say, of individual happiness, social amity and universal peace. Their cultivation would be lead universal brotherhood and social harmony.

(c) **Parmita:** There are Ten transcendental virtues, which in Pali are called parami,[2] that every Bodhisatta practices in order to gain supreme inlightenment, Samma-Sambuddhahood. They are generosity (dana), Morality (Sila), renunciation (nekkhamma), wisdom (panna), energy (Viriya), patience (khanti), truthfulness (sacca), determination (adhistthana), loving-kindness (Metta), and equanimity (Upekkha).

According to the Cariya Pitak commentary, parmitas are these virtue which are cultivated with compassion, guided by reason, uninfluenced by selfish motives, and unsullied by misbelief and all feelings of self-conceit.

(d) **Ariya-Attangika-Magga** on Noble Eight fold path comprising of right understanding (Samma samkappa), right speech (samma vaca), right action (samma kammanta), right lilvelihood (samma ajiva), right effort, (samma vayam), right mindfulness (samma sati) and right concentration (Samma Samadhi).

The above mentioned code of morals has been promulgated by the Lord Buddha on different occasions and does not bear any stamp of particular creed, because he believes that peace, prosperity and harmonization of society can be maintain through this.

3. Code of Social Relations

Buddhism throw proper light on the ideal social relations which are valuable to establish social harmony. In this connection we may quote the discourse given by the Buddha to Sigala, mentioned in Sigalavada Sutta[3] (the code of discipline for laymen). It inculcates instructions whose fulfillment would lead to peace, happiness and prosperity of the individuals and the society. As instance we may mention the last section of the discourse goes into an elaborate explanations of the duties of children and parents, pupils and teachers, husband and wives, friends and colleagues, master and servants, devotees and saints. In each case duties has been specified. This code of discipline for people in general is a short but comprehensive one. The principles enunciated in them are as much as valid to day as they were more than twenty five centuries ago.

Besides, there are scores of Suttas including 'Mangal Sutta', 'Parabhava Sutta', 'Dhammika Sutta', and 'Vyagghapajja Sutta' more or less on the same theme.

4. An Ideal Social Order or System

Another noteworthy Buddhist approach to social harmony is an equality of all human beings. During the time of Lord Buddha, Masses of the country were suffering under the caste system. While a few enjoyed all the rights and privilege the majority were deprived of them. It goes to credit of the Buddha that he was the first great thinker to place before mankind the ideal of social justice and human compassion. In the caste-ridden society of the sixth century B.C., he revolted against the caste system and taught equality of mankind and gave equal opportunities for all to distinguish themselves in all walks of life. His teachings are, therefore, very relevant in the present condition. His path of salvation was open to all. He declared that purity does not depend upon his birth, but upon his action or Karma. For example, we may quote here an emphasis on Karma, said by the Master in very clear words[4]:

> *"Na Jacca vasalo hoti, Na Jacca hoti Brahmano,*
> *Kammuna vasalo hoti, Kammuna hoti Brahmano."*

Besides, there are several instances available in Pali chronicles, which throws lights on the subject.[5]

We may take into consideration regarding the social equanimity which Buddha adopted or recommended as a rule of 'Sapadanacariya' (going form door to door for alms without leaving any house between on grounds of caste, rank and position). As far as Buddhist sangha or order is concerned, it was based on equality and democratic principles. Tathagata used all means for the promotion of equality and brotherhood among the members of his order. In this connection we may quote the instances mentioned in Anguttara Nikaya.[5a]

"Just as, brethren, the great rivers Ganga, Yamuna, Acirvati and Mahi—when they have fallen into the great ocean, lose their different names and are known as the great ocean, in the same way brethren, do the members of these four caste—Kshatriyas, Brahmanas, Vaisyas and Sudras—when they begin to follow the Doctrine and Discipline as propounded by the Tathagata, they renounce their different names of caste and rank, and became members of one and the same order."[6]

Thus, the Buddha organized the society as a whole as well as Buddhist Sangha in the true light of democratic system which is very much relevant for the social harmony in the present Global context.

5. Essence of Social Harmony in Asokan Inscription

The concept of social harmony in Buddhist perspective was promulgated by Emperor Asoka in all over India. Asokan rock edicts and pillar edicts reveal great emphasis on social harmony. Asokan rock edicts and piller edicts reveal great emphasis on Social hamony. Asokan rock edicts VII, XII, XIII as well as pillar edict VI and VII are particularly important as records of social harmony. Rock Edict XIII informs us as to how he became a thoroughly changed person shortly after the kalinga war which took place in his eight year of reign after cornation. We may quote here the R.E. of Shahbazagarhi—"Yo asti anusocana devanampriyasa vijitini Kalingani." In Rock Edicts XII Asoka introduce the term Samavayo or concord which was very much significant in religious and social life. The term samavayo meant religious toleration among various religious and social group included—"all sects, both ascetics and house holders." The Pali term Samavayo means 'coming together, combinations[7] signifying unity of heterogeneous groups or communities. In Girnar version of Rock Edict XII Asoka proclaims that there should "be the growth of the essential elements of all religious sects." It is also stated in the Rock Edict of Asoka that "All religious sects should live harmoniously in all parts of my dominations."[8] In his inscription Asoka proclaimed "that wise counsel is not possible where there is no unanimity in decision and no unity of purpose."[9]

Thus, the Emperor Asoka a great Buddhist king had marvellous approach to harmonize the contemporary society in the light of Buddhist doctrine which is very much relevant to modern or present context.

It is not out of mention that the Buddhist ideal of social harmony has influenced countries beyond Indian Territory, particularly in Japan. Like Emperor Asoka of India, prince Shotoku, the real founder of Japanese Buddhism of A.D. 604 issued the seventeen Article constitution based on Buddhism.[10] It is still relevant to the life, not only of the Japanese people, but also of other peoples of the world from the point of view of national harmony.

On the basis of the facts as mentioned above, it may be observed that in the present Global unrest, Buddhism is the only remedy of the social harmony, peace, happiness and prosperity. At the end of my discussion, I would like to mention the first Sermon preached by Lord Buddha, while revolving the wheel of Dhamma at Sarnath:

Charath Bhikkhave Carikam bahujan
Hitaya bahujana sukhaya,
Lokanukampaya Atthaya hitaya
Sukhaya devamanussanam.[11]

"Wander, O Monks, for the gain of the many, for the welfare of the many, for showering forth compassion on the world; for the good, for the gain, for the welfare of gods and man.[12]

Thus, it is universal truth that Buddism can play historical role in creating a new social order by harmonizing man with society.

Notes and References

1. Khuddaka Path, Metta Sutta.
2. Sutta Nipata.
3. Siggalovada Sutta, Dighanikaya.
4. Digha Nikaya, Awag Sutta, p. 245 (Hindi tr).
5. *Ibid.*, Vol. III, p. 80; Sutta Nipata, pp. 26-28; Vaseth Sutta, (Sutta Nipata), p.138.

5a. Majjhima Nikaya, Ashvalayam Sutta, No. 93, etc.

6. Anguttara Nikaya, p. 101.
7. Rhys Davis, T.W. and Stede, William ed., Pali-English Dictionary, P.T.S., London, 1966, p. 684.
8. Sircan, D.C., Inscriptions of Ashoka, New Delhi, Ministry of I. and B., 1975, p. 48.
9. Barua, Beni Madhava, Ashoka and his Inscriptions, Pt. 5, p. 159.
10. Barua, Dipak Kumar, Role of Buddhism in National Integration Homage to Bhikkhu Jagdish Kashyap, Nava Nalanda Mahavihara, 1986, pp. 121-134.
11. Shotoku, Princ, The Seventeen Article Constitution, trans. By Hajime Naka Mura, pp. 1-5.
12. Vinaya Pitaka, Maha Vagga, ed. Bhikkhu J. Kashyap, Nalanda, 1956, p. 23.

References

Goyal, S.R., *A History of Indian Buddhism*, Kusumanjali Prakashan, Meerut, 1987.

Narada Maha Thera, *The Buddha and His Teachings*, published by Singapore Buddhist Meditation Centre.

C. Mane (ed.), *The Social Philosophy of Buddhism*, C.I.H.T.S., Sarnath, Varanasi, 1995.

Chopra, P.N., *Contribution of Buddhism to World Civilization and Culture*, S. Chand and Company Ltd., Delhi, 1983.

Buddhism and Social Harmony, Proceedings of the 12th International Conference, Bodh-Gaya, 1986.

Buddhism and Himanism, proceedings of the XXI International Buddhist Conference, Nalanda, 1996.

Ecological Ethics and Buddhism, Proceedings of the XXIV International Conference, Bodh-Gaya, 1999.

Singh, S.B., *Prachin Bharat Men Kshatriya*, Janki Prakashan, Patna, New Delhi, 1999.

Mahavagga, ed., Bhikkhu Jagdish Kashyap, Nalanda, 1956.

Dhamma Pada, S. Radhakrishnan, London, 1950.

Relevance of Buddhism and other Religions in Modern Society, Proceedings of the XXII International Conference on Buddhist Studies in India, Nalanda, 1997 etc.

2

Buddha's Economic Concept for Human Welfare

Prof. Angane Lal

'Shakyamuni Buddha' havc generally been considered as a social reformer and a religious prophet. It is a sheer irony that his revolutionary contributions in the field of economics have yet been not exposed to the world attention fully. Buddha probably was the pioneer in contributing the theories of 'Need Based Distribution', the 'Balanced Production' and the 'Income and Expenditure' etc.

He propounded that hunger is the greatest ailment, and poverty is the root of most sins. He also showed to mankind the path to save themselves from such ailments and improve their economic lot. Here, in the following pages, I have tried to throw some light on the economic ideas and ideals which Buddha preached for the happiness and prosperity of human society.

Gautama Buddha, the 'Light of World', was born as Siddhartha to his mother Mahamaya at Lumbini[1] (presently in Nepal), where a Lumbini village[2] was also situated. His father Shuddhodan was a headman of the Shakyan republic of Kapilvastu, which has been identified with the ruins excavated at Piparahava in the district of Siddharthanagar in Uttar Pradesh. Shakyan economy was basically agrarian. They used to celebrate a 'Krishi Mahotsava'[3] in which even the head of the clan, known as Raja, used to take plough in his hands and plough the land. Siddhartha had witnessed many such functions, and was pained to watch the happy birds swallowing small worms and insects which used to come out from the ploughed surfaces.

This treatment of 'Matsya Nyaya' moved the tender heart of the child (Samvignamanah). He has also observed the daily life of wealthy (Mahaddhana), prosperous (Mahabhoga)[4] and of the poor people. He very keenly and minutely observed the miserable life of the slaves and servants, and reached to the conclusion that poverty was a curse to mankind.[5] Therefore, after Enlightenment, the Buddha instructed his Bhikkhu disciples to wander from village to village and preach the people for their welfare (hitaya), happiness (sukhaya) and economic well being (atthaya). Not only this, he also instructed the monks to preach the masses to recognise and do such thing which were good for them in the beginning, good in the middle and good even in the end. They should not preach any other thing except well-being for them.[6] Thus, the Buddha started his mission for human welfare and prosperity.

HUNGER IS THE GREATEST AILMENT

Once Buddha stayed for his Varshavasa at 'Aggalava Chaitya' (Vihara) at Aalvi, the capital city of king Aalavaka.[7] He used to preach there daily. One day it so happened that a cultivator reached the chaitya late because his bullock was lost. After the bullock was found and put back to the house, he rushed to attend the Buddha's sermon which was still going on. The cultivator, being very hungry, was unable to concentrate on the sermon. Lord Buddha knew it by intuition, and so he told a monk to feed him first. After taking food, the cultivator was able to concentrate on the sermon being delivered by the Buddha. Later, monks asked the Buddha for its reason. Tathagata Buddha, narrating the whole story of the cultivator, said, 'hunger is the greatest ailment' (jighiccha parama roga).[8]

The problem of hunger can only be solved by food, which is the primary need of all living beings. The survival of living beings depends solely on food (Sabbe satta aharatthitika).

PROTECTION OF FOODS AND ANIMALS

Food stuffs and grains were collected from agriculture, which was done with the help of bullocks, and bullocks were obtained from cows. Hence, cows were the most important animals for agriculture. Therefore the Buddha gave special emphasis on the protection of cows[10] and bullocks.[11] Agriculture produce was considered as unparallel wealth (natthi dhanya samam dhanam).[12]

'Yajna Sutta' of 'Samyukta Nikaya' reveals an animal sacrifice where 500 bullocks, 500 calves, 500 she-calves, 500 goats and 500 sheep were gathered to sacrifice in that yajna.[13] When Buddha came to know this, he forbade King Prasenjit from doing so, in lieu of the animal sacrifice, he suggested a yajna which gives greater peace and happiness (mahamangala). He asked the king that hungry person should be provided with food, cultivators who have no patch of land to cultivate should be given land,[14] businessmen should be given financial assistance to start their business, unemployed person should be given productive work to do. 'Thus, on one hand, O king! you will not be the killer of animals but rather their savior, and on the other hand, you will make the country richer in economy and production'.[15]

PRODUCTION AND DISTRIBUTION

Gautam Buddha used to say, "those who, without producing anything, take meals on the earth, swallow hot balls (Lohagulam) in the form of food."[16] He laid special emphasis on the growth of production. He said that a man should practice good moral conduct in daily life (seele patitthaya).[17] After due consideration, he should invest his money in such a productive work in which he should not be put to a loss:

> "*Tathatmanam nivesseyya*
> *yatha bhuri pavaddhati.*"[18]

The Buddha underlined the special importance to the small-scale and cottage industries. The craftsmanship was considered as one of the 38 acts leading a man to greater peace and happiness (sippan cha, . . . etam mangal muttamam).[19] It was considered unique and was appreciated in society:

> "*Slipam loke prasansati*
> *slipam loke anuttan.*"[20]

Various craftsmen organized themselves in their respective unions knows as 'Silpa Sreni' and was headed by 'jetthaka'. The head of the federation of such unions was called 'Mahajetthaka'. These guilds were so powerful and important that they were able to issue their own currency.[21]

As the production is important, so is the distribution too. Lord Buddha propounded the theory of 'Need-Based Distribution'. He was against the hoarding of wealth and property. He had, therefore, made a rule that a bhikkhu should not keep with himself more than two pairs of chivaras.[22]

Considering different situations, equal distribution was also not fruitful. Once the King 'Sud Vachan Gampo' of Tibet made an equal distribution of wealth among his people in order to make them happy,[23] but after sometime, he observed that some people became richer and richer , whereas some became poorer. Later on, he realised his mistake of equal distribution. So he applied the Buddha's theory of 'Need-Based Distribution' and consequently found his people in a happier state.

Mahavira Swamy, the contemporary of Lord Buddha, was also against hoarding of wealth and property. He therefore made a rule of 'not-hoarding' (aparigrah).

Digha Nikaya throws some important light on the genesis of hoarding. It states that the desire (tanha) to acquire and accumulate more and more food grain of 'shali' the hoarding was started.[24] But the Buddha discarded even the thinking of hoarding because it was against the principle of 'live and let live'.

INCOME AND EXPENDITURE

Shakyamuni Buddha was, probably, the pioneer personality who formulated the rule of 'income and expenditure' or the 'Production and Utilization'. "It is essential for a man to earn, but much more important than that is how he utilizes his earnings'. According to Buddha, the earnings should be divided into four equal parts. With one part he should support his family, with other two parts he should do some business for his livelihood, and the last one should be saved for the rainy days and the future needs.[25] One who does not follow this principle goes towards poverty (daliddiyam) and was considered as a curse for the society. Living on loan was considered to throw oneself in troubles.[26]

Digha Nikaya reveals that poverty encourages a man for sinful acts like stealing, looting, killing and what not.[27] If such poverty-based sinful acts persist for a longer period, the state of anarchy would prevail in the state. It has been rightly said that when the king is weak, the thieves would become powerful, and when the king is strong, the thieves will be weak. Therefore, it is the pious and worthy duty of a king to keep his masses satisfied and contented.[28] The ruler should feel happy only if his people are living in peace and happiness (praja sukhe sukhi raja).

ECONOMIC STANDARD IN SOCIETY

Indian society is caste-based society. Caste is fore-runner of a man. One's honour and dishonour depends on his caste. Buddha was opposed to this birth-based caste system and he said that it was only according to one's deeds and occupation that one become a Brahmana or a downtrodden (vasala):

"Na jachcha vasalo hoti
Na jachcha hoti Brahmano
Kammana vasalo hoti
Kammana hoti Brahmano."[29]

The Sramana literature of that period tells us about social change. The 'Khattiya' (Kshatriyas) have attained the supreme and first position in the social order in lieu of Brahmanas.[30] Bhadant Upali, though was born in a low community, yet was able to become the reciter of the 'Vinaya Rules' formulated by the Buddha.[31] Although the social positioning of classes seem to have changed, yet the economically poor man had no respect in the society. A poor person, in the eyes of a wealthy man, was as dwarf as a man sitting on the top of a mountain beholds a person standing below on the ground.[32]

WHEN AND HOW A MAN BECOMES POOR?

'Digha Nikaya states that the six reasons responsible for the poverty of human beings are:

1. Drinking, or taking other types of intoxicants.
2. 'Untimely walking'.
3. Indulging in lustful and worthless songs and dances.
4. Gambling.
5. Friendship with vile and anti-social elements.
6. Avoiding hard labour.[33]

Ignorance is another prominent factor for poverty. Buddha calls it as the greatest enemy of human being.[34] It is because of their ignorance that men seek shelter on hills, forests, groves, trees and shrines to get rid of their fears. Such ignorant fools are unaware of the rational fact that such type of refuges cannot protect them from their sufferings.[35]

Idleness is like death standing before a man (pamado machchuno padam), whereas activeness is a symbol of immortality (appamado amatapadam).[36] Therefore, people should keep themselves away from the blind-beliefs and idleness in order to become economically self-reliant.[37]

People who did not follow the rules of 'Income and Expenditure', as was preached by Gautama Buddha, become extravagant, and so to meet their daily needs, they take loans.[38] The loans increase day-by-day and hence, their domestic life becomes miserable.[39] Therefore, it is necessary for a man to maintain his economic position by 'Right Efforts' of livelihood.

'Parabhava Sutta' also throws ample light on the reasons leading a man towards his downfall and poverty. A few of them are religious jealousies, love towards a bad man and hate a good man, practice of blind-beliefs, untimely sleeping, avoiding labour, lying idle, taking meals alone in the presence of others, showing arrogance of wealth, indulging in adultery, drinking and gambling, being greedy etc. These reasons for the downfall of a man have been in the past, are still prevalent in the present, and will be present in the future. Thus, those who wish to lead a happy and peaceful life should keep themselves away from these misdeeds.[40]

'Vasala Sutta' also inumerates such misdeeds which lead a man to a disgraceful life.[41]

HOW TO IMPROVE THE SOCIO-ECONOMIC LOT?

'Samyukta Nikaya' clearly mentions the six factors responsible for economic and social degradation of man. These are idleness, inactiveness, unenthusiasm, indiscipline, excess sleeping and ignorance. The text calls them as a hole (chhidda) through which the riches flow down. Therefore, a man who wants to improve his economic and social position in the society keep himself away from these acts and try to cover up these holes.[42]

The Buddha preached the path of 'Panchsheela' to householders for their happy and prosperous life. The 'Fifth Sheela' saya 'abstain from intoxicants and gamble'. We are aware of the fact that not only families, but kingdoms also have lost their existence because of drinking and gambling.[43]

We must keep in mind the saying of Lord Buddha that if a man longing for a company, does not find a wise and prudent friend, then, like a king who leaves behind a conquered kingdom, or like alone elephant in the elephant forest, he should go his way alone.[44] It is better to live alone rather than to keep the company of a bad or foolish man:

> '*Ekassa chatitam seyyo*
> *Natthi bale sahayata*'.[45]

'Firm Determination' (Adhishthana) and right efforts (samma vayamo) make a man successful. He should never feel discouraged or stumbled even by facing the difficulties in the way of his goal.

Under the 'Astangika Marga', Tathagat Gautama Buddha had preached about those right characteristics which make human beings happy and prosperous. If one treads on this path, he is bound to reach the goal of peace and prosperity. The eight steps of that path are:

1. Right perception or vision, view (Sammadithi)
2. Right (firm) determination (Samma sanikappo)
3. Right speech (Samma vacha)
4. Right action, right behavior (Samma kammanto)
5. Right livelihood (Samma asivo)
6. Right efforts (Samma vayamo)
7. Right remembrance (Samma sati)
8. Right concentration on one point, or one-pointedness.(Samma samadhi)

It is necessary for one who is striving for a peaceful life that he should overcome the angry by non-anger, wicked by goodness, miser by generosity and the liar by truth:

'Akkodhena jine kodham
Asadhum sadhhuna jine
Jine kadariyam danena
Sachchena alikavadinam.[46]

The path which Buddha has shown to humanity for social and economic welfare should always be controlled by 'karuna' and 'prajjna'. "There must be 'dana', but without 'prajjna', 'dana' may have a demoralizing effect. There must be 'karuna', but without 'prajjna', 'karuna' may end in supporting evil. Every act of 'Paramita' must be tested by 'Prajjna Paramita which is another name for wisdom.[47]

Buddha was a person of theory and practice both (vijja charan sampanno). Whatever he said he had done it himself, and what ever he did he preached the same to his followers. In 'Dhammapada', he has very clearly emphasised "You yourself has to make an effort, Buddha would only show the path."[48]

Countries which have followed the rational and progressive socio-economic teachings of the Buddha are in sound and stable position today. India, where Lord Buddha was born and preached, is still busy in beating about the bush of irrational and unscientific customs and practices in the name of traditions. Hence, our country is still in the list of 'Developing Countries' rather than the 'Developed' ones. For seeking ways towards the upliftment of society, we must once again peep in to our valuable legacies which are in the form of Buddhist Literatures and which have already opened the eyes and enlightened the whole of the world.

"*Sabbe Satta Sukhi Hontu*:
May all Beings be happy."

Notes and References

1. 'Lalite Vistara' (Sanskrit), p. 61/5, 8 (Mithila Vidyapeeth, 1958).
2. Ashoka's 'Rumminidei Pillar' inscription, line-4 (D.C. Sircar, 'Select Inscriptions', Vol. 1, p. 67, Delhi, 1993).

3. Lalita Vistara, *op.cit.*, p. 90.
4. 'Samyukta Nikaya', Vol. 1, p. 167.
5. 'Chakkavatti Sihanath Sutta', 'Digha Nikaya', Vol. III, pp. 54-56.
6. 'Mahavagga', p. 23 (ed. Bhikkhy J. Kassap, Pali Publication Board, Bihar Govt., 1956)
7. 'Dhammapada', pp. 361-62 (Biblothica on Indo-Tibetan series No. XX, Sarnath, 1986).
8. *Ibid.*, p. 15/7.
9. 'Khuddaka Patha' (in 'Sutta Nipata'), 'Khuddaka Nikaya, p. 4, (Pali Publication Board, Bihar Govt., 1959).
10. 'Samyukta Nikaya, Part 1, p. 7 (Hindi tr. By Dharmarakshit, Mahabodhi Sabha, Sarnath).
11. 'Samyukta Nikaya', Vol. 1, p. 8.
12. *Ibid.*, Vol. 1, p. 8.
13. *Ibid.*, Vol. 1, p. 79.
14. 'Digha Nikaya' (Hindi tr. By Rahul Sankrityayan), p. 50.
15. 'Samyukat Nikaya', Vol. 1, p. 72, 'Kutadanta Sutta' (in 'Digha Nikaya' Vol. 1, p.104). For the importance of agriculture, 'Kasibharadvaja Sutta' should also be seen.
16. 'Dhammapada', 25/12. (ed. Acharya Buddharakknita, Buddhavacharm Trust, Bangalore, 1986).
17. Seen, 'Visuddhimagga'.
18. Dammapada, 20/10.
19. 'Mahamangal Sutta', Gatha No. 3.
20. 'Mahavastu Avadana', Vol. III, p. 35/12 (ed., E. Senart, Paris, 1882-97).
21. 'Gupta Abhilekha' (hindi) by Vasudev Upadhyaya, pp. 61-63 (Bihar Hindi Grantha Academy, Patna, 1974).
22. 'Vinaya Pitaka (Hindi tr. By Rahul Sankrityayan) pp. 279-81.
23. 'Bharat Aur Videshon Me Bauddha Dharma Prasarak (Hindi) by Dr. (Smt) Yamuna Lal, p. 204 (Pratiba Prakashan, New Delhi, 1997).
24. 'Agganna Sutta', 'Digha Nikaya', Vol. III, pp. 70-71.
25. 'Sigalovada sutta', 'Digha Nikaya', Vol. III, p.145.
26. *Ibid.*, p.143.
27. 'Chakkvatti Sutta', 'Dighja Nikaya', Vol. III, pp. 51-56.
28. 'Digha Nikaya', pp. 48-51.
29. 'Vasal Sutta', Getha No. 27, 'Sutta Nipata', p. 34.
30. 'Chullavagga' p. 356/17; 'Avadana Shataka', Vol. I, p. 248, 311, Vol. II, p.14; 'Mahavastu', Vol. II, p. 139: 'Chatvari Me Bhikshavah Varnan Katame Chtvarah Kshatriyah, Brahmnnah, Vaishyah, Shudrah'.
31. 'Vinaya Pitaka' p. 543.
32. 'Dhammapada', 2/8.
33. 'Sigalovada Sutta', Digha Nikaya', Vol. III, p. 141.

34. 'Dhammapada', 3/10.
35. *Ibid.*, 14/10-11.
36. *Ibid.*, 2/1.
37. 'Kutadanta Sutta', 'Digha Nikaya', Vol. I, p. 109: 'Simyukta Nikaya' Vol. 1, p.74.
38. 'Samyukta Nikaya', Vol. 1, p. 72.
39. 'Digha Nikaya'; p. 273.
40. 'Parabhava Sutta' (in "Sutta Nipata"), 'Khuddak Nikaya Pali', pp. 285-87.
41. 'Vasal Sutta' (in 'Sutta Nipata'), 'Khuddak Nikaya Pali', pp. 287-289 (Pali publication Board, Bihar Govt. 1959).
42. 'Samyukta Nikaya', Vol. I, p. 40.
43. 'Buddha Charita' 11/31; Footnote: 'Andhaka Vrishni' were destroyed due to drinking and 'Kurus' were destroyed due to gambling. Also see, 'Sanskrit Baudha sahitya me Bharatiya jeevan' (Hindi) by A. Lal, p. 187. (Kailash Prakashan, Lucknow, second edition, 1972).
44. 'Dhammapada' 23/10.
45. *Ibid.*, 23/11.
46. *Ibid.*, 17/3.
47. 'Buddha and His Dhamma' by Dr. B.R. Ambedkar, p.130 (Buddha Bhumi Prakashan, Nagpur, 1997).
48. 'Dhammapada' 20/4.

3

APPLIED BUDDHIST PHILOSOPHY AS A PANACEA FOR SOCIAL EVILS IN MODERN SOCIETY

DR. V.V.S. SAIBABA

Even though the Buddha placed *Nibbanā* as the Summum bonnum before Mankind, he had lot of concern about the demands and attractions in the secular world by which his lay disciples and common householders were confronted. The whole teachings of the Buddha are motivated how to organise their lives in accordance with the Buddhist ethical principles. The Buddha is quite aware of the limitations of his lay disciples who are more interested in day to day life rather higher philosophical teachings. Hence, he gave discourses on the themes of social interest viz., social harmony, family obligations, corporate activities, better livelihood and so on.

There are three types of discourses[1] addressed by the Buddha to the laity which are conducive to their happiness and well being. A study of these discourses addressed to the householders and Buddhist laity provides us an idea of socio-ethical and religious life of the lay devotees. We find in many Pali Nikaya passages the Buddha's appeal for ethical uplift of the people. A householder should abandon four vices of conduct i.e., destruction of life, taking what is not given, licentiousness and lying.[2]

I
THE BUDDHA'S TEACHING ON SECULAR MATTERS

The first of the four Pāli Nikayās are the veritable mines of information about the social conditions of the people of pre-Christian years of India. This reservoir of information contains rich information on how the common folk led their lives, family and marital relations, the conception of the caste system prevalent in those times, the status of women and slavery etc.

The Pāli Nikayās provide us the disastrous effects of Caste system from the ethical, social and political points of view.[3] The Buddha refuted the hereditary character of caste system in the Dīgha and Majjhima Nikayās by declaring that all human beings are born from their parents. Since no one is superior, all are equal before the moral law and have to experience the consequence of their deeds. According to the Assalayana Sutta the Buddha taught the members of the four castes were equally eligible to attain the spiritual heights of inner purity. The Vesettha Sutta states that since human beings biologically have no differences unlike animal and plant lives, the caste system based on any kind of discrimination are of arbitrary character. The Agganna Sutta while rejecting the divine origin of caste system shows that class and caste are of conventional nature. During his life time the Buddha had shown neither favour nor prejudice against anybody and he always preached justice, brotherhood, peace and happiness. In view of scholars like D.K. Barua[4] it is thought that Buddhism was basically a protest against caste-system sponsored by the Brāhmana class and declared that superiority is based not by one's birth but on one's own spiritual and moral attainments.

From Buddhist viewpoint the existence of caste was purely a secular and practical affair, a kind of hereditary division of labour which had become essential in the distant past. In Buddhist thought caste did not possess a religious significance as in Brahmanism. Further more in Buddhist Sangha all Worldly distinctions including those of caste had ceased to exist. According to the Buddha all classes of people irrespective of their caste should abstain from murder, theft, unchastity, lying, slandering, gossiping, greed, malevolence and false opinion. Since virtues and vices were distributed among each of the four classes the claims of Brahmanas for socio-ethical supremacy were refuted as baseless.[5]

The *Dighā Nikāya* provides an interesting Buddhist interpretation of caste on the origin of the four social circles according to which *the lord of the fields* was known as Khattiya (noble), the people who put away (bahanti) evil and immoral customs were known as Brahmanas who used to dwell in wood-lands meditating (Jhayanti) seeking alms in villages and towns and were also called *repeaters of Vedas* (ajjhāyaka); those who adopted the married life and engaged in various trades were called as trader folk (Vessa) and still others who dwelt on hunting and such like trifling pursuits were known as *Sudda.*[6] But some group from all the above classes subsequently went forth from home to homeless life finding fault with their respective ways of life and formed as a body of recluses.

On the grounds of character the Buddha rejected the superiority of the Brāhmanas. The Buddha condemned the exclusiveness and pride born out of caste. We may conclude from several descriptions of Pāli texts that even though the general frame work of the caste system was recognized the superiority and high position of the Brahmanas were questioned. In Buddhist perspective caste had nothing to do either with material success in life or with one's spiritual upliftment. But it is significant to note that neither the Buddha nor his disciples were keen in totally abolishing caste distinctions but were stopped at the point of maintaining the Upanisadic viewpoint that one can be called a Brāhmana or Candala not by means of one's character. Hence, scholars like Fick opined[7] that the Buddha cannot be called as a *social reformer* and his doctrine as revolt against the then existing caste system. In some instances like the *Ambattha Sutta* of the *Digha Nikaya* the Buddha was reported to have said that the *Khattiya* were higher than the Brahmanas (Khattiyā vā setthā hina Brāhmana). Among men and women the Khattiyas were looked as superior than the Brahamanas who were inferior.[8]

The Buddha had only proclaimed that one cannôt become a Brāhmana or a Vesala (out caste) due to mere birth since it does not hinder them from their spiritual realisation. According to early texts like the *Suttanipāta* a virtuous out-caste was higher than even an immoral Brāhmana. Thus, it appears that the Buddha placed morality and virtue over and above caste without interfering to abolish the caste system itself. Further, as against the Brahmanical tradition, there existed no distinction among castes imparting education to the people in Buddhist order. For instance Jīvaka the son of a harlot received the highest education in medicine and rose to the status of a royal physician of king Ajātasattu. Similar in the case with a royal slave who became a monk.[9] From sociological point of view the classification of social groups was based mainly on the mode of their living but not connected with their trade or profession.

II
BUDDHA'S ATTITUDE ON THE STATUS OF WOMAN

In the days of Buddha two forms of marriage Avāha and Vivāha were widely prevalent. As far as the Buddha was concerned with the marriages; with reference to woman one's birth (Jati) or clan (gotta) or the prestige (mana) was not taken into consideration and between the Groom and the bride one was not held as superior over another on the above basis. Besides marriages of the same caste inter-caste marriage was also prevalent in Buddha's times. There are sundry evidences of unusual unions such as marrying one's sister for the maintenance of the purity of blood which was encouraged among the Sakyas. According to the *Dīgha Nikāya*[10] through the fear of injuring the purity of their lives they intermarried with their sisters. In the Nikayās we come across incidental references to inter-caste marriage between the Brāhmana girl and the Kattiya gentleman and vice-versa. It should be noted that the Buddha did not pass any adverse remarks against such inter-caste unions.[11] Besides we come across references to the prevalence of polygamy. In such cases as Mahā Govinda, High Steward, the Brāhamana who liberated his forty wives who were placed in the same status before his renunciation.[12]

In the Singalovāda Sutta, the Buddha while exhorting that a householder should worship six quarters, referred to the mutual obligations between a husband and wife which reflects his attitude towards woman. A husband should minister his wife by respect, courtesy, faithfulness and giving her authority over assets and making her happy by providing to her adornments. In return a wife should serve her husband by showing hospitality to the kith and kin and by successfully managing home affairs by her skill.

In one of his discourses addressed to Sujāta, the daughter-in-law of Anāthapindaka, the Buddha refers to seven types of wives viz, one who is like a slayer, a robber, a mistress, a mother, a sister, a companion and a handmaid. Of the above, the first three due to their immoral character suffer a miserable life in hells. On the contrary a wife who behaves like an affectionate mother, as a sister, as a companion or a 'slave' will be reborn after death in heaven.[13]

According to the Buddha womenfolk shall win over power in this world being endowed with four qualities namely the capability at work (susam vihita kamman to), management of servants (sanghahita parijjano), ability for being lovely to husband (bhattu mānapām) and protection of wealth (sambhattam anurakkhati). By means of these four virtues a woman becomes accomplished in faith, virtue, charity and wisdom (saddha, silā, cāga and pānna) and attains peace and prosperity.[14] According to the Anguttara Nikāya[15] in his discourse to the married girls of Uggahā, a householder, the Buddha enumerates certain duties and obligations of a married woman wherein he advises the girls to train themselves in attending their husband's property, to rise up early from their bed and to retire last of all, to work willingly, to order sweetly and gently, to honour all whom their husbands revere i.e., parents, recluses godly men and to offer seats and water to such respected persons. The girls are further admonished to be active and expert at their husbands' home crafts, to know the work of each servant; to realize the strength and weakness of the sick; to divide the hard and soft food each according to his or her share and to keep safe watch over her husband's wealth. By possessing these virtues such woman will be born among gods of lovely forms.

III
BUDDHA'S ATTITUDE ON SLAVERY

Apart from the four social categories referred above, slaves form a separate groups,[16] were divided into two types[17] viz., (i) Those captured in predatory raids and having been reduced to slavery and thus had been deprived of their freedom as a judicial punishment and (ii) Those who had submitted themselves to slavery of their own accord. The Nikayās frequently refer to both male and female slaves employed in the kings' palaces, households of rich people in capital cities and under the well-to-do villagers. In the times of the Buddha slavery was hereditary and even the children of the slaves were used to become slaves. But it is significant to note that the Buddha prohibited the bhikkshus from accepting the gifts of male and female slaves.[18] Regarding the position of the slaves of those times most of them were household servants with the exception of stray instances of punishing female slaves by beating them.

As regards the freedom of slaves either they might be manumitted[19] or could be made free by payment. Besides these, there were instances in the Pāli Canon where slaves were liberated from their slavery either when they embraced an ascetic life[20] (or entered the sangha) and as soon as their servile status terminate, they were to be greeted with reverence and were provided with all requisites. Another solitary case was when a slave was liberated for bringing happy news for the master.

IV
BUDDHIST ETHICS AS THE PANACEA FOR SOCIAL EVILS

All the above mentioned social evils are due to the collective domination of our sense faculties which spring from the greed, hatred and delusion produced by the wrong notion of 'self' which is like a strong post to which we are tied by the rope of carving (tanhā). The Buddha taught that by the observance of the five precepts viz., the abstention from killing, stealing, illicit sex, falsehood and intoxicants, and by the cultivation of positive emotions known as Brahma Viharas viz., Loving-Kindness (Metta), Compassion (Karuna), Sympathetic joy (Mudita) and Equanimity (Upekkhā) and by means of Right livelihood (Samma ajivā) the Buddhist laity as well as the householders will not only enjoy peace in this world but also shall become eligible for higher spiritual life. By adhering to the Middle path they can lead a comfortable life by avoiding the two extremes of miserliness and extravagance. By training their minds through the meditative techniques of Samatha and Vipassana (calm and insight) by maintaining equanimous outlook towards the vicissitudes of gain and less, fame and lack of fame, praise and blame, happiness and sorrow; they can lead simple, peaceful and contended lives. By cultivating the Buddhist ethical precepts our attitudes towards the world can be changed.

Lord Buddha taught the four Noble Truths, the Law of Dependent Organisation, the Doctrine of Karma and Rebirth and constantly exhorted the world to practice the Noble Eightfold path which is the only effective means for uprooting all social evils, for establishing global peace and universal happiness. The Karaniya Sutta reflects this Buddhist notion:

"Let his thoughts of boundless love pervade
the whole world above, below, across
without any obstruction, without any
hatred, without any enmity."[22]

Notes and References

1. Dipak Kumar Barua, An Analytical Study of the Four Nikayās, Calcutta: Rabindra Bharati University, 1971, pp. 74-75.
2. *Ibid.*, p.75.
3. B.C. Law, *Studies in the Digha Nikaya of the Sutta Pitaka,* in the Journal of Indian History, Vol. XLII, April, 1964, p.16.
4. D.K. Barua, *op.cit.*, p. 224.
5. Digha Nikaya, Vol. III, pp. 82-83.
6. See, *Ibid.*, p. 95.
7. R. Fick, *Social Organization in North-East India in Buddha's Times*, p. 32.
8. Digha Nikaya 1, p. 98.
9. *Ibid.*, Vol. I. pp. 60-61.
10. *Ibid.*, Vol, I, p. 92: "Te Jatisambheda-bhaya sakahi bhagini hi saddim sambasam Kappesum."
11. *Ibid.*, I. p. 97.
12. "Maha Govinda brahmanoyana cattarisa bhariya sadisyo ten upasamkami," Digha Nikaya, II, p. 239.
13. Anguttara Nikaya, Vol. IV, pp. 91-94.
14. *Ibid.*, Vol. IV, pp. 269-71.
15. *Ibid.*, Vol. III, pp. 37-38; IV, p. 265; Gradual sayings Vol. III, pp. 29-30.
16. Digha Nikaya, I, pp. 60, 72, 921; 104.
17. Shmangala Vilasini, I, 168; Vinaya, I.72.
18. Anguttara Nikaya, Vol. III, p. 209.
19. Digha Nikaya, Vol. I, p.72.
20. *Ibid.*, pp. 60-61.
21. See, Ratthapala Sutta of Majjhima Nikaya, Vol. II, p. 62.
22. "Mettam ca sabha-lokasmin-manasam bhavaye aparimitam.
    Uddham adho ca tiriyanaca-asambhadham averam aspattam."
    Karaniya Metta Sutta, Verse.

4

Social Philosophy of Buddhism: Relevance for Modern Times

M. Rajagopal Rao

Gautama Buddha appears a radical in thought, a reformer in approach and a revolutionary in spirit when understood in the social scenario of his time. Northern India (uttarapātha) of the time was experiencing severe stress and strain due to the cross currents of thought buzzing around. Traditionalists, on the one hand, were trying to uphold the prestige of household life (gārhastya) to perpetuate the performance of yājnas (sacrifices) homās (fire worships), vratas (rituals) and so on, with the help of rulers and rich people, promising happiness here (iha) and here after (para); while hoards of freelance thinkers and propagandists wandering about the country were condemning these practices, upholding the ideal of asceticism as a sure way of getting rid of the sufferings of the world and attaining permanent happiness, on the other, landing people in utter confusion of what was right and wrong, good and bad and proper and improper.

It goes to the credit of Gautama Buddha to have striven on his own and obtained that perfect knowledge (sambodhi) and see things in their original nature (yāthābhita) and communicate his understanding to everybody, outlining the practical way (magga) following which anybody could obtain such knowledge and decide for himself what is right and wrong that made him the popular figure of the time and his dhamma a popular movement attracting all sections of society necessitating the organisation of a sangha (community) of his own.

It is well known that the Buddhist Community, even in its early stage of development, had to be distinguished between the Bhikkhu sangha and the Upāsaka sangha and a fixed set of rules had to be worked out to regulate the life and work of the Bhikkhu sangha which made it the first organised society of its kind in the country. This made it shine better as compared to the disorganised society of the Upāsakas that consisted of a coglomeration of groups pursuing a variety of vocations differing widely in aims and objectives, leading to the conception that bhikkhus are the elite of the Buddhist community and that these communities are exclusive of each other. But a perusal of Sutta pitaka would have us understand that neither these sections are that exclusive nor the upasakas were left uncared for, and that the two sections of the Buddhist community interact and depend on each other. The bhikkhus depend on the upasakas for their requirements and the upāsakas depend on the bhikkhus for guidance and for the teaching of the Saddharma (true dhamma). Both sections, it can be understood, had to conform to the conditions of the society in which they live. It is this requirement that made Gautama Buddha think beyond the requirements of his community and take care of the situation of the society and try to tone it up.

Buddha evolved a composite method of theory and practice (dhamma vinaya) basing on his personal experience that was open to everybody to adopt and practise and elevate himself from the lower state of life (lokīya) to the higher state (lokuttara), and went about teaching the same. He taught the same dhamma vinaya to the different sections of the society adopting different methods in tune with the requirement of the assemblies he was addressing.

His exhortation was brief (samkhitta) sometimes, expository sometimes (vitthara), gradual sometimes (ānupārvika) and elaborate (bahulam) sometimes. But all the time, it was the same dhamma vinaya that would help annihilate the inner (ajjhattā) and the bahiddha (outer) asavas (inflows) that would result in the total removal of dukkha (suffering) and release (vimuttī) from samsara, the never ending series of birth and death and enjoy that ananta sukha (infinite happiness) of Nirvana, though it was received differently by different sections according to the abilities of their understanding. Thus, it can be seen that the goal of Nirvana was open to all sections of the society if they undergo the required discipline and make themselves fit for undertaking meditation (jhāna), the means of wisdom (pāññā) which in turn leads to release and the enjoyment of release by wisdom (pāññā vimutti).

It was towards the realisation of this goal that Gautama Buddha tried to streamline the society. The society of his time was steeped in blind faith, outmoded practices and undesirable, harmful division of the society based on Jṭti (birth) gotra (lineage) kula (family) riches and so on resulting in mutual hatreds that disturbed social harmony. Buddha wanted to develop a social order in which everybody would enjoy equal status having equal opportunity to pursue his/her material and spiritual advancement. In addition Buddha preferred to teach in the language of the people (Sakaya nirutti) and encouraged everybody to understand what was taught and question and clarify doubts and decide for himself it would help achieve the desired goal. This deviation of Buddha from the established tradition, accounts for the hostility built up against him in the opposite camps.

ORIGIN AND DEVELOPMENT OF SOCIETY ACCORDING TO BUDDHISM

Society, according to Buddhism, develops naturally and gradually. It trace the way life naturally develops, the emergence of the female-male being (saitthi puma) from which develop man and woman in along course of time. It is from them the human race develops. As they go on increasing in number and go on living together there develops some unwelcome tendencies among them forcing them to look for some controller. They select or elect by common consent the best among themselves and make him the Mahasammuta and conduct themselves according to the regulations laid down by him in the best interest of the management of the group or society. Thus, evolve the society and its organisation which amply establishes the fact that all members of the society are equal and that there was no scope for the heirarchy of the high and the low, the lord and the sevile the privileged and the under privileged. We can discern in this social format three factors that contributed to this development.

(a) Man-woman Relation

There is that natural tendency among men and women to like, love and attach themselves to each other fostered by rupa (form), sadda (speech), rasa (taste), gandha (odour) and phassa (touch). Addition factors like sympathy, empathy and the efforts made to generate them would help unite them. This forms the key for the development of family and attachments between parents and children, brothers and sisters, friends and relatives and so on. The grouping and living together of these families and the mutual relations that follow make the society. Thus, the kernal of society would be the man-woman relation.

(b) Individual-group Relation

It is unusual to find a man or a woman living alone. There is that natural tendency or instinct among all living beings to group together and to live together which is being attributed to the gregarious instinct. But mere grouping would not make a society. The occasional grouping of human beings and their temporary interaction as on festivals would not make it a society. It was described as 'samaja' in Buddhist texts. Thus, what we call society or samaja would require the permanent living together and closer intercourse. Thus intercourse (sannivāsa), worthy intercourse (santa sannivāsa) would fold the key for the formation of society and the maintenance of its harmony. All men are sociable (samsattha) by nature and they tend to live in society and share in all its activities as well as the pleasures and pains. Thus develop that social bonds between them, that make them identify with it. There may be some that are not sociable (asamsattha) and prefer to keep away from the society and lead a lonely life for several reasons but that would be rare.

(c) Sense of Mutual Protection

Social life is not confined to the fulfillment of physical needs. Protection, therefore, should not be limited either to physical protection or property protection.

The maturity of a man makes him think not only of himself and of his requirements but also of others and his mind comes to dominate his body. He goes on extending his thought beyond the limits of his family and society and comes to realise the identity of all men, their happiness and sorrows. Thus, a man becomes a great man (māha purusa) or a deva even. Such men extend their friendliness (maitri), compassion (kāruna), pleasure of the doings of others (mudita) and indifference (upekkhā) for his gain or loss, pleasure or pain and see his protection entails the protection of all and the protection of all entails his protection. For such men society means universal society.

CONDITIONS OF SOCIAL HARMONY

The survival of a society depends on the continuity of harmonious relations between its individual members and groups that would result in the unity of the society. This unity would be reflected in the unified activities of its members, the way they think together, take decisions together and sort out the differences, if any, in mutual discussions. These conditions conduce to the development of the society as well. Buddha himself cited the example of such harmonious living among the Licchavis there was a confederacy of eight clans, which they could run in unity and progress. This consists in their meeting often in harmony (samaggā sannipatanti), in their rising together in harmony (samāgga vutthahonti) and in carry out their duties together (samāgga vijjikarana karonti). In addition they did not try to enact new laws in undue haste and continued keeping old traditions in all respect. This makes clear the position of Buddha regarding the continuity of good traditions.

BUDDHIST CONCEPTION OF IDEAL SOCIETY

Equal treatment of all (Samanatthata), equality in the conduct of all (samācariya) were set as the highest ideals that foster unity amity and the welfare of all. Equality of treatment was made one of the four important conditions of the conduct of a learned man. He has to share whatever he has with others (adanā), maintain cordial relations with others by kind words (peyyavajja) conduct himself in a noble way (attha cariya) and treat all equally (Samanatthatā). Samacariya was acclaimed as dhamma cariyā and kusala cariyā. Even samajīvitā taken in its wider connotation as the equality in living could be taken as the third ideal principle of an ideal society. These ideals hold good for any society at any time.

BUDDHA'S EFFORTS AT RECONSTRUCTING THE SOCIETY

Buddha tried hard to transform the society of his time to this ideal state. But it was rooted in several unfounded beliefs convictions and notions that he had to reject some outright, reinterpret some and offer new ideas to regenerate that confidence and independent attitude that is the prerequisite of reformation.

He rejected faith in the Creator (Īsvara) who was held responsible not only for the creation of the world but also the in equality of the society. He pointed out that the traditionalists of the time nor of the seven generations of their ancestors, whom they cite as evidence for upholding their purity, had seen Īsvara. He ridiculed the idea that the four varnas were born of the four parts of the body of Īsvara pointing out that all men at all times were born of their mothers only, and explained that it was built up by later teachers through he say which was being continued form generation to generation without any examination and understanding.

On the hierarchy of the higher and lower varnas and the claim of Brahmanas for the first place on the basis of their first origin he explained that in that case the Khattiyas would occupy the first place and had to be rated as the best of all men for they were the geneological successors of mahasammuta who was accepted as the best of men and elevated to the high position. He, however, ruled that those that have right knowledge which they put into practice were the best of men and devas-vijjacarana saṁpanno settho deva manussati.

Buddha held that it was the conduct and character, kamma, that should be taken as the criteria of deciding the best and the worst. Those of good conduct or pure conduct or sukka kamma should be rated high and these of bad conduct or impure conduct or kanha kamma should be held low. He rearranged the four varnas on this basis—sukka-sukka or of perfect conduct in all respects sukka-kanha, pure in some and impure in others; kanha-sukka, of bad character basically but do good sometimes and kanha-kanha of complete bad character in all. He presented these four types in a different popular format also as joti joti parayano, those that move from light into light; joti tamo parayano, those that move from light into darkness; tamo joti parayano, those that move from darkness into light; and tamo tamo parayano, those that move from darkness into darkness.

He ruled out the consideration of Jati or birth, gotra or lineage or kula or family as the basis of deciding the high and the low, pointing out that there would be good and bad people in all the classes of society and insisted that none should enquire of birth but enquire of conduct- na jatim puccha, caranam puccha, citing the example of the same fire from different logs of wood-kattha have jayatu jatavedo. He illustrated the same point further by pointing out how men of higher classes crammed to serve Matanga of the lowest class because of his famous character—so yasam paramam patta matangoyam sudullabhām, aganchum tassupatthanam khattiya brāhmānā bahū and asked them to realise that a saint could emerge from the lowest of men-nīcā klulinopi muni dhītimā.

Buddha did not stop at that. He redefined the four varnas and reclassified them according to their professions, disapproving the sanity of the division of four varnas and the support adduced in their favour by their professions. He emphasised on kamma and held that men were born of kamma (karajakaya), heirs of kamma (kamma dayada), world and people follow kamma, controlled by it as the linch-pin controls the movement of the chariot-kammanā vattati lokē, kammāna vattatī paja; kamma nibandhanā sātta, radhassanivato yada. He advised everybody to care for the present without wasting time looking into the past that cannot be recaptured and expecting the future of which nothing can be known and lead good conduct and character mindful of the fact that one has to reap good or bad results of their own good or bad actions in this very life.

EXPLORATION AND EXPOSITION OF NEW DIMENSIONS

We find Buddhism delving deeper into the activities of the individual and the society and come forward with measures of correction and improvement.

Buddhism examined the constitution of man minutely and came out laying emphasis on the internal or psychological mechanism rather than the physical mechanism or outward behaviour. It pointed out that in man the physical constituent (rūpa) was one of the five constituents, remaining four vendana (feeling), sanna (perception) samkhara (confections) and vinnana (knowledge) were mental (caitasika) hence the conduct and character of man could not be considered on the basis of his outward appearance of behaviour. It is the mind that leads the behaviour of man-māno pubbāngama dhamma,' mind is chief and men are mind-made (mano settha mānomaya). It is not only man but the whole world is under its control and guided by it citten loko niyati, cittena parikassati, cittassa uppannassa vasasm gacchati. This understanding of the importance mind led to the closer analysis of the conduct of man and society.

The character of man lies in the way he thinks, speaks and acts and so there should be complete syncronisation or correlation between thought, speech and action. The tendency to keep his thinking for himself, talk something palatable to others and act compromising with the situation and try to pose good while feeling reluctant all the time, did not find favour with Buddhism. These three factors were explained as mental factors. One should think of the welfare of others, express what he thinks and act accordingly and that makes a man a perfect man. Buddha was known for that yatha khameyya tatha vadeyya, yatha vadeyya tatha kareyya or yatha vadi tatha kari, the standard set as a model to be emulated by others.

We find enough evidence in the texts that Buddhism wanted the adoption and implementation of this principle in all the institutions of the society. This can be clearly seen in the way Buddhism tried to bring about a change in the tone and tenor of the judicial system. The order of the day was to depend completely what was done without any consideration of the motive of the action or of the situation and decide it to be right or wrong and punish. In addition discrimination of justice was rampant. Different types of punishments were being awarded for the same offence on the basis of varna. Members of Brahmana community were getting exempted even for serious offences like murder. It was Buddhism that situated against this discrimination in justice and propagated equal justice to all and emphasised the psychological side of an action.

FAMILY: MICRO UNIT OF THE SOCIETY

We find the social structure of Buddha's time in the structure of the family and its relations with the members of the family and outside. Family was sufficiently large consisting of mother, father, children, friends, relatives, advisors and workmen. It was the responsibility of the householder, the gahattha, to earn and maintain social relations while the management of the family was the responsibility of his wife gharani or gahapatani. She attends to the requirements of the members and assigns duties according to their abilities. It is here, perhaps for the first time, we find the duties a housewife specified and the equality of a husband and wife in the management of a family. In addition they had to take care of the wandering ascetics that could call on them any time of the day for their requirements. The householder allots one-fourth of his earnings for this purpose. Thus, family of the time appears a micro unit of the society.

Two things arrest our attention in this connection. Here we find it made incumbent on the gahapati to take care and serve his parents-mata pitu upatthānam, in which mother finds the first place. We find several passages in the texts highlighting the sacrifices made by parents to their children as well as the breast-feeding of the mother, to impress upon the need to serve them best. We also find the banner of monogamy raised to its heights here where not only Gautama Buddha but all the early Buddhas (purva Buddhas) were said to have married one, while their parents like suddhodana could marry many. This assumes significance in the context of the tradition of Brahmanas allowing the Brahmanas to marry four women of the four varnas; ksatriyas marrying three from three varnas excluding the brāhmana vārna; vaisyas marrying two leaving of the two upper varnas and sudras marrying one from their own varna, opening the floodgates for the development of mixed varnas making it difficult for the Dharmasastra writers of later times to account for them properly.

THE IMPORTANCE OF THE INDIVIDUAL AND INDIVIDUALITY

Buddhism recognises the importance of individuality as the

means of developing oneself and work for the development of the family and society. It encourages everybody to exert himself in all directions without depending on anybody—navayameyya sabbattana'nnā purusosia, na'nna nissayā jeeveyya. The same was carried in the last advice of the Buddha-strive on your own, depending on yourself, without depending on anybody else-attā dipā viharatha atta saranā, nā'nna saranā. Any householder would have that freedom to get over the life of desire (kamabhoganu-vartanā) by the observation of the householders celibacy (gahattha brahmacariya) by means of cultivating panca sila, attha sila and nava sila in a progressive manner and arrive at that state of brahmavihāra which rids him of his selfishness, and elevates him to that state of extending friendliness, compassion, pleasure and equanimity in all directions of the world and to all men which is the last stage of the attainment of nirvana.

Thus, the social philosophy of Buddhism provides a unified system of discipline that would conduce to the welfare of the individual, family, society and humanity at large.

RELEVANCE OF BUDDHIST SOCIAL PHILOSOPHY FOR TODAY

The ideals of equality, the necessity of getting over unfounded beliefs, outdated harmful practices; the need for ridding selfishness, and extending help to parents, elders and respectable ascetics; the need to eliminate all divisive tendencies and aim at the establishment of a unified society and so on, are as relevant now as it was at the time of Buddha. That commitment to do what we profess and profess what we think right would find relevancy for any society at any time.

5

Buddhism and its Impact on Society

Dr. N. Kanakarathnam

We have a rich history, philosophy and literature. The Vedas, Upanishads, Vedanta,[1] and Six systems (Sad-darshanas) on one hand and the Carvaka, Jainism and Buddhism on the other have enriched Indian culture. The Hinduism deals with metaphysical concepts viz., God, rebirth, belief, moksha and Karma theory.[2] On the other hand the Jainism [3] and Buddhism have special attention on axiological doctrines viz., ethics, non-violence, compassion, love, and socio-religious philosophy. Brahminism as an offshoot of Hinduism has given more attention to ritualism and casteism where as Buddhism contributed to the Neo-Hinduism. Since the beginning of rationalist movement in Greece, France, and philosophical religious movement in Germany, the sociological approach to the problems of religion has become very significant. In this paper I will attempt to discuss the Buddhist religion and its relevance to the modern society.

Let us know the meaning of the religion. Religion is based on the view of an ordered, organic and spiritual nature of the universe.[4] This organic teleology is not merely functional but is the consequence of the presence of a supreme divine truth.[5] Lord

Buddha was the Supreme monastic wanderer and preacher.[6] He was a prophetic religious leader. He had renounced the pleasures of a royal home and had accepted the begging bowl.[7] Hence, by this supreme example of self-negation he had conformed to the traditionally venerated path of religious men.[8]

Buddha was a great ethical teacher.[9] Lord Buddha's basic problem was the emancipation from the entanglements of the world.[10] The Buddha was opposed to metaphysics because he was preoccupied with the problem of immediate release from the sufferings of the world.[11] His stress was on the healing of a wound caused by an arrow and not dialectical discussions about the structure of the arrow. He is supposed to indicate his pragmatic and positivistic temper. He started the concept of suffering at physiological, psychological and transcendental levels. It is eternal in the sense that death, disease and disaster are the permanent distinctive of all human beings.[12]

Buddhism was the most potent religious movement in the whole of Asia.[13] The emergence and growth of this religious system was an indication of the great advance of the human intellect. The philosophical and sociological study of this religious system is a very great intellectual enterprise.[14] The concept of suffering repents on the dominant aspects of Buddhist religion and philosophy.[15] Man's capacities for fulfillment and realisation are limited. The Buddha was a believer in equality of all human beings irrespective of gender, caste, creed and economic or social status. He was a social revolutionary. He rejected caste system.[16]

The Buddha believed in intellectual enquiry, freedom of thought and action and dignity of labour. The Buddha was one among the great Indian religious leaders but unique in one respect.[17] While he shunned metaphysics and speculative thought for its own sake he enthroned reason. Reason constituted the very gist of Buddhism. He was a true philosopher, a rationalist and a social reformer. Buddha's teaching was primarily ethical he wanted to make men perfect among the religious thinkers of India,[18] the Buddha was almost the first to realise the importance of practical ethics in personal as well as in social life.

Buddha was a social and radical humanist. He did not preach any open crusade against the caste system. But social ethics was designed to enshrine the concept of merit in place of birth as the criterion of social stratification. "A man dose not become a Brahmana by his plated hair, by his family, or by birth; in whom there is truth and righteousness, he is blessed, he is a brahmana. I do not call a man a brahmana because of his origin or of his mother. He is indeed arrogant and he is wealthy; but the poor who is freed from all attachment, him I call indeed a brahmana."[19]

Buddhist's ethics is more comprehensive than the traditional and brahminical identification of ethics. He feels that there is no boundary of human desires and therefore the people in society are addicted to a custom with non-ethical or undemocratic behavior in the society for their temporary happiness.[20] Gautama was a symbol of true mankind. If we implement and practice his philosophical message with great commitment and devotion then we can create an ideal society. Buddha explains to his monks that "O my dear monks your birth is not the welfare of your self it is the welfare of the society wherever you read traditional texts and believe the concept of God you will never get attainment or liberation or Nirvana."[21]

In his first sermon at Benaras the Buddha preached his famous doctrine of the Noble Truths [22] *(Airyasathyani)* and Eight Fold-path *(Astangamarga)*. The purity of mind can be achieved only by the practice of noble eight-fold path. To quote the Buddha "O Ananda, do not grieve for the Master in dying, work out for your freedom, follow the noble eight-fold path, work out your salvation by diligence."[24] Further Buddha says there is no supreme power, which manifests controls and preserves the universe. No supreme power will come and help one in attaining freedom from Dukkah. Man alone is responsible for his deeds, and he is alone in his pursuit for freedom. Man has to work out his freedom all by his himself."[25]

Buddha told his disciples, "we must strive to avoid extreme addiction to pleasures that is meaningless and worthless and the extreme of self mortification, which is painful and fruitless." The importance of the Buddha's teaching was to make men perfect and to free them from the wheels of samsara.[26] The Buddha said 'one must not accept my Dharma from reverence'. First try it as gold is tested by fire.[27]

He believed in the dignity of labour. He established a new religious order. The Buddhas Sanga was very important and in the Buddhist form of worship, Sanga is included as one of the trinity—Buddha, Dhamma, and Sangha.[28] The Buddha was compassion incarnate. Metta (universal love). Karuna (Compassion), Mudita (Sympathetic joy), and Upekkah equanimity) are the four sentiments which know no bounds of time, space or class.

Albert Schiweitzer said that when the Buddha exalted compassionate love to the fundamental principle of morality, he breathed into Indian ethics a new breath of life.[29] The religion of India has experienced three changes, Vedic religion which was practiced first gave way, in course of time, to Brahminism and this in turn to Hinduism. From the times of Brahmanism there were disparities in the society viz; caste-system, inequality, and untouchability. Under these circumstances Buddhism was born. This was because Buddhism was opposed to inequality, authority and division of society.[30]

The Buddha did not lay the foundation of his religion either on God or on soul or any super natural powers. He says, 'no monk shall have a private property'. The reason is that, if we have property, ultimately it leads to suffering. Buddha upholds his view that the world cannot be reformed except by the reformation of the mind of the man and the mind of the world.[31]

During the Buddhist period different sects of the people were attracted to the teachings of Buddha in India. The non-aryan races like, Koliyasa, Moriyas, Haryanka, Mourya, Kushana, Pushyabhuti, Naga, Malla, Ikashvaka and kings like, Bimbasara, Ajatasastruvu, Ashoka, Milinda, Nagasena, Gautamiputra Satakarni, Yajanasri Satakarni, Virapurushadatta, followed

Buddhism. Historically there were various Buddhist schools which propagated Buddhist teachings and the scholars like Asanga, Vasubandhu, Parsva, Asvagosha, Narayanadeva, Dharmakirti, Manoratha, Vasumitra, Isvara, Kumaralabdha, Deva, Nagarjuna, Madhyantika, Samghabhada, Skandhila, Purna, Bodhila, Vinitaprabha, Katyaniputra, Gunaprabha, Srilabdha, Buddhadasa, Devasaraman, Gepa, Dharmapala, Gunamati, Sthiramati, Dinaya, Bghavaviveka, Achara, Jainaputra Bhadrabuchi Mahakatyana, distinguished themselves as great teachers.[32]

The monasteries were like colleges to which students were admitted on completion of their preliminary education. A child is first introduced to a Siddham (Which forms the expression Siddhir-astu, May there be success!) After his mastery of the Siddham, he was introduced at the age of Seven to the "great Sastras of the Five Sciences." Viz.: (1) Vyakarana (Grammar), (2) Silpasthanavidhya (The Science of Arts and Crafts), (3) Chikitsavidhya (Science of Medicine), (4) Hetu-Vidya (Logic or Tarka) which included "the metaphysical and argumentative treatises of the great Doctrines of Abhidhamma."[33]

The Buddhist qualification for the religious teacher or leader, having knowledge of craft, art was necessary in serving humanity. Huen-Tsang, a Chinese Pilgrim, visited Nalanda University and studied for a long period (A.D. 638-648). During that period, he collected there some 400 sanskrit texts of 500000 Slokas. This shows that Nalanda possessed a well equipped library.[34] Fa-hien, Huen-Tsang and Itsing studied in Nalanda. The university was sustaining on the income of huge estates. Today modern universities are providing boarding facilities on the lines of these Buddhist universities.

The father of Indian Constitution Dr. Ambedkar incorporated the philosophical messages in our constitution viz., Fundamental Rights, Directive Principles, and the meaning of secularism etc., Ambedkar rejected caste distinctions and inequalities. Rhys David also stressed that Buddhism ignores, completely and absolutely all advantages and disadvantages arising from birth, acquisitions or social status and sweeps away all barriers and disabilities arising from the arbitrary rules of mere ceremonial and social impurity.[35]

There are two kinds of religious schools in Buddhism[36]—Hinayana and Mahayana. They are also called northern and southern Buddhism. Countries like, Mangolia, China, Korea, Japan and Tibet, represents Mahayana Buddhism where as India, Burma, Siam and Cambodia belong to Hinayana school. Though these two schools appear as independent but their philosophical contributions are the same.

The aim of these two schools was to propagate the Buddhist teachings. They established educational institutions and Sanghas. Most of the Indian and the Western rulers, scholars and writers were attracted to the Buddhism. In Ceylon and Burma influence of Buddhism could be found in all the educational activities exhibited by the Buddhist's monks. Every village of these countries had Buddha—Vihar where monks resided and propagated Buddhist religion.[37]

Buddha's first sermon started in the Banaras city and started his ethical teaching to the public. The first follower of Buddha was Kondanya The famous aristocratic family in the city of Benaras by name Jasa was attracted by the Buddha's discourses. Jasa's family and his friends were ordained as lay-disciples.[38]

Ancient History reveals that the Magadha King Bimbisara alongwith twelve myriad's of Maghadha Brahmins also joined as disciples of Buddha. The king Bimbisara is mostly respectable ruler invited Buddha Bikshus and provided food to them. He cleaned Buddha's bowl and hands and he sat down at Buddha's feet. Bimbisara donated 'Veluvana Garden' to the Bikshus. Buddha blessed him and accepted the gift. Along with Bimbisara , many noble youth of Magadha territory joined themselves into the Buddhist order. Similarly the followers of Nanda and his princess, Janapada-Kalyani and his relatives the Kolyans among those predecessors like Anadas, Devadatta, Maggalan, and Anuradha, followed the Buddhism.

Buddha went from place to place delivering discourses. Through his teaching the famous robber by name Angulimala changed his mind and joined as disciple of Buddha. One hundred years after Nirvana of Buddha, the Mahayana school became more powerful and spread the Buddhist religion. The first and important author of the book '*Manikambum*' by name *Thumi Sumbhota* (632-35, AD) came to India and learned Buddhist sacred books and established an independent school by name *'Tibetan Buddhism*-called *Kadampa*[39] which propagated Buddhist message in the Tibet.

To conclude that though Buddhism was born in our motherland, it was attracted by the entire Asian Continent. Buddhism faded away in India because of the rise of Vaisnavism, Saivism and the Muslims invasions on India. The Islamic rulers ruthlessly killed Buddhist monks and destroyed Buddhist historical monuments. When Alla-ud-din marched into Bihar, he killed five to six thousand Bikshus. The remaining Buddhist monks fled to the neighboring countries like China, Nepal and Tibet.[40] Hence, Buddhism could not survive in India and slowly declined. Another reason is that unlike Hinduism, Buddhism is a religion and it is difficult to practice. Besides the political climate in India had also been inhospitable to its advancement.[41]

Notes and References

1. David, R., *The Relation between Early Buddhism and Brahmanism,* International Encyclopaedia of Buddhism, Vol. 32, p. 4051.
2. E.B., *Subjective Idealism in Mahayana Buddhist Thought,* International Encyclopaedia of Buddhism, Vol. 34, p. 4583.
3. Johannes Bronkhorst, *The Two Traditions of Meditations in Ancient India*, p. 36.
4. Lama Angarika Govinda, (Tr), by Maurice Walshe, *Buddhist Reflections*, pp. 25-27.
5. Sharma, J.B. & Sharma, S.P., Buddha the Light of Asia, p. 47; Verinder Grover, *B.R. Ambedkar: A Biography of His Wison and Ideas*, p. 413.
6. Yumkomiyajaki, (Tr.), *Buddhism for World Peace*, p. 186.
7. Monier-Williams, M., *Buddhism*, p. 79.
8. *Ibid.*, p. 310.
9. Sharma, J.B. & Sharma, S., p. 45.
10. Sastri, M.N., *The History of Buddhism*, p. 22.
11. Yumiko Miyazaki, p. 42.
12. Jtava, *Philosophies of Buddhism and Marx*, p. vii.

13. *Ibid.*, p. 4.
14. Jyot Devasthan, Theology of Buddhism, Vol. I, p. 10.
15. Jatava, pp. 43-44.
16. *Ibid.*, p. 4.
17. Hermann Oldenberg, (Tr), by William Hoey, *Buddha His Life His Doctrine His Order*, p. 72.
18. Krishnamurthy, K. and Padhmanabha, K., The Buddha His Nirvana and Mahaparinivana, p. 73.
19. Edward, J. Thomas, *The History of Buddhist Thought*, pp. 108-109.
20. Law B.C., Jainism and Buddhism Influence of the Five Heritical Teachers, *International Encyclopaedia of Buddhism*, Vol. 27, p. 2666.
21. Jafar Mohamud, S., *Buddhism Religion and Meditation*, p. 228.
22. Sastri, M.N., *The History of Buddhism*, p. 45.
23. *Ibid.*, p. 43.
24. Hermann Oldenberg, p. 106.
25. Bond, G.D., Meditation on Death and the Symbolism of Initiatory Death, *International Encyclopaedia of Buddhism*, Vol. 29, p. 3171.
26. *Ibid.*, p. 3170.
27. Howard, H., *The Essential of the Dhamma*, *International Encyclopaedia of Buddhism*, Vol, 26, p. 2365.
28. E.B., *Orthodox Saints in Buddhism, International Encyclopaedia of Buddhism*, Vol. 30, p. 3537.
29. Albert Schieveitzer, *Indian Thought and its Development*, p. 121.
30. Verinder Grover, p. 64.
31. Jafar Mohamud, S, *Buddhism Religion and Meditation*, p. 229.
32. Radhakumud, S., *Ancient Indian Education*, p. 426.
33. *Ibid.*, p. 527.
34. *Ibid.*, pp. 526-574.
35. Rhys, T.W., *Buddhism its History and Literature*, p. 8.
36. Jyot Devasthan, *Theology of Buddhism*, Vol. I, p. 79.
37. *Ibid.*, pp. 107-08.
38. Sastri, M.N., p. 47.
39. *Ibid.*
40. Jatava, p. 7.
41. Verinder Grover, p. 64.

6

Buddhism and Modern Society

C. Anjaneeya Reddy

Ven. Bhikkus and Learned Scholars assembled here for the two-day seminar on Buddhism and Modern Society.

Let me confess at the outset that I have no credentials whatsoever to be the Chief Guest at the inaugural meeting. I am no academic of any standing in Buddhist studies. I owe the honour to the generosity of the organizers and perhaps my association with Ananda Buddha Vihara. I came to Buddhism fascinated by its profound understanding of the human condition and the humane approach it adopts in suggesting solutions. What appeals to me in good measure is the fact that it is a homocentric or man-centred religion in a world dominated by theo-centric or God-centred religions. It would appeal to the modern mind that it avoids all speculation about super-natural forces and places die responsibility of elevating or degrading oneself in one's own hands in its unique Doctrine of Karma. All this can be understood clearly if we appreciate the origins of Buddhism.

There have always been two distinct religious traditions in our country—sacrificial tradition with its origins in the Vedas and ascetic tradition which is both pre-vedic and non-vedic. Early

Buddhist literature frequently makes references to Sramanas and Brahmanas. While the Brahmin priests continued down the ages as custodians of the Vedic tradition including the right to conduct sacrifices and confer ritual status on their benefactors, the Sramanas belonged to the other stream of religious life with its origins in the non-vedic cultures of India. The Sramanas in ancient India were renunciates who abandoned the world and opted for the homeless life of wanderers or Parivrajakas. Often, the two groups were rivals in religious life but were received with equal respect by people.

Some among the Sramanas took to austerities in the hope of acquiring paranormal powers or purifying the spirit, while some others propounded different theories about the world and nature and delighted in disputation. The teachings of the Sramanas were many and varied: "some very wise, some exceedingly foolish, some loftily spiritual and some crudely materialistic." The Pali canon introduces us to six well-known contemporaries of the Buddha in this tradition: Purana Kassapa, an amoralist, Makkhali Gosala, a determinist, Ajita kesa Kambal, a materialist, Pakudha Kacchayana, a categorialist, Nigantha Nataputta (Mahavira) who was a relativist and eclectic and Sanjaya Belaputta an agnostic, sceptic or positivist, all older than Gautama. It is obvious that die Sramanas were not a homogeneous group; they were free thinkers and preached what pleased them. It is note-worthy, the Sramanas received no less respect than the priests from all classes including kings. They played an equally important role in shaping the early religious thought and tradition of this country. It is said that they were the propounders of the original secret teaching incorporated in early Upanishads which came to be later grafted on to orthodox Brahminism to form the core of the later Vedanta System. Buddhism and Jainism belonged to this stream of religious life. In early Buddhist texts, both Jain and Buddhist monks are referred to as Sramanas and Buddha is hailed as Maha Sramana.

Not only the Sramana content of the Indian thought has not been properly appreciated, attempts have been made to underplay, if not belittle their contribution. There is an oft-quoted but ill-informed comment that the 'Buddha was a Hindu, who sought to reform the orthodox religion. Apart from the anachronistic use of the term Hindu, it is wrong because he rejected ritual sacrifice and claims of the priests as religious authorities and assigned to the gods of those days an unimportant role in his scheme of things insisting that the gods themselves were unenlightened beings and were in need of the teaching as much as men. Yet another comment that 'Buddhism rose out of the Upanishadic thought and later merged into it can be easily dismissed. It would suffice to say that what is central to Buddhism is the doctrine of anatma which denies the existence of the individual self and is indifferent to the Universal Self with which the Upanishadic thought is largely concerned.

The Sramana thought, as it has come down to us in both Jain and Buddhist tradition has had no concept of a creator God; they believed in the doctrine of Karma which is an impersonal natural law that operates in accordance with our actions and without the intervention of any external agency. Karma in Buddhism is a substitute for God. In his profound insight of dependent co-origination (Pratitya Samutpada), the Buddha explains the arising, abiding and ceasing of all phenomena, physical and mental, due to configuration of causes and conditions. This implies the absence of any permanent or inherent essence or Self in any phenomena. Buddhist and Jain traditions strongly believe in man's capacity to raise himself spiritually by his own effort.

Coming to Buddhism, Siddhartha Gautama, in his enlightenment not only understood the human predicament but found a way out of it. The first sermon of the Buddha, commending the middle path and defining the four noble Truths and the Eight Fold path for man's salvation is the very essence of the Dhamma. The Eight Fold Path encompasses the three pillars of the Dhamma: Sheela, Samadhi and Prajna.

Sheela is the moral life which a practitioner has to adopt: Panchashila for householders, Astasheela for Anagarikas homeless ascetics and Dasha Sheela Samaneras who are admitted to the Sangha.

Samadhi is a self-cleansing process of rigorous self-observation and purification. In its Vipassana tradition, it demystifies meditation and enables the practitioner to hold mirror to himself. The practitioner trains his mind to recognize *kushala* and *akushala* Dhammas or wholesome and un-wholesome thoughts. By fostering the former and eliminating the latter, he launches on a long process of self-purification and finally attains Prajna in which the three taints—lobha (greed or lust), dvesha (hatred or aversion), and moha (delusion or ignorance) are eliminated and the practitioner is in a position to see the good as good, evil as evil—Yadabhuta Jnana Darsanam.

As can be seen, the thrust of the Dhamma is to unfetter man and help him rise above himself. In making man, the object of all attention and concern and stressing the fact that Tathagatas are there only to show the way and one has to endeavour along the marga or the way, the Dhamma not only promotes a humanistic approach to religion but seeks to make man self-reliant. Says the Dhamma pada:

> By oneself alone is evil done
>   by oneself is one defiled
> By oneself is evil avoided
>   by oneself alone is one purified
> Purity and impurity depend on oneself
>   no one can purify another.

In the four noble truths—the existence of sorrow (dukkha), the cause for the existence of sorrow (samudaya), the dissolution of sorrow (nirodha) and the way (marga) leading to the dissolution of sorrow, we have perhaps the earliest approach to a rational understanding of the human situation : recognition of the problem, comprehension of its causes and a prescription for its solution. This approach is consistent with modern scientific methods. It is not without reason that Albert Einsten observed "if there is any religion that would cope with modern scientific needs, that would be Buddhism."

In its avoidance of all extremes and adoption of the middle path, the Dhamma provides many solutions to world's problems. We can see it at work in His Holiness Dalai Lama's approach to the resolution of the Tibetan problem. He proposed an autonomous status for Tibet within the Chinese Republic reconciling the two extremes of total Independence and abject surrender.

Buddhism has promoted an enlighted approach to religion from the very beginning. It assures freedom of conscience to all practitioners. The world has been witnessing increasing violence in the name of religion and is still not free from religious bigotry. Several hundred years after major religions made their appearance, man is yet to secure freedom of conscience. Most religions, frozen in time as they are, seek to hold man in their thrall negating in a way man's intellectual advancement. Buddhism seeks to set man free and encourages him not to accept anything unless it is tested and found to be beneficent to oneself and for all others. In the well-known Kalama Sutra, the Buddha advised the Kalamas not to accept even what he said out of regard for him but after examining it, "as the wise test gold by turning, cutting and rubbing on a touch-stone." Buddhism insists that we zealously guard our spiritual freedom and not throw it away by accepting an authority. This idea has been carried forward in the teachings of J. Krishnamurthy, India's best-known philosopher of the 20th Century. Buddha compared Dhamma to a raft. As a raft is useful to cross the river so is Dhamma to cross the ocean of Samsara. After the river is crossed, the raft becomes a burden and is best left behind. If this analogy is understood and appreciated, all religious bigotry would come to an end. Now the world needs these ideas more than anything else.

Dhamma aims at creating harmony in die lives of people here and now. One does not have to wait till die end of one's life to benefit from the fruits of its practice. The disease is here and die cure is also here and now. Nirvana is not necessarily at the end of a virtuous life. Upadhi-sesha-nirvanam is here and now, if you are rid of those three taints, lobha, dvesha and moha.

Rhys Davids, a great: pioneer of Buddhist studies, launched on his endeavours about a hundred. and fifty years ago to gather material to expose and if possible condemn Buddhism. After he read through die ancient Pali texts, he became a great Buddhist and recorded:

> "I have examined every one of the great religions of the world and in none of them have I found anything to surpass in beauty and comprehensiveness, the noble eight fold path of the Buddha."

The relevance of Buddhism is obvious. Its approach is scientific and its essential concern is man and his material and spiritual well-being. Buddhism places humanism on the high pedestal much before human rights were thought of. Buddhism goes much further and seeks the well-being of all sentient beings. In a 4th Century inscription near Amaravati, the aim of the Dhamma is defined as 'sarva satvanam nikhila dukkhopasamanam' i.e. relieving die sorrow of all living beings.

Inaugural Address by C. Anjaneya Reddy at the National Seminar on "Buddhism & Modern Society" held on 1.2.2004 at Kakatiya University, Warangal, Andhra Pradesh.

7

Buddhism: The Way to World Peace in Modren Society

Gali Vinod Kumar

It is necessary to understand the History of the Saints and Gurus who made significant contributions towards giving a right direction to the Human Society from time to time. If the words of Buddha and Dhamma inspire us to reconstruct a social order into one based on equal values, we should opt for it. In the larger interest of the country and the world at large, to encourage humanity and humanism, we should not hesitate in following such religion. In other words, since Buddhism has valuable lessons for the today's global village we should take full advantage of such a religion. This approach might be misconstrued, as if we are trying to preach a particular Religion. All religions have to be equally respected. But the shortcomings of each religion in so for as they fall short of what is "Dhamma" have to be clearly understood and practiced today. There are people who profess different religions. All political parties should bear in mind the principles of secularism, and instead of misusing Religion for political benefits, they should use Religion in the best interests of the country, for giving correct direction to the Society. Now the question arises, as to which are the religions, which help us to preserve the Unity and Integrity of the Society. To arrive at an answer to this question, we will have to study the History of all Religions as was done by Baba Saheb Dr. Ambedkar. After an in depth study of all Religions, he described the Teachings of Buddha as appropriate for building an equality based social order. A glimpse of this belief of Baba Saheb is visible in his historic speech delivered on 14th October 1956, in Nagpur. It becomes necessary to make a special mention of that speech so that, not only the Majority People but the whole society as such will realise some truths about the teachings of Buddha. This teachings, will helps in the reconstruction, of the society on equality based order.

It is important to throw some light on the significant things which are essential for reconstructing the social order on the basis of equality, and which Gautam Buddha emphasized in his sermons, before we come to the principles highlighted by Baba Saheb in his speech at Nagpur. Gautam Buddha said, "Do not believe in traditions merely because they have been handed down for many generations and in many places; do not believe in anything because it is rumored and spoken by many. Do not believe because the written statement of some old sage is reproduced. Do not believe in fancies, thinking that because they are extraordinary, they must have been implanted by a deva, or a wonderful being." Only after careful observations and analysis, when a thing agrees with reason and is conducive to the good and benefit of one and all, accept it and live up to it. (Kalma Sutta, Anguttara Nikaya)

Gautama Buddha announced a social revolution for the first time in India. He taught the lesson of equality, comradeship, mercy and brotherhood to the entire human society, and laid the foundations for an independent conscience, delivering the society from the slavery of spiritualism. Atmvad, Ishwarvad, Shastravad, and religious scriptures. It is due to his saddharam that the Country scaled heights of art and culture. But those professing Brahmanism did not like it since the interest of their section of society were served only by perpetuating inequalities, through Iswarvad and shastravad. As a result, Brahmins used all possible conceits and even State power, to extinguish Saddharma and Buddhism from the very land on which it was born, while it kept flourishing abroad, beyond the boundaries of our Country. On 14th October 1956, Baba Saheb Dr. Ambedkar gave a call to this oppressed and deprived class to return to their own culture, namely Buddhism. He showed the path to comprehensive Dalit Revolution and Independence. By leaving Hindu religion, and returning to Buddhism alone, is emancipation and progress of Dalits possible. Not only this, the welfare of entire society of India and the welfare of the whole Country as such, lies only in adopting the high human values professed by Buddhism.

Dr. Baba Saheb explained why Buddhism should be embraced in his speech at Nagpur.

'Those who have studied the ancient history of India, and the Buddhism connection, know that the credit for propagating Buddhism in the beginning goes to Nagas. Nagas were non-Aryans, and there existed a fierce enmity between the Aryans and the non-Aryans. Aryans wanted to completely annihilate the Nagas. There are many legends, to be found in the puranas in this connection. The Sage 'Agastya' is said to have saved one snake deity, symbolic of Nagas. You are all supposed to the descendents of Naga. The Nagas, who were suppressed and oppressed by the Aryans, were on the look out for a great man to liberate them, and they found the great man in the person of Lord Buddha. Nagas spread the Religion of the Buddha throughout India. Nagas were predominantly the inhabitants of Nagpur. A river following at a distance of 27 miles from Nagpur is also named Nag. It appears that the Nagas lived on the banks of this river. This is mainly the reason for selecting Nagpur for this occasion.

RELIGION HAS USE FOR THE POOR

It is the poor who need Religion. The suffering and the oppressed need religion. The poor live on Hope. Hope is Foundation of Action in Life. Life cannot go on it Hope is demolished. Religion affords this Hope to everyone. Religion gives solace to the poor and the oppressed, and assures that life is full of Hope. This is the reason why the poor cling to Religion.

Some people will, no doubt, say that the Buddhism is the Religion of the untouchables. Brahmins used to irreverently address Lord Buddha as "Bho-Gautama'. They used to insult and disrespect him with such name. But as you know, if the idols of Rama, Krishna, or Shankara are kept for safe in foreign countries, nobody would buy them. But if the images of Buddha are kept for sale none will be left. So much has happened and has been witnessed in India. Let us look outside the Country also. If there is an Indian God whose name is popular abroad, it is Lord Buddha.

We shall follow our path, undaunted. Let others follow their own path. We have found a new way to life and we shall follow it. This path symbolises Hope. This path leads to progress. In fact we have not imported it from outside. Buddhism is the Religion of this country. It is more than two thousand years old. I feel sorry for the fact that I did not embrace this Religion earlier. The teachings of Buddha are eternal, but even then Buddha did not proclaim them to be infallible. The Religion of Buddha has the capacity to change according to times—a quality, which no other Religion can claim to have.

Buddhism has hope for this Country and for the World:

> There is no salvation for anybody in Hinduism. According to the tenets of Hinduism only the so-called higher castes have been benefited. There is no exaggeration in my statement. What has the Shudras or the Ati-Shudras gained? As soon as the wife of a Brahmin conceives, she thinks of the High Court, whether any post of a judge has fallen vacant, but when our woman becomes pregnant, she cannot

think anything better than a sweeper's post under the Municipal Committee. This deplorable situation exists only because of Hinduism. How can we gain by staying in this system? It is only by embracing Buddhism that we can hope to gain anything.

Brahmins and Shudras alike embraced the religion of Lord Buddha. While delivering a sermon to the original Bhikkus, Lord Buddha said, "O Bhikkus, you have come from different countries and various castes. Great rivers when they flow in different countries maintain their individual flow, but, after falling into the ocean, they loose their separate identities. Buddhism is like that ocean. All are one and equal in this ocean. It is not possible to identify the waters of Ganga or Yamuna when they have merged. Similarly after embracing Buddhism, you are all one." Such was the teaching of Lord Buddha.

You must bear in mind, some facts while accepting Buddhism. You must not think that the Teaching of Buddhism are of temporary value, and are not likely to last longer. Even after a lapse of 2,500 years, the world respects the teaching of Buddha. There are as many as 2000 Institutions of the followers of Buddhism in the United States of America. In England, a Buddhist Vihara has been built at a cost of Rs. 3,00,000. There are some 3000 or 4000 Institutions founded in the name of Buddha in Germany. The Principles of Buddha are Eternal, but in spite of this fact Buddha did not claim any Divine Status for himself, nor did he claim his faith to be Infallible. Buddha did not say that he was the Son of God, or the last Prophet Messenger of God. On the contrary he said, "My Father and my Mother are ordinary mortals." Only those people should embrace this Religion who earnestly believe in it. For, such high principles are not to be found in any other Religion.

There is a world of difference between this Religion and other Religions of the world. Main Principles of Buddhism form no part of theistic Religions. According to other Religions, God created the world. This Earth, and thereafter he created Heaven, Air Moon and other planets. God has done all that was required to be done, and there remains nothing for us to do. All that we are required to do is, just to sing the praises of Almighty God. According to Christianity, there will be a day of judgment after death. Everything will be determined on the basis of that judgment. This does not appeal to rational man today.

Buddhism denies the existence of God and Soul. The real basis of Buddhism is, rational way to eradicate suffering. "There is", Buddha said, "suffering in the world-suffering wide spread." Ninety-percent people are afflicted with suffering or misery of some kind or the other. The main object of Buddhism is to emancipate the suffering humanity. The question arises then, what is the use of Das Kapital? I believe that Karl Marx was behind Buddha. For, he did not say anything that had not been brought to light by the Buddha himself, some two thousand and four hundred years before Karl Marx was born. Whatever Buddha said was simple, and the path he showed was straight.

At one place, speaking about the universal applicability of Buddhism, Dr. B.R. Ambedkar said, "This religion can serve not only this country but the whole world. At this juncture in the world affairs, Buddhism is indispensable for world peace. You must pledge to day that you, the followers of Buddha, will not only work to liberate yourself but will try to elevate your country and the world in general."

What Baba Saheb Dr. Ambedkar has said once is still relevant today, when the world is passing through the danger of nuclear weapons and highly advanced warfare technology. Today the world, led by America, is dead set to overpower in international domination and consequently utilize and apply different tactics to extend the sphere of its influence. This mad race of international domination demanded on their part to posses highly sophisticated weapons to exhibit superiority in the warfare and accordingly large sums of its national budget is being diverted for manufacture of these weapons. In this context possibility of atomic war is hanging on the head of human race. The world has already seen the evil and dangerous effects of these highly sophisticated nuclear and chemical weapons on the human race in Hiroshima, Nagasaki and Vietnam and would never be in a position to witness another. If by chance and unfortunately it so happens the world will be reduced to ashes.

The superpower, which is mad to control the large part of the world to fetch maximum economic benefits to their countrymen, design their foreign policies accordingly. The play of international relation is, thus the manipulation by these two super power.

Lord Buddha gave this world the message of "Bahujan Hitai, Bahujan Sukhai," 2500 years back. His teachings are more relevant today than any time before. It was Buddha, who initiated the first attack against all sorts of exploitation and discrimination against human beings. It was Buddha who gave the message of world brotherhood. His teachings are based on sound and scientific reasoning. There is an element of flexibility inherent in it, which is not to be found in any other religion. That is why in context to the communist success, Baba Saheb said "I am quite confident that if we all become one tenth as enlightened as the Buddha was, we can bring about the same result by the methods of love, of justice and good will."

Emperor Ashoka, after Kalinga, war denounced the use of military power and extended the reigns of his kingdom through love, justice and good will. If we really desire to save the world from being destroyed, it is Buddha's teachings alone which can help us. The Panchshila, the principles which were made the base India's foreign policy and adopted by large number of countries in Banding Conference in 1955 can still play an important role in reducing the tension in world affairs and minimizing the dangers of nuclear war.

Buddhism is not a dogmatic religion but the great social philosophy, which can be, practiced anywhere and everywhere. The society based on Liberty, Equality and Fraternity where justice will prevail is the society Buddha wanted to establish through his teachings. If we look at the world map we see a great part of humanity is still denied liberty and equality, what to talk of justice!

As long as, the great part of humanity is deprived of these rights, Buddha's message need to be taken there. Those who desire sincerely to see the human race live the life in peace and enjoy the fruits of human birth, they should come forward to spread the message of Buddha throughout the world, which is the only way and which alone can establish peace in the world.

8

BUDDHISM AND SOCIAL JUSTICE IN AMBEDKARIAN PERSPECTIVE

DR. LELLA KARUNYAKARA

Historically speaking modern society is a society equipped with democratic institutions. In other words, institutional structure of a society including polity and religion adhering to the democratic principles of social justice and equality and making the impact of the same over all the spheres of life of its members can be called as a modern society. Ambedkar has located the relevance of Buddhism in its purpose to spread the principles of modernity in order to integrate historically deprived sections of the society with the ethos of his time, i.e., culture of rationality of post enlightenment modernity. The major thesis of this paper is that Buddhism provides the space for social justice by the denial of caste system and recognition of social equality, which made Ambedkar to lead the deprived classes of Indian society, particularly Dalits to embrace Buddhism to regain the lost self-respect. The paper is a pioneering attempt to understand Ambedkar's reinvention of Buddhist tradition for the social and political empowerment of Dalits.

Buddhism in Ambedkar perspective is basically a social gospel. The Buddha's gospel is a collection of doctrines and social reforms. Unfortunately his teachings have not been interpreted and understood in the social context by particularly the dominant modern Buddhist streams. Buddhism has rarely been studied as a social movement. For many it is just the name of a religion. This paper aims to study the contribution of Ambedkar for reinventing the philosophy of social justice in the Buddhist tradition.

B.R. Ambedkar redefined the meaning of social justice in Buddhist context. He expressed meaning of 'liberty, equality, and fraternity'[1] in the social context unlike understood in the political philosophy of French revolution. The philosophy of social justice propounded by Ambedkar is very much rooted in the religion of the Buddha.[2] He aimed to achieve social justice for Dalits in two different ways namely: (I) religious conversion and (II) political power.

I. RELIGIOUS CONVERSION AS A MEANS

Conversion to Buddhism is the means to achieve social justice for Dalit Community. Ambedkar preferred Buddhism because it gives three principles in combination, which no other religion does. "Buddhism teaches prajna (Understanding as against superstition and supernaturalism). It teaches karuna (love), it teaches samata (equality)."[3] These are the main constituents of what we now term as social justice. At a time when Dalits started aspiring to chieve by religious conversion or turn to Marxism, Ambedkar preferred Buddhism, a religious system for Dalits instead of Marxism, a secular system. He felt that secular system could not last very long unless it had the sanction of the religion.[4] He claimed that Buddhism was a complete answer to Marx and his Communism.[5] Marxist communism aims to bring social justice through a bloody revolution whereas the Buddhist communism brings it through a 'bloodless mental revolution'.[6]

The world cannot be reformed except by the reformation of the mind of the man and the mind of the world. If the mind accepts any ideology or belief and loves it loyally and carries it out it is a permanent thing, it does not required a police or a soldier to keep a man or a society in order. If state is the biggest enemy of society, withering of state is not the solution but change in the character of the state is required. If a man is bad we should not kill him but a change in the mind or the mental transformation makes him to see the reason. After all, state reflects society. Change in the thinking of minds that is social transformation of society guarantees responsible state. Ambedkar wanted to bring change in the character of Indian state by the social transformation of Indian society. He adopted religious revolution as the means to achieve his goal.

Ambedkar believed that religion is absolutely necessary for the progress of mankind. Religion may be opium for the masses. But religion has significance and meaning for the human life.

Poverty had not made Ambedkar irreligious.[7] He was not against economic progress of Dalit community. He very much desired mankind to become economically strong. One must have a healthy body in order to be free from disease, so in order to keep the body healthy one must also develop the sentiment mind, or else it would be futile to say that man is developing and making progress.

Many think that the life means 'eat, drink and be merry'. All that they want is bread and butter for breakfast, delicious meals in the afternoon, nice comfortable bed to sleep on and cinema to while away their time. In their life there is no place for religion. Ambedkar did not agree with the people believing in this kind of life.[8] There is a difference between life of man and animal. Mind must be developed side by side with the body and mind should be filled with pure thoughts. Religion played key role in developing mind with thoughts of pure and impure.

Now the question is about religion of good or bad ideas. Ambedkar finds Buddhist ideas good for mankind so as to society and state. Buddhism believes in equality of all beings. That is why Ambedkar emphasised on the importance of religious system over secular system. Materialism for Ambedkar is not the only solution for the progress of mankind. A prostitute could have good meal every day bought out of her earnings. Material gain what a prostitute acquired would not bring honour and self respect to her. People who madly rush for material benefits even at the cost of their self-respect are not less than prostitutes. "Self-respect is more important than the material gains, Ambedkar asserts, our struggle is for honour, for self-respect, not only for the economic progress alone."[9]

Self-respect is very much related to social justice. In Ambedkar's perspective religious conversion alone assures Dalits' self-respect, which ultimately results into social justice. Dalits could gain self-respect in the society and social justice from the state by the religious conversion. Ambedkar once asked his Hindu friends, on the practice of the removal of the dead bodies of animals by Mahars and Chamars, "You take the milk form the cows and buffaloes and when they are dead you expect us to remove the dead bodies. Why? If you carry the dead bodies of your mothers to cremate, why you do not carry the dead bodies of your 'mother-cows' your-self? . . . If you let us remove the dead bodies of your mothers we shall very gladly remove the dead bodies of your cows and buffaloes as well."[10]

A Hindu wrote a letter to Ambedkar explaining financial loss to untouchables who stopped removing the dead bodies of animals. According to him every Chamar who removed the dead bodies of the animals earned between Rs. 500 and Rs. 600 per annum from the sale proceeds of the skin, horns, teeth, hoofs and bones of the dead cows. Ambedkar's answer was befitting to expose Hindu hypocrisy, "if you are so much anxious about our losses, why not send your friends and relatives to live in the villages and do this dirty job of dragging the dead bodies of animals so that they may earn Rs. 500 per annum. In addition to that amount I will pay Rs. 500 from my pocket. They will gain doubly. Why miss this opportunity. True, we will suffer a loss but you stand to gain."[11]

There is a linkage between self-respect and change of religion in Ambedkar's scheme of social justice. Valuable part of

Ambedkar's scheme is that it identifies the problem and provides alternative to solve it. He with firm belief says, "No change in our status can be expected if we continue to be slaves of Hinduism. If we have any hope it is by renouncing the Hinduism and following the path of the Buddha."[12]

Social justice is part of the religious emancipation. Social transformation of the society is possible only through the firm belief in ethical culture. What lacks in Hindu society, according to Ambedkar, is ethical character. Absence of concept of equality means no concern for humanity. If a religion is not for human welfare it is devoid of social justice. Ambedkar finds failure of Hindu philosophy to pass the test of social justice and utility. He concludes that Hindu religion contains no space for social justice hence there is no utility of its philosophy for the progress of individual and society.[13]

Religion is a social force. Ambedkar's meaning of religious revolution is not a revolution in the religious organisation of society; it is a revolution in the norms. Religion may not be necessary for the well to do. Those who are holding high positions in life, have nice bungalows to live in, money to buy all comforts of life and servants to attend them, perhaps, have little use for religion. Ambedkar taking support from German scholar Winterniltz claims that it is only the poor who need religion. He says, "Hope is the spring of action in life. Religion affords this hope. Therefore mankind finds solace in religion and that is why the poor cling to religion."[14]

Ambedkar aimed to bring change in the norms of Indian society by reviving Buddhism. He felt that religion of the Buddha has capacity to change according to times, a quality which no other religion could claim to have.[15] Religious conversion as a means of social justice has two aspects. One is material and the other is spiritual. It is a struggle related to social status. It is a struggle for equal treatment. Conversion gives mental strength, sense of oneness and identity and no wastage of finances on unnecessary religious rituals. The object of Ambedkar's movement of religious conversion is to gain social freedom. Ambedkar says, "To get human treatment, convert yourselves. Convert for getting organised. Convert for becoming strong. Convert for securing equality. Convert for getting liberty. Convert so that your domestic life may be happy."[16]

Ambedkar's mission was not to liberate Dalits alone but the whole India as a nation from the culture of inequality. Ambedkar felt, "There is no salvation for anybody in Hinduism . . . This religion and this social order has ruined us. But this is not going to stop here. This would ruin the Hindus themselves and ultimately India. I don't accuse the Hindu religion in vain. This religion cannot save anybody. It has no life left in it."[17] Therefore, he aimed to bring religious revolution in Indian society to establish 'just society'.

II. POLITICAL POWER AS AN END

Ambedkar wanted Dalits to acquire political power through social democracy. Political democracy, in Ambedkar's project of political power, must be based on social democracy for its survival. Ambedkar's meaning of social democracy is a way of life, which recognizes liberty, equality and fraternity as the principles of life. To divorce one from the other is to defeat the very purpose of democracy.[18]

Liberty cannot be divorced from equality; equality cannot be divorced from liberty. Nor can liberty and equality be divorced from fraternity. Without equality, liberty could not become a natural course of things. Ambedkar found complete absence of equality and fraternity in Indian society. On the social plane, Indian society is based on the principle of graded inequality, which means elevation for some and degradation for others. On the economic plane in Indian society there are some who have immense wealth as against any who live in object poverty. In politics because of democracy there is equality. There is one-man one vote and one vote one value. But there is no principle of one-man one value in Indian society. The absence of equality forbade fraternity in the society.

Fraternity, in Ambedkar words, a sense of common brotherhood of all Indians.[19] It is the principle, which gives unity and solidarity to social life. Division in the name of caste is a division of nation. Ambedkar maintains, "the castes are anti-national."[20] Caste is basically an identity. Caste brings about separation in social life. They are anti-national because they generate jealousy and antipathy between caste and caste. There cannot be a unified nation without fraternity.

Political freedom is of no utility without equality and fraternity. Social democracy of Ambedkar aims to achieve social freedom i.e., social justice by the establishment of equality and fraternity in all spheres of life. Ambedkar had rightly visualised that political power was the key to all social progress of Dalits. He emphasised on ethical value in the exercise of power. It is not enough to have independent state but it should be a good state.

Ambedkar in *Muknayak* says, "a class holding the state should have the will to perform the good job for the people. If this class is unselfish then it can serve the society properly. Efficiency of governing class is not enough to run the government because such class if plagued with selfish motive, however, efficient it may be, may exploit the poor sections of the society. But the protagonist of democracy seldom understand the need to have impartial governing class."[21] In India the governing class (Brahmin and Banias) has misused the political power with no sense of responsibility. This power hungry insatiable class posed a serious threat to democracy and created imbalance in the political field.[22]

Ambedkar wanted representative democracy with ethical character. He wanted political democratic set-up to represent positively identified comprehensive ideals like freedom, justice and equality. This institutional arrangement for him was a mechanism to empower the Dalit and to make them the ruling race in this country. Ambedkar's goal to capture power through social democracy leads Dalits to the seizure of power through compromise rather than conflict. It is not the conflict model of capturing power. He suggested a seizure of power through sharing it with the Muslims.[23] He also suggested the broad political unity of the SC, ST and the OBC s in the country, to organize for the purpose of capturing political power because of adult franchise.[24]

Political power in the liberal set up as exists in India goes much deeper than what one could experience at the peripheral of power institutions. There are centers and little known points of support within the liberal structures like the very democratic space that the liberal system provides.[25] Therefore, Ambedkar, apart from adult franchise and political reservation provided Buddhism as a path to political power.

CONCLUSION

Buddhist society is Ambedkar's ideal society, consists of a state apparatus and ethical culture as core of its behaviour. Withering of the state is not in Ambedkar's agenda. Change of state's character from oppressive and exploitative nature to modern, liberal, progressive and particularly to democratic is the goal of Ambedkar's project of social democracy. His suggestion of social alliance with other oppressed groups for the realization of political power is the secondary strategy. The basis of his project, which aims to gain social justice by capturing political power, is Dhamma of the Buddha. Conversion to Buddhism becomes the main strategy of his project.

Critical examination of Ambedkar's project of Dalit liberation reveals that the recovery of self-hood for Dalit is still waiting to be actualized. Buddhism should be more than emancipatory project to realize the lost Dalit self-hood. Dalit assertions are of two types: for identity and for secular gain. Ambedkar's legacy is restricted to secular realm—resources, education, jobs and power that remained limited. This had led the Dalit to treat the state as some thing as neutral arbitrator and not discriminatory and exploitative. The Dalit have placed the state above the contradiction in the civil society unlike communists of Marx. The Dalit have become the ardent supporters of the Constitutional liberalism that exists in India, because they treat the state as the Constitutionally mediating force among the different competing social groups.

Dalit society at large has the faith in Constitutional mediating for simple reason that the father of Indian Constitution is B.R. Ambedkar. They have an emotional attachment to it. Recently constituted committee for the review of working of Constitution is looked with suspicion by Dalit intelligentsia. Dalit in general time and again in the past fifty years reposed faith in the belief that Constitutionalism would help them to gain social justice. Their major activity is not to demolish the Constitutional structures of the state but to bring change in the attitude of the state by social transformation of the society. For social transformation, there is a need of change in the culture and belief and value system. Buddha Dhamma, thus plays a dominant role in the Ambedkar's project of Dalit liberation.

For Ambedkar's project actual solution lies in opting out and conversion. Social justice will remain unachieved goal till Dalits opt a religious system different from Hinduism. Buddhism as a religion with positive social values like equality, brotherhood and freedom is the alternative proposed by Ambedkar. The realisation of social justice by Dalits in Ambedkar's project is possible through the Buddha Dhamma. Exclusion of religious conversion or Buddhism paralyses the Dalit emancipatory project. Political status to Buddhism is the main theme of Ambedkar's idea of social justice. The combination of religious and secular projects is the fundamental feature of Ambedkar's project of Dalit liberation to realise a society based on justice.

Notes and References

1. Dr. Ambedkar discussed his social philosophy in a talk on the All India Radio, Delhi in the series "My Personal Philosophy" on 3rd October 1954.
2. *Ibid.*
3. On the B.B.C., London on 12 May 1956, Ambedkar talked on why he liked Buddhism and how useful it was to the world.
4. *Ibid.*
5. *Ibid.*
6. *Ibid.*

7. On 14th October 1956, Babasaheb Ambedkar embraced Buddhism, along with half a million of his followers, at a historic conversion ceremony at Nagpur. On 15 October 1956, he gave a speech in Marathi and explained the causes for his conversion to Buddhism. See D.C. Ahir, Dr. Ambedkar on Buddhism, People's Education Society, Bombay, 1982, pp. 31-43, 47-50.
8. *Ibid.*
9. *Ibid.*
10. *Ibid.*
11. *Ibid.*
12. *Ibid.*
13. Ambedkar, B.R., Philosophy of Hinduism, compiled by Vasant Moon, Vol. 3, Dr. Babasaheb Ambedkar Writings and Speeches, Education Department, Government of Maharashtra, 1987, p. 22.
14. *Op.cit.*, D.C. Ahir.
15. *Ibid.*
16. *Ibid.*
17. *Ibid.*
18. Constituent Assembly Debates, Vol. XI, 25 November 1949, pp. 972-81.
19. *Ibid.*
20. *Ibid.*
21. Muknayak (Marathi) 14 February, Mumbai, 1920.
22. *Ibid.*
23. Ambedkar, B.R., What Congress and Gandhi have Done to the Untouchables, Thacker & Co., Bombay, 1945, p. 240.
24. Bhagvandas, (ed.), Thus Spoke Ambedkar, Vol. I, Buddhist Publishing House, Jalandar, p. 87. And also see C.B. Khairmode's Bhimrao Ramji Ambedkar (Marathi), Maharashtra Sahitya Sanskriti Mandal, Vol. 10, and p. 164.
25. Guru, Gopal, "Ambedkar Concept of Political Power" a paper presented at a National Seminar on Ambedkar in Retrospect held at Jawaharlal Nehru University on 29.8.1998, p. 24.

9

Ambedkar Views on Buddhism and Applicability to the Modern Society

G. Laxmaiah and P. Ramakrishna

Bhimrao Ramji Ambedkar was born on April 14, 1891 in a small village at Ambewada in Maharashtra, and he Spent his childhood at Mahu of Madhya Pradesh. His parent were Ramji Shagal and Bheema Bai and were of low caste named as 'Mahar'. Since his childhood he encountered destute poverty and hardship. With so many hurdles before him, he worked hard to come up as a brilliant student. With his knowledge and humbleness he gone to abroad, to complete his Post-Graduation and doctorate there itself and return to India there after. Being a person from low caste, he suffered humiliation many times in the hands of upper caste Hindus. He raised his voice against untouchability and discrimination against low caste people, for this, he used media as a powerful weapon.

Ambedkar certainly possessed a multi-dimensional and multifaceted personality. He was a great soul with a spirit of sacrifice and scientific outlook, who led and whose followers continüe to lead movements of self-respect through out India. It took two decades for him to embrace Buddhism, a momentous decision indeed. But his choice of Buddhis... in 1956 unfolded a new life before millions of exploited untouchables.

When Ambedkar declared in 1935 that he was going to renounce Hinduism, some Hindus including Mahatma Gandhi felt that religion was not a thing which could be ordered at the whims and fancies of the person concerned. Mahatma Gandhi said: It is unfortunate that Ambedkar has declared his resolve to abandon the Hindu religion. But conversion is not going to serve his purpose. Religion is not like a house or coat which can be changed whenever one feels like it. Ambedkar, on the other hand, felt that man is not born for religion. Religion is created by man and, therefore, it should work for the welfare of man. A religion which does not respect equality, liberty and fraternity among all its adherents is not a religion but a felony. It sounds strange but yet it is true that Hinduism shows love, respect and sympathy for the animals, birds, stones, woods, etc. but it does not consider man as man and even the co-religionists are not shown any sympathy and love.

While speaking at the Mahar Conference in 1936 on the question of conversion to some other religion, Dr. Ambedkar said: I have decided once and for all to give up this religion. My religious conversion is not inspired by any material motive. There is hardly anything that I cannot achieve while remaining an untouchable. There is no other feeling than that of spiritual feeling underlying my religious conversion. Hinduism does not appeal to my conscience. My self-respect cannot assimilate Hinduism. In your case, change of religion is imperative for worldly as well as spiritual ends. Do not care for the opinion of those who foolishly ridicule the idea of your conversion for material ends. Of what avail is the religion that deals with life after death. A rich man's sense may be tickled by this idea in his leisure time. Those who are well placed and prosperous in this world may pass life in contemplation of life after death. But why should you live under the fold of that religion which has deprived you of honour, money, food and shelter? The result was confusion for those people who feared that change of religion by the untouchables was going to divide the Hindu society, Ambedkar believed that since there was no social relationship between them in matters such as dining and marriage, there was no need to be disturbed about it. He thus said in the same conference: Therefore, nobody can say that by change of religion of the untouchables, Hindu society would be divided into two pieces. You will be just as different to them after conversion as you are to the Hindus today. Nothing new is going to happen.

He had gone through the literature of Hindus and made his own comments and out rightly rejected the theory of "karma". He felt than Hindu upper caste people cleverly used this weapon against the low caste people to realize their own ends. He was also against worshiping the gods by sheerly neglecting the welfare of mankind especially the downtrodden. To set right this he had chosen Buddhism has best alternative. Ambedkar gave considerable time to study various religions, especially Hinduism, Christianity, Islam and Buddhism. He found that Hinduism offered no succor to the untouchables. According to him, both Lord Christ and Prophet Mohammed arrogated to themselves divinity by their emphatic declaration that they represented gods. Lord Christ regarded himself as the Son of God. Similarly Prophet Mohammed claimed that he was the messenger of God and also the last messenger of God on earth. On the other hand, Lord Buddha believed in self-abnegation. He regarded himself as the son of the soil and preached his gospel as a common man. Buddha considered himself merely a "*Margadata*", whereas Christ and Mohammed considered themselves "*Mokshadata*". Whatever Islam and Christianity taught were the words of God and therefore God's words, taught by both Christ and Mohammed, were infallible and beyond question. On the contrary, Buddha told Ananda, his disciple, in Mahaparinibban Sutta that his religion was based on reason and experience and he advised his followers not to accept his teaching blindly without reference to reason and experience. Buddhism was the only option for Ambedkar, because its revival in India had long since begun. The roots of this revival trace back to archaeological discoveries of British civil servants, to the recovery and translation of texts by nineteenth century European scholars, and Anagarika Dharmapala's foundation of the Maha Boddhi Society, dedicated to the rehabilitation of ancient shrines and the renaissance of the faith on its native soil. By the early decades of this century the beginnings of a revived Indian Buddhism were evident-in limited but influential conversions at both extremes of Indian society. These included Tamil-speaking *pariahs* in the South and the emergence out of caste-Hindu society in the North of a trio of Buddhist scholars, Mahapandita Rahula Sankrityayan, Ven. Anand Kauslyayan and Ven. Jagdish Kashyap. The writings of the Tamil Buddhist, especially of P.L. Narasu, made a strong impact upon Ambedkar, while the leading and enduring role played by the latter three is continued today by Ven. Anand Kausalyayan in his training center for bhikkhus in Nagpur. The convert's background, as Untouchables in a caste society, colors their views of the faith they espouse-casting into bold relief the social teachings of the Dhamma and those interpretations of the Buddhist past that speak to their need for self-respect. These perspectives were afforded them by "Babasaheb" Ambedkar, whose authority is unquestioned by most converts. A few oven refer to him as a "Second Buddha" and the Nagpur *diksha* has been described as a new turning of the Wheel of the Law. This new turning gives the Law a distinctive flavor. As a scholar of political theory and champion of the downtrodden, Ambedkar projected upon the Dhamma his own faith in rationalism and his over-riding concern for social reform. The chief vehicle for transmitting and interpreting the new faith is his book *The Buddha and His Dhamma,* written in English at the end of his life, published posthumously and subsequently translated into Hindi and Marathi. His aim was to produce a "Bible", and so it has served and continues to serve in modern Buddhist India, where it is held in reverence and gratitude. For many of the literates it is the sole Buddhist text they own or have read. For the illiterates it is the one they hear, read aloud to them in villages and city slums, bearing in their eyes the authority of sacred scripture.

In his Hindi translation of the volume, Bhadant Anand Kausalyayan has identified the original texts from which Ambedkar drew. Queried about departures from canonical *The Buddha and His Dhamma* represents a "new orientation, but not a distortion" and that all central doctrines are present. Ambedkar himself offers a rational by which differences can be explained. He points out that oral transmission of the teachings gave scope for error even during the Buddha's lifetime. Identifying five such cases in the Suttas, he notes that mistaken views appear "common with regard to karma and rebirth," and are likely to have continued, especially, since they represent Brahmanical reinterpretations. "One has, therefore, to be very careful," Ambedkar concludes, "in accepting what is said in Buddhist canonical literature as being the word of the Buddha." Ambedkar sets forth the criteria by which he determines authenticity: There is one test which is available. If there is anything which could be said with confidence, it is: He was nothing if not rational, if not logical. Anything, therefore, which is rational and logical, other things being equal, may be taken to be the word of the Buddha. The second thing is that the Buddha never cared to enter into a discussion which was not profitable for man's welfare. Therefore, anything attributed to the Buddha which did not relate to man's welfare cannot be accepted to be the word of the Buddha (IV.V.12-4).

Ambedkar's chief departure from the traditional view of the historical origins of the Dhamma lies in his account of the circumstances prompting the Going Forth of Gautama and the ethnic character of the mass, of his followers. Both these points of divergence lay emphasis on the nature of the Dhamma as rationalistic social gospel and both dramatize the role of non-Aryan elements in its birth and dissemination. The cause for Gautama's renunciation of his princely life is no longer taken to be the traditional Four Passing Sights, which confronted the young Sakya with the fact of human sufferings. Ambedkar found it an affront to commonsense to suppose that a man of 29 would not have been exposed earlier. It is impossible to the presence of sickness and death. These are common events occurring by the hundreds and the Buddha could not have failed to come across them earlier. It is impossible to accept the traditional explanation that this was the first time he saw them. The explanation is not plausible and does not appeal to reason.

In Budhism Ambedkar found 3-distinct qualities prajna, karuna, samata. Prajna means one's own decisiveness before many alternatives to make a right choice. Karuna is nothing but love of mankind. Samata in other words equality among citizens of the society. Ambedkar felt that the existing Hindu Dharma favours few sections of the society and making others scapegoats by putforthing Karma theory for their present condition. With lot of concern towards the untouchables he organized mass conversions into Buddhism. He openly expressed his anguish against the atrocities on 'Dalits' even in free India. As a true Buddhist he tried to incorporate some of his views while drafting the Constitution of India. Directive principles of state policy of our Constitution clearly directs the state to follow the path of equality and fraternity. In the views of Dr. B.R. Ambedkar Buddhism propagates selflessness, simplicity, humanity, sacrificing nature, concern towards the needy, equality of opportunities to all irrespective of their caste, color and creed. He thought that in modern society where exploitation against the dalits is in crooked and naked way, Buddhism could be an eye-opener to the Hindu fundamentalism. Birth and death are similar for every one and blood that flows in everyone is of the same colar, then one should be discriminated and exploited? Ambedkar opined that the preachings of Buddha can educate the Dalits to understand the happenings around them and the real drama of Hindu fundamentalists in the name of religion. The dalits can get proper direction from Buddhism to set right their own thinking and come-up as a united force to tackle the situation. He found the lack of education, accessibility to the minimum needs and productive assets is the root causes for lower status of dalits. Thus, he preached and argued for equal rights to the downtrodden. He advocated unity among dalits to fight against evils of the society through he maintained report with the national leaders he maintained his own identity. As a true representative of crores of dalits he had never taken a back step to put forth his ideas in true spirit to protect the interests of low caste people. Dr. B.R. Ambedkar, a true Buddhist not only preached but followed the principles through out his life. He appealed to the Dalits that by adopting Buddhism, they can realise that their sufferings are not due to their 'karma' but because of wrong doings of Hindu fundamentalists in the name of God and they can fight these forces with their education and unity.

Dr. Ambedkar recognised Buddhism is the best religion for peace and happiness of both man and society. Buddhism is a universal religion which does not allow itself to be passed into oblivion, as it is based on reason and experience as opposed to the sterile and static doctrines of other religions. Dr. Ambedkar stated that Buddhism was also an integral part of our social system. Buddhism laid emphasis on non-violence and morality. It was true that in Buddhism there was no God but Ambedkar held that Buddhism had substituted morality for God. He had prepared his followers psychologically for a conversion by declaring in 1935 that he "would not die a Hindu." But the conversion was held suddenly, dramatically and without much organizational preparation on October 14, 1956 and within two months Ambedkar was no more. He had died a Buddhist, and he had set in motion a movement that soon involved over three million people.

With his strong faith in Buddhism and concern towards Dalits in his words and deeds, he became champion of the downtrodden forever in the history of modern India.

References

Kadam, K.N., Dr. Babasaheb Ambedkar—Significance of his Movement—A Chronology, Popular Prakashan, Bombay, 1991.

Kumaraswamy, B., The Role of Dr. B.R. Ambedkar in Freedom Struggle—Understanding in Perspective, 1920-40, *op cit.*, p. 42.

Dhananjay Keer, Dr. Ambedkar Life and Mission, p. 19.

Khararde, D.K., Mythree Gurus and Three Deities who Influenced My Life, translation of a speech by B.R. Ambedkar in Dalit Voice, Vol. 9, No.15, New Delhi, 1990, p.6.

Romilla Thapar, A History of India, Vol. I, Penguin Books, New Delhi, 1968, p. 66.

Lokhande, G.S., Bhimrao, Ramji Ambedkar—A Study in Social Democracy, Sterling Publishers Private Ltd., New Delhi, 1977, p. 4.

Romilla Thapar, *op.cit.*, pp. 67, 68.

Romilla Thapar, Asoka and the Decline of the Mauryas, Delhi,1961, p. 141.

Lokhande, G.S. Bhimrao Ramji, *op.cit.*, p. 5.

Kharat, S.R., *"Dr. Babasaheb Ambedkarnchi Patran"* quoted in Chandra Bharill's *Social and Political Ideas of B.R. Ambedkar,* 1977, p. 242.

Dhananjay Keer, *op.cit.*

Quoted in Chandra Bharill, *op. cit.*, p. 252.

Ambedkar, B.R., *Buddha and the Future of his Religion*, 1975.

B.R. Ambedkar, *The Buddha and His Dhamma,* 2nd Edition Bombay, 1974.

Ambedkar, Introduction to 1st Edition of *The Buddha and His Dhamma*, 1957.

10

Buddhism and Modern Society

Dr. Manjual B. Chincholi

Buddhism, a distinguished historian declares, is the most important product of Indian mind, in the history of the world. Various grounds for such a judgement can be adduced. Although born on Indian soil, Buddhism is one of the three great religions of the world. With a great following at the height of its influence, Buddhism was followed by a third or a fourth part of the human race and which even now is not negligible.

Its founder, Gautama Buddha is universally recognized as the perfect embodiment of the ethical and spiritual ideals. Buddhism is the greatest of the non-theistic faiths whereas both Christianity and Islam are forms of theism. Its influence upon the other systems of belief has been profound and Buddhism affords the unique spectacle of a doctrine of salvation propagating itself on a hitherto unprecedented scale entirely by peaceful means.

During the last half of the century Buddhism has received the increasingly respectful attention of western students of comparative religion as well as of psychologists, philosophers and lovers of art. As exemplified by current expositions, there are a number of alternative approaches to Buddhism. The scientific approach, which is of a modern western origin is exemplified in the works of the great classical orientalists. The traditional approach is that of the Buddhists, who whether learned or unlearned takes refuge in the three jewels (Triratna) the Buddha, the dharma and the Sangha, the sectarian approach is, in fact, only one part of the total Buddhist tradition. The synoptic approach recognizes the essential authenticity of the entire Buddist-tradition. "The doctrine of the Buddha, conceived in its full breadth, width majesty and grandeur comprises all those teachings which are linked to the original teaching by historical continuity and which work out methods leading to the extinct of individuality by eliminating the belief in it."[2]

As a teaching aiming at the experience of enlightenment, Buddhism has no direct connection with the collective life of man on the social and political teachings and therefore, scattered here and there throughout Tripitakas. Matters of every day social ethics apart, the social teaching of Buddhism concentrates upon two vitally important issues—caste and means of livelihood. Buddha rejected the system of hereditary caste.

Modern Buddhist revival begins about a hundred years ago. 1891, Anagarika Dharmapala, a Sinhalese, founded the Maha Bodhi Society in India, which ever since its inception has worked for the revival of Buddhism in the land of its birth, this appreciation was symbolized, when, upon the attainment of independences in 1947 the Ashoka Chakra was inscribed upon the national flag. In 1956-57, the 2500th Buddha Jayanti was celebrated on a Nation-wide scale. 1958 saw the flight of the Dalai Lama from Tibet to India and the influx of about 50,000 Tibetan refugees, among them more than thousand monks. From the point of view of Buddhist revival however, the most (active) and far reacting event of modern times occurred when the late Dr. B.R. Ambedkar the untouchables' leader embraced Buddhism at Nagpur on October 14th 1956 along with half a million followers. Despite his untimely death a few weeks later the movement of mass conversion among the untouchables snowballed to such an extent that whereas the census of 1951 returns 1,80,000 Buddhists for India and census of 1961 returns 3,250,000 the greatest gains having been made in Maharashtra.[3] This spiritual movement the value of the individual.[4]

The essence of Buddhism consists not in the removal of sufferings, which is only negative and incidental, but in the attainment of perfection, which is positive and fundamental. The Bodhisattva not afraid of suffering accepts it joy fully if he thinks it will assist him to the attainment of his great goal of "Enlightenment for the sake of all sentient beings.[5]

What is the position of Buddhism as of today? It is considered part of Hinduism. According to RSS-BJP Hindu revivalists everybody except a Muslim, Christian or Parsee in India is a Hindu. Buddhism has ceased to be a force having been swallowed by Hinduism. Ambedkar had admitted this weakness of Buddhism in his speech in Colombo in May 1950.

Repudiating all suggestions that Buddhism has disappeared from India, he said "Buddhism in its material form had disappeared. I agree, 'but as a spiritual force it still exists'." As regards Hinduism, he said that "it went through three stages: Vedic Religion, Brahminism and Hinduism, it was during the period of Brahiminism that Buddhism was born."[6]

Buddha is considered the greatest Indian and the influence of Buddhism on the modern Hindu mind is something great. Buddhism was responsible for the stress the Government of Independent India lays on socialism, secularism and humanism. On the religious side the influence is pronounced, it has checked excess of ritualism and helped to stress the substance aspect of religion and its humanism.[7]

Coming to the impact of Buddhism on the Orissa culture and civilization. Hare Krishna Mehtab, a freedom fighter and Governor of Orissa wrote in his book "History of Orissa," that "There is no doubt that at one time the symbols of Buddha, Dharma and Sangha were being worshipped all over India. Recently a stone of Asokan polish with the symbols of Buddha, Dharma and sangha at the top has been found out at Bhubaneshwar and it is now preserved in the Museum at Calcutta. The symbols are little different from those found at Sanchi and other places but the Bhubaneshwar symbols are almost exactly like the images of Jagannatha, Bolabhandra and Subhadra." The Bhubaneshwar discovery proves that in Orissa the worship of the symbols was prevalent since the Asokan period.

From the foregoing we may conclude that during the reign of Asoka, the Savaras of Orissa were converted to Buddhism.[8] Similarly, the historic importance of the place, Karumady, 20 km away from Alapuzzha, is that it has a Buddha Statue. The local people call this Buddha as Karumady Kuttan, a name which sounds indigenous and closely associated with the Dalits living in this area. Kerala was once a Buddhist state. The dalits and Backwards caste people of this state were all Buddhists. There are several Buddhist monuments in Kerala but the upper caste call (Aryans) them Hindu monuments. The most famous is the Ayyappan temple at Sabarimalai which was a great Buddhist centre.[9]

E.J.Mills, author of "Buddhism" says "In no other religion are the values of knowledge and evil of ignorance so much insisted upon as they are in Buddhism." Prof. W.T. Stace says in his "Buddhist Ethics that the arhat, had to be both morally and intellectually great. He had to be a philosopher as well as a man of good conduct and knowledge. This was always stressed by the Buddhism as essential to salvation and ignorance as one of the two main causes of failure to attain it.[10]

Notes and References

1. Mahasthavira, Sangharakshita, "A Birds Eye-view of Indian Buddhism". Sihanad Publication, Pune, 1987, p. 1.
2. *Ibid.*, p. 3.
3. *Ibid.*, p. 35.
4. Mahasthavira, Sangharakshita, The Individual and the World Today, Sihanad, Pune, 1991, p. 16.
5. Mahasthavira, Sangharakshita, The Path of the Inner Life, Reprint, Pune, 1983, p. 43.

6. Rajshekhar, V.T., Ambedkar and His Conversion, Dalit Sahitya Akademi, Bangalore, 1983, p. 40.
7. *Ibid.*, pp. 109, 110.
8. Rajshekhar, V.T., Dalit Voice, Vol. 18, Bangalore, July 16-31, 1999, p. 20.
9. Rajshekhar, V.T., Dalit Voice, Vol. 19, Bangalore, July 16-31, 2000, p. 20.
10. Ambedkar, B.R., The Buddha and His Dharma, VIII, Bombay, Siddharta Publication, Fourth Edition, 1991, p. 427.

11

Gauthama Buddha, Father of Social Revolution—A Study

B. Kumara Swamy and P. Swaroopa Rani

In the later Vedic period caste system has developed into water tight compartment. There is difference of opinion amongst the scholars regarding the origin of caste system. Prof. Rapson believes that the Varna or colour was the basis of caste system. According to him the caste system took its birth when the white races poured into India.[1] In the ancient literature we have conclusive reference to four castes.[2] Further, it is difficult to accept this view because the Aryans were themselves divided into Brahmanas, Kashatriyas and Vaishyas.[3] Therefore we can say that the caste system originated as a result of four fold division of duties for the convenient working of the society different persons adopted different professions. With the lapse of time the people belonging to different professions formed separate entities. As these professions became hereditary, the caste system assumed definite shape. However, it may be noted that at that stage it was not that rigid.[4] But in the later period the caste has become the structural basis of the Hindu society. Caste is not merely a principle of social division, but a comprehensive system of life dealing with food, marriage, education, association and worship. Caste is defined as a hereditary, endogamous, usually localised group, having a traditional association with an occupation, and a particular position in the local hierarchy of castes. Relations between castes are governed, among other things, by the concept of pollution and purity, and generally commensality occurs within the caste.[5] The basic principles of caste can be summarised as under: (1) inequality of mankind based on birth, (2) inequality of professions, and (3) absolute and rigid social exclusion between the four main castes and the equally rigid sub-divisions between themselves. The whole system permeates the dogma of Brahmanic superiority. In short, "caste is social imperialism perfected by experience and maintained by religious sanction." This system functioned best in a feudal, stationary economy with minimal occuapational and spatial mobility.[6]

The stratification of a civil society on the basis of socio-economic status enjoyed by the people had been a worldwide phenomenon. The people belonging to the lowest strata are called differently in different countries. The Romans had their slaves, the Spartans their helots, the British their villeins and the Americans their Negroes. So the Hindus have their Untouchables.[7]

The Buddha's teaching begins and ends with enlighten-ment. On the whole he concentrates on moral aim and purpose. His religion was very simple and practical. It aimed at moral uplift of the people and encouraged the people to attain 'nirvan'. Because according to him "Dharma is supreme in this life as nirvana can be achieved only in his life."[8]

Buddhism profoundly influenced the political life of India. (1) Buddhism promoted a feeling of peace as most of the rulers who adopted Buddhism followed a policy of non-violence. In this way peace reigned in the country for quite a long time. (2) Many books were written for the propagation of Buddhism. Though these books were part of religious literature yet they are valuable source of information about the contemporary social and political life and institutions. (3) The Indian rulers who embraced Buddhism took several projects for the welfare of their subjects. They built hospitals not only for the treatment of men but also for birds and animals. Wells and tanks were dug. All these measures made their life happier. (4) According to Havell the spread of Buddhism throughout India promoted a sense of political unity in the country. (5) Buddhism inspired the idea of universal brotherhood.[10]

In the twentieth century Buddhism has taken a new birth in India. Its new birth has various hidden dimensions in modern India since it is functioning more as a social movement than as an institutionalised religion. In this respect this modern Buddhism come closer to the teaching of the Buddha than the medieval times which functioned merely as an orthodox institution. Modern writers recall the Buddha as a symbol of national prestige and as a crusader for the oppressed and the down-trodden.[11] The leaders of the Dravidian Movement Periyar E.V. Ramasamy and Arinar Anna have made use of Buddhist ideals as a weapon to fight against social oppression. It was utilized as a political and social weapon by Dr. Ambedkar. In his speeches and writings he mentioned Buddha as his authority in his movement against the evils of the caste system.

Great Buddha gave solace to women. Fallen women were raised by his compassion to high levels in society. The noble acts of the Buddha in this regard have become a powerful theme in modern feminist writings. Modern writers who propagated their feminist gospels have made the best use of such episodes narrated in ancient Buddhist literature and Jataka tales. Gautama Buddha wants every individual to pass judgement on the basis of rational thinking. This attracted rational writers who also accept the no-soul theory of Buddhism. Social laws in a democratic set-up are made with a rational frame-work, rejecting a metaphysical base. Dr. Ambedkar's movement which fights for the down-trodden and Gandhiji's non-violence movement are influenced by Buddhism in many respects.

Dharmanand's book Bhagavan Buddha was taken up by the Sahitya Akademi, New Delhi, for translation in thirteen Indian languages, on the occasion of 2500th anniversary of Buddha's Mahaparinirvan, in 1956. The same book was declared as the official text on Lord Buddha's life and work, when Dr. B.R. Ambedkar embraced Buddhism along with his two lakhs followers, at Nagpur, on 14th October, 1956.[13]

Lakhs of the lowest strata of society placed in humiliating positions and suffering mentally and physically in the set up of Hinduism for thousands of years now got their chance. They took the step of freeing themselves from the clutches of the deep-rooted structure of casteism and the escapist philosophy of karma prevailing in the land. Answering the call of Dr. B.R. Ambedkar, whom they had unquestioningly accepted as their leader and saviors, they found solace in Buddhism, where there were no castes, no disparities amongst human beings and no karma theory to whitewash the inhuman behaviour of a few fortunate high-castes. On the contrary there was a message for the entire world to eliminate sorrows and agonies by taking the course of compassion, friendship and love. By embracing Buddhism along with their adored leader, the down-trodden people of India in general and those of Maharashtra in particular, rose from the darkness of their position into the light of a new equality, promising new hopes, aspirations and expectations.[14]

Thus, it would be clear that Ambedkar's acceptance of Buddhism was not just an attempt to break away from unwanted Hinduism. It has a plus value of its own. Ambedkar had studied Buddhism thoroughly and deeply, and he was honestly impressed by its greatness. But with the lakhs of his followers, ignorant of the Buddha's teachings, the motivation was just faith in the leader and revolution against Hinduism. If Ambedkar had chosen Islam or Christianity for his purpose, they would have gone along behind him in the same manner.[15]

With the transformation of Indian life under the new secularism caused by British rule, the injustice of old practices of untouchability in Hindu society, moved the hearts of Indians. The revival of Buddhism happening at the same time made people understand that love towards fellowmen, irrespective of caste and creed, can be the only base for an ideal society, where every one can be treated equally. Buddhist literature translated from many other languages like Tibetan, Pali, Sanskrit etc., made people well-versed with Buddha-dharma and emphasised social equality and compassion. The 2500th Buddha Jayanti celebrations held on 25th May, 1956, and the mass conversion for Dr. B.R. Ambedkar with his two lakh followers on 14th October, 1956.[16]

So far as the Andhra area is concerned, the relics discovered during the construction of Nagarjunasagar Dam in 1955 also reminded people of the past glory of Buddhism. As a result, the Purna-kumbha became the symbol of the Andhra Pradesh Government.[17] The world-wide movement showing sympathy and kindness for the suffering and the weak, called 'humanism' has the same message as that of Buddhism-universal love. Buddhism's ideals of ahimsa, self-sacrifice, compassion (karuna), universal love and equality in society impressed Telugu writers who said: "All the living beings in this world are equal. Caste differences are the evil creations of men, forming chains, obstructions to the fulfillment of human destiny devised by selfish people." Buddhism only can bring harmony to the world. Writers wished for the re-birth of Buddha in this world.[18]

A humanist society moved by love, compassion and self-sacrifice, without divisions of rank and birth has become the modern ideal; these requirements stressed in Buddhism. "Today we hear the cry of humanity, as violence is ruling nations and the only hope lies in the Buddhist Way." Modern sense of the importance of man leads to credos like "God is also a human with blood and soul. We won't accept any religion not based on this value". Buddhism is the only religion which accepts this principle of elevating man. It says "There is no hell or heaven. The acts done by us and the sorrow of happiness attained by our acts alone is heaven or hell.[19]

Buddhism pays respect to human values and tries to protect human rights. Its "Trisaranas' (Buddha, Dharma and Sangha) are words of peace. It begins with the message of peace and the truth of life throbs in it. "Forgiveness is Buddhism." Buddhism created a history without bloodshed. Once we understood the Buddha Dharma as a social thought, the rebirth of the Dharma will become permanent. Though Buddhism was not visible for a few centuries in India, it remained in the minds of the people and in this modern age it has come out with new vigour and recognition at all levels. In the modern Telugu literature we see that works touching social problems resort to the discussion of preachings of the Buddha and the religion of Buddhism. All the Buddhist literary works in Telugu in the form of poetical compositions. Novels, plays including one-act plays, street dramas like burra-katha, and dance-dramas, translations, essays, critical, descriptive and reflective and research work and all allied writings on arts and customs and travels, constitute a steady stream, flowing full with varied contributions.[20]

P. Laxmi Narasu, a Buddhist writer and missionary who worked as a Professor of Physics and Chemistry at Madras Christian College, Under his leadership a small community of Buddhists came into being in Madras. He published a well-known book "The Essence of Buddhism" in 1907, reprinted in 1912 with an introduction by Anagarika Dharmapala. The third printing came out in 1948 with a preface by Dr. B.R. Ambedkar himself showing the prestige of the book and the subject.

Leaders like B.R. Ambedkar (1891-1956), Narayana Guru (1856-1928) and Periyar E.V. Ramasamy (1879-1973) were sociopolitical activists who worked for the emancipation of the down-trodden in different ways. They were inspired by the principles of Buddhism. Though Periyer E.V. Ramasamy, as an atheist, did not have any faith in any religion including Buddhism as such, he celebrated the birth-anniversary of Buddha every year, because he looked upon him as a great reformer who challenged the supremacy of Brahmins and varna system and thus strengthened his movement against them. Buddha is state. by Periyar E.V.R. to have denounced God and Atma as a rationalist and condemned rituals and superstitions.[21] Influence of three great personalities of modern India. Mahatma Gandhi, Rabindranath Tagore and Sri Aurobindo. The Buddhist ethos merged beautifully with Gandhian thought.[22]

During the Pandit Age, we get in direct touch with Buddha through Narsimharao Divetia's translation of Edwin Arnold's. The Light of Asia entitled Buddacarita.[23] 'Impact of the Light of Asia'. The role of Edwin Arnold's Political Masterpiece in English. The Light of Asia (1879) on the life and teachings of Buddha in stirring world-wide interest in Buddhism is well known.[24]

For the socio-economic and political benefits to reach the deprived, the Buddha's philosophy serve as an effective weapon empowering the hands of the social reformers to fight against social injustice and evils in the modern society.

Notes and References

1. S.C. Roychowdhary, Social Cultural and Economic History of India: Ancient Times, Surjit Publications, 1989, p. 78.
2. Kundra, Bawa, History of Ancient and Medieval India, Neelam Publishers, Jullunder, pp. 78-79.
3. S.C. Roychowdhary, *op.cit.*, p. 47.
4. *Ibid.*, p. 48.
5. W.N. Kuber, Builders of Modern India, B.R. Ambedkar, Ministry of Information and Broadcasting of Government of India, 1987, p. 1.
6. *Ibid.*, p. 2.
7. Dr. B.R. Ambedkar, Mr. Gandhi and the Emancipation of the Untouchables, Bheem Patrika Publications, Jullunder, p. 11.
8. S.C. Roychowdary, *op. cit.*, p. 78.
9. Vidyadhar Mahajan, History of India, Chand Company Pvt. Ltd., New Delhi, pp. 104-105.
10. Kundra, Bawa, *op. cit.*, p. 90.
11. Dr. Shuhiko Sankar & Dr. G. John Samule, (Editors) Buddhist Themes in Modern India Literature, Navalar Nedunchezhian, Institute of Asian Studies, Madras 1992, p. 11.
12. *Ibid.*, p 11.

13. *Ibid.*, p. 154.
14. *Ibid.*, p. 154.
15. *Ibid.*, p. 155.
16. *Ibid.*, p. 169.
17. *Ibid.*, p. 169.
18. *Ibid.*, p. 171.
19. *Ibid.*, p. 179.
20. *Ibid.*, p. 180.
21. *Ibid.*, p. 208.
22. *Ibid.*, p. 138.
23. *Ibid.*, p. 138.
24. *Ibid.*, p. 216.

12

Philosophical Approach to the Buddhism

K. Yesudasu and S. Venkataiah

In his *Six Systems of Indian Philosophy* Max Muller appropriately observes that the spirit of the doctrines preached by the ancient thinkers of India should be pursued aright. In his own words, "What I feel is, that it is not enough simply to repeat the watch words of any ancient philosophy which are easily accessible in the Sutras, but that we must at least make an attempt to bring those ancient problems near to us, to make them our own, and try to follow the ancient thinkers along the few footsteps which they left behind." What he points out is that mere understanding of the meaning of the statements recorded in the texts is not sufficient. Hegel rightly points out that in thought, and particularly in speculative thought, comprehension means something quite different from understanding the grammatical sense of words alone, and also from understanding them in the region of ordinary conception only. Interestingly, Hegel compares such non-philosophical historians of philosophy to 'animals which have listened to all the tones in some music, but to whose senses the unison, the harmony of their tones has not penetrated.

A philosopher looks at all the questions in a way different from that of historians and other researchers. Remaining indifferent to all other aspects the philosopher counts mostly on reason. Philosophy accordingly is the foundation of all other sciences and acts as lamp to unveil the mysteries of the universe. In India we notice the practical application of the concept maintained by Plato that philosophers must be the rulers and directors of the society. The ultimate truths are the truths of spirit and in the light of them actual has to be refined. It is interesting that the hard task of interesting the multitude in metaphysics is achieved in India.

India is fortunate in the sense that religious leaders here had always been the philosophers and seers with an endless quest in mind for realizing the realities of life. Buddha was one such seer in the true sense of the term, who made his august appearance on the soil of India at a time when the Upanisadic thoughts were still prevalent in some form or other. The loft idealism of the *Upanisads* could hardly influence the society as a whole, sacrificial religion being still the dominating force.

It may be presumed that in case the idealism of the *Upanisads* had permeated the masses it might have contributed to the remodeling of the racial character and regeneration of the social institutions. 'The conservatism of the religious institutions and contempt of the masses lived side by side with a higher spirit adopted by a few votaries of the perfect life. It was an age of spiritual contradiction and chaos'.

Radhakrishnan in his *Indian Philosophy* presents before us a picture of the society in the following lines.

This period was one of spiritual dryness, where truth hardened into tradition and morality stiffened into routine. The mind of man moved within the iron circle of prescribed formulas and duties. The atmosphere was choked with ceremonialism. Reconstruction was the greatest need of the hour. A deeper and more spiritual religion which could come down to the common life of man was what the times were waiting for.

What the masses eagerly sought as a religion understandable

and dear to them was supplied by Buddha, the perfectly Enlightened One, who was principally stirred by the pathetic force of fatality. Impressed by the emptiness of the objects of the universe, he unhesitatingly renounced the ease, power and wealth of the royal life to mediate on the eternal and to open for his fellowmen an easy device for escaping from the meanness of life and illusion of flesh. Truth was yet a problem and life an interrogation. Enlightenment was attained as desired after strain and the great seer of the Sakya (Sakyamuni), the Tathagata declared finally the nature of the reality. Buddha thus typifies for all time to come, the soul of the East. In fundamental ideas and essential spirit Buddhism approximates remarkably to the advanced scientific thought of the nineteenth century. The modern pessimistic philosophy of Germany that of Schopenhauer and Hartmann, is only a revised version of ancient Buddhism. As far as the dynamic conception of reality is concerned, Buddhism is a splendid prophecy of the creative evolutionism of Bergson.

We notice therefore that in the second century after the Great Decease of Lord Buddha, no less than eighteen varieties of Buddhist doctrines can be traced. Besides these internal changes there were the great factors like conflicts with the teachers of the Brahmanical schools who instead of driving Buddhism out of their territory with the help of swords, preferred to undo the doctrine through arguments and reasonings and quite interestingly we notice that as a result of such duels between the two intellectual parties—the Brahmanical teachers and the Buddhist teachers, the academic world has been fortunate to have before them a good number of Sastras in both the fields specially in the field of Nyaya (logic). Special mention may be made of the following: *Madhyamakasastra, Pramanavartika, Tattvasangraha, Pramanasamuccaya* on the side of the Buddhists; and Sankarabhasya, Nyayavartika, Slokavartika, Atmatattvaviveka, Nyayakusumanjali on the side of the Brahmanas.

In this background the theory of momentariness as advocated by the Buddhists deserves our attention for the simple reason that this theory has become the subject of discussion and criticism by the Hindu philosophers of ancient India. Madhavacarya in his *Sarvadarsanasangraha* refers in general to the four principal doctrines of the Buddhists, namely, all the objects are momentary, all are of the nature, painful; all is like itself alone and are void.

We refer here to the statement recorded more than once in the *Upanisads* that anything other than the Great One (Bhuma) is to be deemed as mortal.

Yo vai bhuma tad amritam atha yad alpam tan martyam.

What is intended is that all the bubbles in the water. There is not finality or rest within the universe, only a ceaseless becoming and a never-ending change. In the words of Shelley 'Naught may endure but Mutability'.

The doctrine of impermanence held in common by the *Upanisads* and the early Buddhism has been developed by later Buddhism into the view of momentariness. But to say that things are impermanent is different from saying that they are *ksanika.* Oldenberg in very short analysis brings out the difference in attitude between the Brahmanical and the Buddhist concepts in the following lines:

> The speculation of the Brahmins apprehended being in all becoming, that of the Buddhists becoming in all apparent being. In the former case, substance without causality, in the latter, causality without substance.

The description exaggerates the dominant aspects of the two systems which one agrees are the fundamentals, though there is the distribution of emphasis.

The Upanisads excluded the idea of absolute change by calling attention to the fact that there is a permanent underlying the flux. But the Buddhists deny this. They hold that all existence is momentary. Permanent existence, they argue, is a self-contradiction. Their argument is that existence or sattva stands for practical efficacy or arthakriyakaritva. Existence is the capacity to produce some change in the order of things (arthakriyakaritvam sat). A seed, for example causes the shoot and its capacity as a seed to produce the shoot must manifest in itself at once. The Buddhists are of opinion that a thing should be capable of producing something and yet should not produce it or do so only bit by bit, is inconceivable. So we should admit that whatever capacity a thing has, is at once and fully manifested; and since a thing is only when it acts, it must be momentary.

Existence is defined in terms of causal efficiency (arthadriyakaritya) which however deserves an interpretation. Dharmottara, the expositor of the logical text, Nyayavindu by Dharamakirti speaks of it as action with reference to undesirable and desirable objects (heyopadeyarthavisayatva). But with Ratnakirti the term arthakriyakaritva has an entirely different sense. It means efficiency of producing any action or event and as such it is regarded as the characteristic definition of existence (sattva). Whenever Hindu writers after Ratanakirti refer to the Buddhist doctrine of arthakriyakaritva they usually refer to the doctrine in Ratnakirti's sense.

In other words, an object is described as ksanika or momentary in as much as it has existence for a moment only.

Change is ordinarily understood to imply something that extends through it. If we represent a changing subject by XA, it becomes, according to the common view XB under certain conditions, where X stands for the element common to the two phases. This view that a changing object persists amidst varying features does not commend itself to the Buddhist; and he maintains that all change is necessarily total. That is, change means revolution, not evolution.

It has been urged that as a thing is seen to perish in a determinate place and time its destruction must be contingent upon an extraneous cause and so long as this destructive agent does not appear, it will naturally continue to exist. The hypothesis of spontaneous destruction is opposed to experience and hence unacceptable, but the Buddhists answer by saying that the whole argument of the opponent however, is vitiated by misreading of facts. The theory of an external destructive agent gives rise to logical complications. As regards the so-called non-perishable entities such as space, time, God and the like, they are mere fictions of imagination and do not exist as objective realities, as the connotation of reality is causal efficiency (arthakriyakaritva) and no causal efficiency is predictable of them. An objection has been raised about the criteria of reality. The objection is that reality cannot be supposed to consist in causal efficiency, as causal efficiency exists even in such unreal fictions as sky-lotus and the like. These fictions certainly generate an impression in the mind and thus have causal efficiency in that respect, but they cannot be accepted as real on that account.

The Buddhists defend their criteria by maintaining that prediction of causal efficiency relates to an objective reality and does not include subjective fictions. In dreams and illusions the objects that are experienced are not real objective facts, but are evolved from the imagination. It will be a sheer perversion of facts to apply to these mental fictions the standard of reality which belongs to objective reality, it cannot have any application to these fictitious representations of the imagination.

The Buddhist conception of reality is criticized in several ways by the exponents of the other Indian philosophical systems. If everything be a flux and is being continually renovated, no recognition would be possible. The Buddhists meet this objection by answering that the things in the two moments of our cognition are only similar and that we mistake them to be the same. In other words, all recognition is erroneous since similarity is mistaken in it for identity. Another criticism is that if the self be also changing every moment, it becomes difficult to account for the fact of memory. Here also the Buddhist has his explanation. He holds that each phase of experience, as it appears is wrought up into the next so that every successive phase has within it 'all the potentialities of its predecessors', which manifest themselves when conditions are favourable. Hence, though a man is not the same in any two moments, yet he is not quite different. The definition of the real as the causally efficient is also criticized. Though commonly, according to Buddhism, a series never ends, but may only be transformed into another as in the case of the seed becoming the shoot, certain exceptions are admitted of which one is the cessation of the ego-series when an Arhat dies and attains Nirvana. Here the question arises as to whether the final member of the ego-series in question is real or not. Since by hypothesis it gives rise to no successor, it is not causally efficient and cannot therefore, be real. And if that is unreal it must follow that the next previous one is unreal and so on backwards until the whole series disappears as a figment with the result that either the ideal of nirvana should be given up as never achievable or the ego-series representing the aspirant for Nirvana should be admitted as absolute non-existent.

As indicated earlier, the followers of Buddha at a later age in their earnest zeal to defend their doctrines against the attacks of the thinkers and logicians belonging to the Brahmanical school, followed subtle lines of argument for proper comprehension of which it is absolutial that a scholar will have to be fully conversant with the terms and technicalities of Nyaya applied both by the Buddhists. Within the short space of a paper it is not at all possible to present a fully convincing account of the rival schools against the theory of momentariness may be shown to be imaginary and fanciful being based on short-sighted logic and surface-view of reality. They do not at all affect the solid foundations of the doctrine of momentariness. On the contrary, they find their solution in it, which other systems have failed to afford.

Notes and References

1. Satkari Mookherjee, The Buddhist Philosophy of Universal Flux, (Calcutta 1935; Reprint, Delhi, 1975). Specially pp. 39-86.
2. Bidhubhusana Bhattacharya, K., Sanabhangavada (in Bengali), (Calcutta, 1975).
3. *Buddha*, p. 251.
4. Slokavartika, pp. 728-745.
5. Aspects of Buddhism.
6. Buddhism in Comparative Light.

13

Buddhism and Modren Society

P. Abbai

An attempt is made in this paper to explain the following aspects of Buddhism and their relevance to the modern society.

1. The concept of Dhamma,
2. Social organization in India at the time of the Buddha,
3. Buddhism and Economic operations, and
4. Political setup.

1. WHAT IS DHAMMA?

The teachings of the Buddha are known as Dhamma. The Buddha has divided his teachings into three categories. The first category is known as Dhamma, the second one is called Addhamma and the third one is Saddhamma.[1]

The functions of Saddhamma are:

1. To cleanse the minds of impurities, and
2. To make the world a kingdom of Righteousness.

How to Clean the Impurities of Mind?

What are the Impurities of Mind? The thoughts those generated from the mind, which harms the individuals as well as others are called evil thoughts or unwholesome thoughts. We can say that the mind which fills with evil thoughts, is called impure mind. Once evil thoughts are removed from the mind then mind becomes pure. The evil thoughts referred here are the three root causes of all evil, namely: thoughts of lust (craving), hate and delusion. All other passions gather round these root causes. How to remove these evil thoughts from the mind? Through right efforts these will be eliminated from the mind. The functions of right effort are: be vigilant and check all unhealthy thoughts and to cultivate, promote and maintain wholesome and pure thoughts arising in man's mind. To establish kingdom of Righteousness Dr. Ambedker said that by observing panchasila (the five precepts) and the Noble Eightfold path, we make the world the kingdom of Righteousness.

Panchasila

Panchasila (the five Precepts) is the Buddhist code of morality. These are the basic principles for the lay follower of Buddhism. They are:

1. To abstain from killing anything that breathes (including oneself).
2. To abstain from taking what is not given.
3. To abstain from sexual misconduct.
4. To abstain from speaking falsehood.
5. To abstain from liquor that causes intoxication and headlessness.

These percepts indicate the five arterial directions in which a Buddhist has to exercise his self-control. Thus the first rule calls upon him to control the passion of anger; the second the desire for material possessions; the third—the lust of the flesh; the fourth—cowardice and malevolence (the cause of untruthfulness) and the fifth—the carving for unwholesome excitement.

The practice of these precepts helps one to cultivate five ennobling virtues, which correspond, to each of the precepts. The first is the cultivation of compassion; the second—generosity and non-attachment; the third—contentment; the fourth—truthfulness and the fifth—mindfulness and clarity of the mind. By observing these precepts human progress and spiritual advancement will be achieved.

What is the Noble Eightfold Path?

The Noble Eightfold Path is the path leading to the cessation of sufferings. It is the last truth in the group of four Noble truths, which form the central conception of Buddhism. It is also known as the Middle Path because it avoids two extremes: Indulgence in sensual pleasures which is low worldly and harmful is one extreme. Self-torture in the form of severe asceticism which is painful and also harmful is the other.

This Noble Eightfold Path consists of eight factors. They are:

1. Right Understanding,
2. Right Thought,
3. Right Speech,
4. Right Action,
5. Right Livelihood,
6. Right Effort,
7. Right Mindfulness,
8. Right Concentration.

These eight factors are divided into three groups. The first two factors are in one group known as Wisdom (*Pragna).* The next three factors form another group known as Morality *(Sila)* and the last three factors form concentration (*Samadhi)* group. These three go together and supporting together. As in the case of tripod, which falls to the ground if a single leg gives away, so here one cannot function without the support of the others. Sila strengthens the meditation and meditation in turn promotes wisdom. Wisdom helps one to get rid of the clouded view of things to see life, as it really is i.e., to see life and all things pertaining to life as arising and passing away.

This middle path is a way of life to be followed, practiced and developed by each individual. It is self-disciplined in the body, word and mind, self-development and self-purification. It has nothing to do with belief, prayer, worship or ceremony. This is Buddha's Dhamma.

2. THE SOCIAL ORGANISATION IN INDIA AT THE TIME OF THE BUDDHA

(i) Does Hindu social order recognize the individuals?

(ii) Does it recognize his distinctiveness and his moral responsibilities?

These are the questions raised by Dr. Ambedkar in his article 'Hindu Social Order' and 'Its essential principles'. He said, "The Hindu social order does not recognize the individual as a center of social purpose. For the Hindu social order is based primarily on class or varna and not on individuals. Originally and formally the Hindu social order recognized four classes. (1) Brahmins, (2) Kshatriyas, (3) Vaishyas, and (4) Shudras. Today it consists of five classes, the fifth being called the 'panchamas' or 'untouchables'. In the Hindu social order, there is no room for individual merit and no consideration of individual justice . . . ".

Hinduism does not recognize fraternity because they believe that their social order is based on the doctrine that men are created from the different parts of the divinity-from the mouth, from the arms, from the thighs and from the feet. As they were created from different parts of the Devine body, they generated the belief that it must be Divine will, that they should remain separate and distinct. Hence they will not recognize fraternity. How do these castes behave towards one another? Their guiding principle is "be separate", "do not intermarry". 'do not inter dine', and 'do not touch'.

"If the Hindu social order is not based on equality and fraternity then what are the principles on which it is based? Dr. Ambedkar had given an answer for this. He said that the Hindu social order is reared on three principles. Among these the first and fore most is the principle of graded inequality. The second principle is that of fixity of occupations for each class and continuance there of by hereditary. And the third principle is fixation of people with in their respective classes. Because of these principles the lower classes cannot make any progress.

Buddhism and Social Organization

As the Hindu social organization established on inequality, Buddha opposed it route and branch. He was the strongest opponent of caste and the earliest and staunchest up holder of equality. There is no argument in favor of caste and inequality, which he did not refute. No caste, no inequality, no superiority, no inferiority. All are equal. This is what Buddha stood for.

Lord Buddha never preached that any person is super human in the world. He said, 'All are equal'. The aim of human being should be to attain Nirvana, peace and prosperity for all. Buddha preached that, as the water, whether it is from Ganga, whether it is from Jamuna or whether it is from a drainage, when it enters the sea, it is sea water, like wise there is no distinction between men when they enter his religion. All are equal in his religion.

The Buddha freely admitted into the order people from all castes and classes. The Buddha also raised the status of woman in India. During the time of the Buddha, owing to the Brahminical influence, women were not given much recognition. They were deprived of learning, participation of spiritual aspects etc. Let me quote some of the laws made by Manu regarding women.

- Women have no right to study the Vedas (Manusmriti 1X. 18).

- A woman shall not perform the daily sacrifices prescribed by the Vedas. If she dies she will go to hell. (X1.36.37)
- A wife, a son, and a slave, these three are declared to have no property.

The wealth, which they earn, is (acquired) for his to whom they belong (1X.416).

Buddhism has given equal opportunities to all, irrespective of caste, clan or class. The Buddhist social organization depends on Justice Liberty, Equality and Fraternity.

3. BUDDHISM AND ECONOMIC OPERATIONS

In the system of Chatruvarna what was the occupation of Shudra? Manu says that the most excellent occupation of a Shudra is to serve the Brahmins. If he does any thing other than this it profits him nothing. The left over food should be given to Shudra and the old clothes, so too the blighted part of the grain, so too the old furniture. Indeed, accumulation of wealth should not be made by Shudra even if he is able to do so. For the sight of mere position of wealth by a Shudra injures the Brahmin.

These are the conditions of the Shudras and Untouchables in Hindu social order. How they can maintain economic stability, when all doors of opportunities are closed by laws. The Hindus philosophy tells that you are poor and low because you had committed sins in your previous births. Because of those sins you have to suffer in this life. Do good. By your good deeds you may be born in rich and high family in next birth. This is how Hindu philosophy imposed *karma* theory.

What is Buddha's opinion on this? The Buddha discarded this view. Buddha's laws of *karma* applied only in the present life, not life after death. Buddha dislikes the poverty. A hungry man will suffer and he cannot lead a happy and righteous life. The Buddha in one of his discourses stressed the need to improve the economic conditions of the people. He explained to Anathapindica on the necessity to accumulate wealth. He said that the first reason is to make himself and his parents, wife, children; his slaves happy if one should get wealth. The second reason is to make his friends and company, happy and glad. The other reason is to help various social, spiritual organisations if one must acquire wealth. The Buddha supported the need of their earnings through rightful manner. He advised the householders for saving from their earnings. One should divide his earnings into four parts. One part of it is for his daily upkeep and that of his family. Two parts were to be invested in his business and the fourth part aside for any emergency. Buddha also advised the people to spend their income reasonably in proportion neither too much nor too little.

The Buddha not only taught about the mental and moral aspects of the people but also he preached about the social setup and economic stability in the society. There were no restrictions about the selection of occupations in Buddhism. There are no permanent divisions of occupation; anybody can take up any occupation he likes in Buddhism. In Buddhism worth is the measure of man, whereas in Hinduism birth is the measure of man. Because of equal opportunities in Buddhism everybody has taken up his interested occupation and shown their abilities and capacities and improved their social and economical conditions.

4. BUDDHISM AND POLIICAL SETUP

Prince Siddhartha became Parivrajika at the age of 29 leaving his Rajya, Rani and son Rahula. After six years of continuous efforts to study on various philosophies to eradicate the sufferings of humanity, finally he was succeeded in attaining Enlightenment and became the Buddha. Though the Buddha had transcended all worldly affairs, he still gave advises on socio, economic and political fields.

The Buddha once said, 'When the ruler of a country is just and good the ministers become just and good; when the ministers are just and good, the higher officials become just and good; when the higher officials are just and good the rank and file become just and good; when the rank and file become just and good the people become just and good'. (Angutıra Nikaya)

In the jataka, the Buddha had given ten rules for good government, known as 'Dasa Raja Dharma'. These ten rules can be applied even today by any government, which wishes to rule the country peacefully. The rules are as follows:

1. Be liberal and avoid selfishness,
2. Maintain a high moral character,
3. Be prepared to sacrifice one's own pleasure for the well being of the subject,
4. Be honest and maintain absolute integrity,
5. Be kind and gentle,
6. Lead a simple life for the subjects to emulate,
7. Be free from hatred of any kind,
8. Exercise non-violence,
9. Practice patience, and
10. Respect public opinion to promote peace and harmony.

Regarding the behaviour of rulers, he further advised:

(a) A good ruler should act impartially and should not be biased and discriminate between one particular group of subjects against another.
(b) A good ruler should not harbour any form of hatred against any of his subjects.
(c) A good ruler should shoe no fear whatsoever in the enforcement of the law, if it is justifiable.
(d) A good ruler must possess a clear understanding of the law to be enforced. It should not be enforced just because the ruler has the authority to enforce the law. It must be done in a reasonable manner and with common sense. (Cakkavatti Sihananda Sutta)

The king should always improve him self and carefully

examine his own conduct and his deeds, words and thoughts, trying to discover and listen to public opinion as to whether or not he had been guilty of any faults and mistakes in ruling the kingdom. If it is found that he rules unrighteously, the public will complain that they are ruined by the wicked ruler with unjust treatment, punishment, taxation, or other oppressions including corruption of any kind, and they will react against him in one way or another. On the contrary if he rules righteously they will bless him: 'Long live His Majesty.' (*Majjhima Nikaya*)

In the *Kutadanta Sutta,* the Buddha suggested economic development instead of force to reduce crime. The government should use the country's resources to improve the economic conditions of the country. It could embark on agricultural and rural development; provide financial support to entrepreneurs and business, provide adequate wages for workers to maintain a decent life with human dignity. If this advise of the Buddha followed by the rulers of the country, then terrorism will vanish.

The Buddha is said to be the first social reformer. He condemned caste system, recognized the equality of people, spoke on the need to improve socio-economic conditions, recognized the importance of a more equitable distribution of wealth among the rich and the poor, raised the status of woman, recommended the incorporation of humanism in government and administration, and taught that a society should not be run by greed but with consideration and compassion for the people.

References

Ambedkar, B.R., "The Buddha and His Dhamma."
Dhammanada, K. Sri, "What Buddhists Believe."
Ven, Piyadassi Thera, "The Ancient Buddhist Path."

14

Buddha's Teaching of Happiness and its Relevance for the Modern Society

Dr. U.S. Vyas

Several modern writers on Buddhism tend to believe that Buddhism is mystical and a social. One of them observes "Buddhism not being concerned with man and his welfare was equally disinterested in man and his interest. Hence jurisprudence, politics and economy were not within the scope of Buddhism . . ., and the Buddha was indifferent to status quo.[1]

There is yet another question which occurs in the context of the present day high-tech society. The situation of the world view during Buddha's time was totally different from that of today. Man had so many hardships and limitations then, but those have been overcome by dint of boon of modern high-tech. scientific inventions. Therefore what is the relevance of the Buddha's teaching for modern day society?

While encountering such questions it is essential to say at the very outset that on first thought, it might seem plausible to say that the Buddhist way is essentially private and without the concern of the material well-being of society but if we minutely examine and analyse the early and later phases of Buddhist literature, we found that the above mentioned views are unfounded. The Dhamma of the Buddha is a dynamic principle. It is compared to a raft which takes one form this shore to another.[2] The Dhamma is a principle moving towards the generation of complete social harmony in life as a whole. The essential aspects of the Dhamma are, Sila, Samadhi and Panna. Here Sila or ethical aspect of human action; is necessarily of impersonal nature. It entails a great deal of social inter-action. Every follower of the Buddha's way is expected to live within a network of human relationships. This fact is clearly manifested in the teachings of Sila such as the abstention from killing, stealing and adultery etc. There are also many teachings which basically aim at encouraging and promoting an ideal and harmonious social behaviour of a householder. One of such teaching is contained in the famous Sigalovada-sutta. Without entering into the details of the contents of this Sutta it is sufficient to point-out here that in spite of many changes in the pattern of the family life today, such teachings may be used as an efficient instrument for resolving many complicated problems of human relationships.

It is also equally true that machines and high-tech scientific discoveries have now made man's life seemingly more comfortable, happy and more dynamic. But honestly speaking man's hungers or his willing (tanha), always latent in man's consciousness have now come to surface even more. With the high-tech industrial and consumer-culture, the values in understanding of true happiness undergo a drastic change. Henceforth an excessive pressure on bio-physical structure tends to make the human being totally unfit to pace with the fast electromagnetic force of the cosmos. That leads new generation to a fix for the forth-coming days ahead.

Modernism, although contributing a lot for the material growth, has also brought forth anxieties and frustrations by creating environs and exciting explorations. Man invented machines and scientific tools to fulfil his material needs, and thereby to attain happiness, but man has now becomes slave of machines and a prey to consumer-culture. Industrial re-generation throughout the world today indulging in violence, hatred, exploitation and torture upon his fellow-beings, has made man sick of himself. Therefore the Buddha's teaching of the way of attaining the material and true happiness (in general and the Bodhisattva ideal for the way—farer of the Mahayana Buddhism) is neither obsolete nor out of date.

Although the highest conceivable happiness; according to the Buddha, is NIBBANA (Nibbanani Paramani Sukhani), wherein there is complete extinction of all desires; however the Buddha was also interested in the material happiness also. But Buddha's view of even worldly happiness was not similar to the one conceived by ancient hedonists and modern materialists. For him attainment of any form of happiness is not possible without leading a pure and disciplined life based on ethical and spiritual principles of Virtue (Sila), Concentration (Samadhi), and Wisdom (Panna). But being a highly skilful teacher he knew the difference in the mental dispositions, mental aptitudes and intellectual abilities of people. He also was aware of the universal tendency that leading completely pure life is not easy for each and every individual in hostile material and social conditions. Therefore he also pointed out those factors, which are conducive to a layman's happiness.

It is to be kept in mind clearly that the Buddha did not take life out of the context of its social and economic background. He looked at every thing by the eye of conditioned co-originations and considered that although material happiness can not be absolute in itself and is only a means for the attainment of the higher and nobler type of happiness or the supreme bliss, yet it is an indispensable means for achieving a higher form of happiness.[3] He often instructed the householder to improve their economical condition by adopting right means of livelihood and by practicing austerity and simplicity.

In reply to a question by DIGHA JANU, the Buddha, first of

all, tells him about those factors which one should possess for the attainment of the happiness in this visible word. These are:

(1) UTTHANA-SAMPADA, or a man should be skillful, efficient, well-versed and energetic in whatever profession he is engaged.
(2) ARAKKHA-SAMPADA, or he should protect his earnings earned honestly.
(3) KALYANA-MITTATA, or he should have faithful, learning, liberal and intelligent friends who can take him to the right path and help him to take away from the evil one.
(4) SAMA-JIVITATA, or he should spend his earnings in proportion to his income or he should practice the habit of living within his means.

Therefore the Buddha also said that for realizing the nobler type of happiness one should develop four factors or qualities of saddha or confidence in the higher values, Sila or the restrainments in physical and vocal acts, Caga or non-attachment with his wealth and status etc. and Panna or light of the wisdom.[4]

Addressing Anathapindika, his most devoted lay-disciple and famous trader of Sravasti, the Buddha admits four types of happiness for a house-holder:

(1) **Athi-Surha**, the happiness caused by the thinking that I have earned wealth by just means.
(2) **Bhoga-Surha**, the happiness caused by spending his earnings for himself, his family and meritorious acts.
(3) **Anana-Surha**, happiness caused by the feeling that I am free from the debts.
(4) **Anavajja-Sukha**, happiness experienced due to leading a faultless and pure life and committing no evil in thought, speech or physical acts.[5]

The Buddha then reminded the trader that economic and material happiness is not worth one sixteenth part of the spiritual happiness arising out of faultless and holy life.

These few references of the nectar-like words of Tathagata amply confirm the fact that the way of life adopted by the people in the modern society can never help in the realization of true happiness. From this it also follows that modern economical growth, although a prerequiaite for human happiness to some extent, but this progress is not real and true if it devoid of a spiritual and moral values. The Dhamma of the Buddha always lays great stress on the development of values for a happy, peaceful and contended society. Any expectation for leading a happy life with a mental attitude inflicted with social mental factors such as attachment, hatred and false notion is nothing but mere day-dream. Without uprooting the root of desire (Tanha) any happiness caused by material progress and by the satisfaction of the sense-organs would be transitory only.

Modern man must be aware of the truth that any momentary sensation agreeing with our desire can not be called as a sensation of true happiness as after sometime it may lose all its value and may lose all its value and may thereby effect unhappiness. I may be as happy as possible by the satisfaction of my particular will, but when the object conferring this satisfaction of will is taken away, it changes into suffering, which would be even greater. Thus there can be no true happiness in the satisfaction of our desire regarding worldly objects which all are impermanent or transitory by nature.

Following words of the Buddha are to be kept by those who seek happiness in sensuous Pleasures:

(a) "Ko nu haso kimanando
Niccam pajjalite sati
Andhakarena onaddha
Pakasam va cavesatha."[6]

(b) "Sukho viveko tutthassa, sutadhammasa passato,
Avyapajjam sukham loke, panabhutesu samyamo
Sukha viragata loke kamanam samatikkamo
A Smimanassa yo vinayo, etam ve paramani sukham."[7]

Notes and References

1. Milamed Samual, Max, M., 'Spinoja and Buddha'. p. 272.
2. Majjhima-Nikaya, I, p. 179 (PTS).
3. Majjhima Nikaya, attha-Katha, I, p. 290 if. (PTS).
4. Anguttara-Nikaya, 4.281-(PTS).
5. Digha-Nikaya.
6. Dhamma-Pada, 146.
7. Maha-Vagga mucalinda-katha, 1-3 (PTS).

15

Philosophical out Look on Dukkha in Buddhist Tradition

Dr. S. Penchalaiah

"If one speaks or acts with a wicked mind then sufferings follow one even as the wheel, the hoof of the ox. If one speaks or acts with a pure mind, then happiness follows one even as the shadow that never leaves". (Dhammapada—Verse-I).

The present paper is an attempt to understand and interpret Buddhism in global perspective from the earliest times to the present day. Buddhism presents numerous aspects, viz., philosophy, psychology, religion, cosmology, literature, language, socio-economical thought, dance, arts, painting, cultural and historical development in modern global perspective. Human life as a whole is full of suffering (sarvam dukkam). Birth, diseases, old age and death constitute the nature of human suffering. However man is exposed to physical, mental and spiritual suffering.

The philosophical inquiry in Indian tradition had its origin in man's need to extricate himself from suffering of dukka. Indian Philosophy thereby becomes 'a way of life' not merely 'a way of thought'. The aim of a philosophical wisdom is not merely the satisfaction of intellectual curiosity, but mainly an enlightened life led with far sightedness, foresight and insight.[1]

The term 'Dukkha' is derived from the Pāli language (sanskriti-Duhkka) consists of a combination of two syllables 'du' and 'kha'. Etymologically, the term 'dukkha' is said to be derived either from prefix 'du' plus the root 'kha' (du-difficulty; kha- to endure). Dukkha is used in the sense of contemptible (du) and emptiness (kha). Therefore, dukkha means, 'contemptible void'. It is opposed to sukkha or pleasure. Buddhaghosa has given another meaning of the word dukkha. The word 'du' has the sense 'vile' (kucchita), it signifies something bad, disagreeable, uncomfortable. In the ordinary sense dukkha refers to suffering bad, disagreeable, uncomfortable. In the ordinary sense dukkha refers to suffering, sorrow, pain, misery, discomfort, as opposed to the word 'sukkha', meaning happiness, pleasure, comfort, etc,. The philosophical meaning of the word 'dukkha', is imperfection, impermanence, emptiness, lack of wholeness, insubstantiality. It is therefore difficult to find one word meaning to embrace the whole concept of dukkha. Although some times identified with pain, suffering is better understood as a highly unpleasant emotional state associated with considerable pain or distress.[2]

The Vedas formed the source for philosophical speculation in the Indian scene. The Vedic sages prayed for a life free from pain in their daily lives. They began to please their deities either through hymns (mantras) or through sacrifices or both. Their aim was to attain a state of freedom from pain originating in the want of day to day requirements such as food, cattle and so on.

Similarly, in the Upanisadic period a clear demarcation was drawn between the two forms of suffering viz., empirical and transcendental. The empirical suffering refers to suffering of the body and mind viz; fever, injury, and natural calamities like floods, storms, earth-quakes. On the other hand the transcendental suffering is more threatening than the empirical. This kind of suffering arises out of ignorance (avidya).[3]

Avidya is the root cause of all sufferings. It is the failure of discriminating the real, the eternal self from the apparent, impermanent body that leads to the tragedy of man. The self (atman) is neither born nor does it die.[4] The Chandogya Upanisad confirms that it is the self-knowledge or self-realisation that helps us to overcome suffering.[5] Thus, on the whole, suffering is due to ignorance about the true nature of reality. It is due to this ignorance that man performs actions with a selfish motive.

The sixth century B.C. was remarkable for the spiritual unrest and intellectual ferment in India. It witnessed an upsurge of religio-philosophical fermentation and spiritual awakening. A number of teachers[6] both householders and recluses, kept themselves consistently engaged in enquiring into the nature of reality and continued to preach Buddha's doctrines among the people.

Buddha was mainly concerned with the existing problem of life. He advised his followers not to indulge in speculative ideas. He confronted with the basic problem-the problem of suffering. He prescribed a path, which would lead human beings from the state of perpetual suffering to the state of salvation (Nibbana). He was Gouthama Siddhartha or Sakhya Simha or Sakhya Muni, the Light of Asia, the greatest religious teacher of the world. Gouthama was the founder of Buddhism. The life of Buddha is fairly well known. It needs no repetition.

At the ripe age of 80, in the year of 543 B.C.,[8] the Buddha fell ill.[9] On his deathbed under two sala trees in the sala grove of the Mallas, he explained to his disciples that they would not be left without the teacher, for, hereafter 'the doctrine *(dhamma)* and discipline *(vinaya)* would continue to guide them. In the last speech of Lord Buddha said, "I have taught you, that shall be your teacher, when I am gone, behold now, monks I exhort you. Subject of decay or component things. Therefore, work out your salvation with diligence."[10]

Our knowledge about the Buddha's teachings depends today mainly on the three great collections of books called *'Ti-pitikas*[11] viz., The Vinaya Pitika (collection of descriptions, containing the rules of the monastic order), The Sutta-Pitika (collection of discourses consisting of various books of discourses, dialogues, verses, stories and so on and dealing with the doctrine proper as summarised into the *Four Noble Truths*[12] and the Abjidhamma-Pitika (the philosophical collection, asserting the teachings of the Sutta pitika in a strictly systematic and philosophical forms). These three contain information only in Pāli language. In later collections, Buddhism adopted Sanskrit for philosophical discussion and thus the enormous Buddhist literature in Sanskrit came to have developed.

In respect of religious principles Buddhism is divided into the two great well-known schools—The Hinayana or Theravada and The Mahayana (the great vehicle). Further, the Hinayana which is usually regarded as the original orthodox school of Buddhism is followed in Ceylon, Burma, Thailand, Combodia and Vettigon in East Pakistan, while the Mahayana Buddhism developed later and followed in countries like India, China, Tibet, Japan, Mangolia, Korea and so on.

The Mahayana school is divided into two sections: 1. Madhyamika and 2. The Yogacara. Similarly the Hinayana school is also of two kinds: 1. The Soutrantika and 2. Vaibhasika. Even though there are certain differences, with regard to some beliefs, practices and so on, but there is no change on the most important teaching of Buddha.

Buddhism is not dogmatic and does not contain elaborate systems of rites, rules, or prayers. But it is a way of life with purity in thinking, speaking and acting. It is a practical and rational way of life based on morality *(sila)*, concentration *(samadhi)* and wisdom (panna) and culminating in liberating insight. Goutama was known as a man of par excellence because of the perfection of his 'humanness'. To quote the Buddha "O Monks one man whose birth is for the welfare and benefit of the many . . . is the tathagata, who is an arahant, a fully enlightened One."[13]

Man's position according to Buddhism is supreme. Man is his own saviour and master and there is no higher being or power that sits in judgement over his destiny. He has the power to develop and liberate himself from the bondage through his own personal effort and intelligence. Buddha says, the knowledge and wisdom as the key virtue. Wisdom[14] is usually developed by the method of critical reflection. That is to say, one has to learn, to think, to investigate and to understand things for oneself. Thus the Buddha's teaching is qualified as *ehi-passika*, inviting you to come and see but not to come and believe. Buddha advised his disciples 'not to accept any thing by mere report, tradition or hearsay, nor by authority of religious texts, nor by mere logic or inference, nor by considering appearances, nor delight in speculative opinions, nor by seeming possibilities, and nor upon the idea, this is your teacher'.[15] But when you know for yourselves—these things are not good, conducing to lose and sorrow—then reject them. When you know for yourselves—those things are good and conducive to welfare and happiness, then follow them.

The Enlightened One, further says, "one thing only I teach: suffering and the destruction of suffering." "*Now this is the Noble Truth*" of suffering, birth is suffering, disease is suffering, death is suffering, sorrow, grief, pain, lamentations are suffering, union with unpleasant things are suffering, suffering from the beloved objects is suffering unsatisfied. Desires are suffering; in short the world is full of suffering.[16] Buddha advised his followers to cross the ocean of samsara by doing good to others instead of harming others or harming one's own self. The way to nirvana is through self-control, self-restraint and elimination of passions; compassion towards all creatures, men, birds and beasts; and service of the poor and the weak. When the Buddha preceded his noble and glorious doctrine, it attracted people from all walks of life; rich and poor, high and lowly. The Brahmins did not oppose Buddha's philosophical teachings, but they did not like Buddha's concept of equality.[17]

Buddhaghosa in his *Visuddhimagga*, has divided dukkha into

four kinds[18] viz., Concealed suffering (*Paticchanna-dukkha*), Exposed suffering (Appaticchanna-dukkha), Indirect suffering (Pariyaya-dukkha), and Direct suffering (Nippariyaya-dukkha). These provide us with insight into the Buddhist conception of dukkha. Let us know these kinds of sufferings in brief. 1. Concealed suffering (Paticchanna-dukkha): The physical and mental afflictions such as head-ache, tooth-ache, lust, hatred are called concealed suffering. It has also called un-evident suffering. 2. Exposed suffering (Appaticchanna-dukkha): It is opposed to the concealed suffering, the afflictions produced by the thirty two tortures and so on are termed as concealed suffering. The inflictions such as, wound, stroke etc., are exposed suffering. Indirect suffering (Pariyaya-dukkha): Except for painful feeling on 'dukkhavedana', all kinds of dukkha given in the exposition of the First Noble Truth beginning with 'birth' are called 'indirect suffering', because they are the base for one or other kinds of suffering. 4. Direct suffering (Nippariyaya-dukkha): Intrinsic suffering that is painful feeling, which is referred to as 'dukkhadukkha' is called direct suffering. This type of suffering is inherent in us.

In the *Mahadukkhakkhandha-sutta*[19] and in the Culadukkhakkhandha-Sutta, the different kinds of dukkha are explained. Perhaps, a discussion of few more important aspects of dukkha may lead to a comprehensive view of the concept of dukkha. The following, for instance, will be crucial for our discussion hereunder.

KINDS OF SUFFERING

1. Natural Suffering (*svabhava dukkha*)[20]

They are birth, old age, death (jati jara marana). The three are not by themselves suffering, being as they are, but they are natural processes. They are inevitable to all in the sense that having taken birth one must suffer old age and death. Birth is suffering because it conveys the painful and dangerous conditions to the child itself leading to a long road of sufferings and dangers of various kinds. The physical decline is suffering in the manifests with more signs of decay. Death is included in suffering since, it is preceded by severe and unbearable pain. Birth, old age, physical decline, and death are unpleasant to every one.

2. Occasional Suffering (*pakinnaka dukkha*)[21]

Body knows, however, they are unavoidable, sorrow, pain, grief, unpleasant dissociation from the pleasant. Their daily sufferings are regarded as occasional sufferings viz., the rich and the poor; the young and the old; the black and the white; the long and the short and etc. Such a people have under-developed minds, which are vulnerable to influence, which occur to overpower them.

3. Constant Sufferings (*Nibadda dukkha*)[22]

The regular physical needs and the bodily feeling of hunger, thirst, heat, cold are also sufferings. They are constant sufferings. These various aspects of sufferings are undeniable proofs showing, how a person is over loaded by the burdens and still he wants to live and be comfortable.

4. Sufferings produced by Diseases (*Vyadhi dukkha*)

These are also unavoidable some times, the body has contracted some disease from outside and at other times because the systems of the body itself have malfunctioned either through over work or through age. All kinds of diseases bring about to work, and are a drain on money earned with great difficulty.

5. Consuming Sufferings (*Santapa Dukkha*)[23]

These are the sufferings produced by defilement's (*klesas).* Generally, the fires (udhreka) of birth, old age, illness and death consume men and animals. These are the fires connected with the body. These consume their minds—namely-lust, anger, delusion and others. Fires of this kind—those that burn the mind are most powerful in their consuming power.

A mind consumed by lust is tortured by it because, it has

attached itself all the time to that object which stimulates lust. As long as the lust for that consumed by sorrow, grief, or lamentation and depression. In the case of anger, it is an immediate cause of violence and finally it leads to hatred or ill-will and turns to violence or cruelty. Delusion is also another type of fire, which is 'behind the scenes' in all kinds of doings with the wrong cause of action taken. What results is a chain of untold suffering by which the mind is incessantly burnt.

6. Sufferings are Results of Kamic (*vipaka dukkha*)

These are described as being or remorse which results from indulgence in evil doing. As a result, there is downfall and ruin and then the miseries encountered in the various realms of woe. Buddha says that never is there any thing more powerful than forces of *Kamma (karma)*.

7. Sufferings Produced by Quarrel (*Vivada moolaka dukkha*)

This implies sufferings as a result of conflicting ideas and interest. For instance, murders become massacres and a personal feud develops into a national or international war.

8. Sufferings of Characteristic of Aggregates (*Dukkha khanda*)

This kind of suffering refers to the existence of the five aggregates namely—corporeality (roopa), feeling (vedana), perception (sanna), mental formations (sankhara) and consciousness (vijnana), which are the seat of all suffering.

Buddhism is a religion of reason as well as of salvation. The Buddha never rejected whatever is found in reason and is in accordance with objective truth, no matter who stated it. Some of the Indian philosophical systems started their enquiry with metaphysical speculations that these discussions did not seem directly relevant to eliminating man's suffering. It was the Buddha who directly paid attention to man's way of life that leads him beyond suffering. Strictly speaking, the entire Buddhist philosophy is nothing but an attempt to understand human suffering and redeem man from the same.[24]

The very first stanza of Dhammapada says: "mano pubbangama Dhamma ; mano settha mano maya; mannasa ve paduthena; Bhasati va karoti va; Tato nam dukkhamanveti; Cakkam va vahato padam". 'Mind is the forerunner of all existence, mind is the chief, it is all mental, if one evil-mind speaks or acts; suffering follows him like wheels of the cart of the footsteps, of the Bullocks.

The Buddhist way of life is, therefore a training which we have to undergo for the attainment of this high ideal. The practical path is technically called 'Noble-Eight-fold path (Ariya-atthangikamagga), that leads to the solution of the problem of dukka. The Noble-Eightfold path is said to be Buddhist way of life and contains all ethical teachings and practices of Buddhism. Buddha says "the purpose of practicing the Noble-Eightfold path, is to develop full understanding the penetration of greed, hatred, strong language, (angry-speech) delusion, enmity, hypocrisy, malice, envy, avarice, deceit, obstinacy, pride, arrogance, intoxication and indolence and for their complete annihilation, overcoming, vanishing, extenuation, abandoning, destruction, renunciation and the detachment there from." There are five fundamental moral activities (Panca Silas) to overcome the problem of suffering. If we practice pancasilas we do not feel desire, (tanha), envy, anger, pride, and jealousy. Finally, our ignorance is removed. The Buddhist way of life is, therefore, a training which we have to undergo for the attainment of these higher ideals.

Buddha's main objective was to bring about reformation in religious practices and return to the basic principles which are the development of a new type of free man, free from all prejudices, intent on working out his own future with one's self as one's light (attadipa). Further, Buddha says, all human beings are alike and to divide them artificially is a folly. In the case of animal life there are different varieties based on different essential characteristics. So is the case of plants. But there do not exist such differences which justify classification of human beings into watertight compartments as all men are one and the same in their essential characteristics. Therefore, the Buddha asserted in a forceful manner that worth based on deeds, rather than birth, an accidental thing, should be the measure of man. His humanism crossed racial and national barriers and spread all over the world. Thus, desire is the root cause of avarice, anger, hatred, malice, envy, rivalry, jealousy, hypocrisy, deceit, pride, arrogance and ignorance and has ruined individuals and nations. Therefore, we can see that the cause of suffering is within us and the same is in our power to remove this cause and attain happiness. While we have removed the evils from our heart, these will arise the spark called ***Bodhi*** (***Enlightenment***), which bring us serenity, peace, platonic love and perfect happiness.

The great contribution of Buddhism is the establishment of a simple religion, which could be followed and understood by all the people. Rites, rituals, yajnas and caste system have complicated the Vedic religion. Buddha's principles of Ahimsa led to the disappearances of the animal sacrifice from Hindu religion, and complicated yajna etc., became very few and unpopular. Lord Buddha broke the bonds of caste-system and superstitions and paved the way for practical unity of the people.

Finally to quote Jandhyala Papayyasastri (Karunasri), the author of Pushpavilapam, who paid a glorious tribute to Buddha, 'you have been born in the land of Buddha but yet you do not have natural love and compassion for all living beings; you are a killer who have no regard for living things; your life has become impure.' He says, 'only love should be the beginning and the end of all our actions in the world, and selfless service should activate all people.'

> *'The path (magga) without a goal is empty and the goal without path is blind.*
> *Apart from upholding Nibbana as the highest goal of religious life'.*

Notes and References

1. Chatterjee, S.C., An Introduction to Indian Philosophy, p. 12.
2. Edward Craig (Ed.), Encyclopaedia of Philosophy, Vol. VI, p. 214.
3. Chandogya Upanishad, VII. 1.5
4. The Bhagavad Gita, IInd, Chapter, 20th sloka; Kathopanisad, 1.2, 1.8.

5. Chandogya Upanishad, VII. 1.2.
6. When the Buddha began his carrier as a teacher there were many other teachers who preached their own views on the problem of suffering. Of all the various teaches of in time Six of teachers were well known, namely, 1. Puurana kassapa, 2. Makkali gosali, 3. Ajita kesakambala, 4. Pukudha kacchayaka, 5. Sanjnaya belatta putta, and 6. Niganta sata putta.
   Buddha's personal name was Siddhattha (Sanskrit: Siddhartha) and his clan name was Gotama Sankrit: Goutama). He was some times called Siddhattha Goutama.
7. Buddhavamsa, pp. 16, 27, 65. The four sights an known as Deva-Dutta or Divine Messanger.
8. The most of the Modern scholar's take this is to be 483 B.C.
9. According to some scholars opinion that it is poisonous mushrooms.
10. Mahaparinibbana Sutta, No. 16.
11. *International Encyclopaedia of Buddhism*, Vol. 24, Ed, Nagendra Kumar Singh, p. 647.
12. *Ibid.*, p. 1932.
13. Ahir, D.C., *Heritage of Buddhism,* p. 250.
14. Sukumar Dutt, Buddhisit Monks and Monasteries of India, pp. 119-121.
15. Mahadukkhakkhandha-Sutta, Nos. 13, 14.
16. Hermann Oldenberg, Buddhism His life, His Doctrine, His Orders, p. 211.
17. Jafar Mahmud, Buddhism: Religion and Meditation, p. 254.
18. Dasgupta Surendranath, A History of Indian Philosophy, Vol. I, p. 324.
19. *Ibid.*, p. 426.
20. Belvalkar, S.K. and Ranade, R.D., History of Indian Philosophy, Vol. II, p. 455.
21. International Encyclopaedia of Buddhism, Vol. 24 Ed., Nagendra Kumar Singh, p. 6.
22. Rhyas Davids, Dialogues of the Buddha, Part I, pp. 62-63.
23. Nagendra, Kumar, (Ed.) International Encyclopaedia of Buddhism, Vol. 30; Monier-William, M., Buddhism, pp. 126-128.
24. Papayya Sastri Jandhyala, Buddhadevuni-Punarahvamu, Pushpavilapam. (Telugu).

References

Ahir, D.C., *Heritage of Buddhism*, B.R. Publishing, Delhi, 1989.

Barathelemy, Saint—Hilaire, The Buddha and His Religion, Munshiram Manoharlal Publishers, New Delhi, 1997.

Belvalkar, S.K, and Ranade, R.D., History of Indian Philosophy, Vol. II, Bilvakunja Publishing House, Poona, 1927.

Buddhaghosa, (5th century AD) Visuddhimgga (tr) Bhikku Nanmoli, The Path of Purification, Colombo, 1956.

Chatterjee, S.C. and Datta, D.M., An Introduction to Indian Philosophy, University of Calcutta, 1984.

Dasgupta Surendranath, A History of Indian Philosophy, Vol. I, Motilal Banaridass, Delhi, 1997.

David, Buddhism and Brahmanism, International Encyclopaedia of Buddhism Ed., Nagendra Kumar Singh, Vol. 32, Anmol Publications Pvt. Ltd., New Delhi, 1997.

Edward Craig (Ed) *Encyclopaedia of Philosophy*, Vol. VI, Routledge, Co., New York, 1998.

Edward J. Thomas, *The History of Buddhist Thought*, Munishiram Manoharlal Publishers Pvt. Ltd., New Delhi, 1997.

Gandhi, M.K., *My Religion*, Navajeevan Publishing House, Ahmedabad 1958.

Harvey, P., *An Introduction to Buddhism: Teachings, History and Practices*, Cambridge University Press, New York, 1990.

Hermann Oldenberg, *Buddha, His Life, His Doctrine, His Order*, Aryan Books International, New Delhi, 1996.

Iqbal Singh, Goutama Buddha, Oxford University Press, Calcutta, 1998.

Jafar Mahmud, *Buddhism: Religion and Meditation*, A.P.H. Publishing Corporation, New Delhi, 1998.

Jatava, D.R., *Philosophy of Buddhism and Marx*, National Publishing Home, New Delhi, 1998.

Lord Chalmers, *Buddha's Teachings*, Motilal Banaridass Publishers, Delhi.

Monier-William, M., *Buddhism*, Munshiram Manoharlal Publishers, New Delhi, 1995.

Nagendra, Kumar, (Ed) *International Encyclopaedia of Buddhism*, Anmol Publications Pvt. Ltd, New Delhi, 1997.

Schweitzer, Albert, *Indian Thought and its Development*, Wilco Publication 1960.

Shastri, M.N., *The History of Buddhism*, Aruam Books International, New Delhi 1996.

Steeven Collins, *Nirvana and Other Buddhist Felicities*, Cambridge University, 1998.

Sinha Jadunath, *Outlines of Indian Philosophy*, New Central Book Agency, Calcutta, 1992.

Thomas, E.J., *The Life of Buddha*, Routledge & Kegan Pal, London, 1975.

16

The Concept of Astangamarga and its Impact on Modern Society

Dr. N. Susheela

Do we practice *Dharma* where we are confronted with our traditional scriptures? Or do we get the dharma through *Sravana, manana,* and *nididhyasana*? Or where do we find the *Dharma* in this physical world? Or do we find dharma in our ancient Hindu society? All these questions crop up, if we analyse the concept of *dharma*. From the times of *Sruti* to *Smriti*, we find that there is a lot of disparities in the Hindu society. In the ancient times, Hindu society was originally divided into four varnas.[1] The sacred Hindu lawgiver Manu's social system was given psychophysical conflicts among the Hindus. He classified the Hindu caste system and presented rules and duties systematically. Manu and other Law givers have prescribed some rules and regulations for Sudras in general and untouchables in particular.

Goutama Buddha, born in the sixth century BC, found a degenerate society with caste distinctions and other social evils. Goutama was a true researcher of Hindu religion.

Lord Goutama was an ethical teacher and social reformer.

The message of his enlightenment points to man the way of life that leads beyond suffering. He disliked metaphysical discussions devoid of practical utility.[2] Buddha says unprofitable and unanswerable questions are treated as metaphysical questions. They are ethically useless and intellectually uncertain. Buddha says that the most important question is the problem of suffering, its origin and the path leading to its cessation. These four questions are nothing but four Noble Truths.[3]

Buddha introduced Eight-fold-paths for cessation of suffering. The path recommended by Buddha consists of eight steps or rules and is, therefore, called the eightfold noble path (*astanga-margas.*).[4] This gives in a nutshell the essentials of Buddha's ethics. This path is open to all, monks as well as laymen.[5]

1. Right Views (*Samyagdrsti*)

The first factor of the path is known as "right view" or right understanding, which means to understand things as they really are, and not as they appear to be. It is the forerunner of the entire path, the guide for all the factors, enabling us to understand our starting point, our destination, and the successive land makers to pass us practice advances.

To practice right view, one should follow a certain procedure, Usually, an ordinary man develops his wisdom through listening to the suggestions of others. For him, the process of view will start from faith towards the instructor.

There are two kind of views[6] viz; right view and wrong view. The former corresponds to what is real, the latter deviates from the real and confirms the false in its place. If we have a right view, that view will steer us towards right action and thereby towards freedom from suffering.

Now what is Right view? It is the understanding of suffering, understanding of the origin of suffering, understanding of the extinction of suffering and understanding path leading to the extinction of suffering.[7] As ignorance, i.e., wrong views (mithyadrsti) about the self and the world, is the root cause of our sufferings, it is natural that the first step of moral reformation provides right views or the knowledge of truth. It is the knowledge of these truths alone, and not any theoretical speculations regarding nature and self, which according to Buddha, helps moral reformation, and leads us towards the goal—*Nirvana*.[8]

2. Right Thought (*Samyaksankalpa*)

Right thought which is the second factor of the path, is the outcome of right view. It reaches its climax in a direct institution of those same truths. Grasped with a clarity tantamount to enlightenment. Thus it can be said that the right view of the four Noble truths forms both the beginning and the culmination of the way to the end of suffering. Each kind of right thought of *Sammasakappa* counters the corresponding kind of wrong thought. The Buddha discovered this two fold division of thought in the period of his enlightenment. The Buddha describes his teachings as running contrary to the way of the world. The way of the world is the way of desire and the unenlightened who follow this way flow with the current desire seeking happiness by pursuing the objects in which they imagine and they will find fulfillment.[9]

3. Right Speech (*Samyagvak*)

Right determination should not remain a mere 'pious wish' but must issue forth into action. Right determination should be able to guide and control our speech, to begin with. The result would be right speech consisting abstention from lying, slander, unkind words and frivolous talk. According to the Buddha, right speech is divided into four components namely; abstention from false speech, abstention from slanderous speech, abstention from harsh speech and abstention from idle talk. When one abstains form these forms of wrong and harmful speech, one naturally has to speak the truth, has to use words that are friendly and benevolent, pleasant and gentle, meaningful and useful. Thus, speech should not be dominated by unwholesome thoughts by greed, anger, jealousy, pride, selfishness and so on.

Right speech, right action and right livelihood are together grouped under the first course of practical training division, that is moral discipline or *sila.*[10]

4. Right Action (*Samyakkrmanta*)

Right action is the second factor under moral discipline (sila). It means abstinence from three wrong actions viz; killing living beings, stealing what is not given and sexual misconduct. Positively it implies compassion for all living beings; taking only those things that are given; and leading a pure and chaste life.

Right determination should end in right action or good conduct which includes the *panaca-Sila* viz; the five vows for desisting form killing, stealing, sensuality, lying and intoxication.[11]

5. Right Lively-hood (*Samyagajiva*)

Right livelihood is the third and last factor under moral conduct which refers to how one earns one's living in a righteous way. It is an extension of the two other factors of right speech and right action which refer to the respect for truth, life, property and personal relationship. Right livelihood means that one should earn a living without violating these principles of moral conduct. The virtue about right livelihood is designed to bring true happiness to the individual and society and to promote unity and proper relations among people.[12]

6. Right Effort (*Samyagvyama*)

The remaining three factors of the Noble-eight-fold path are factors for the development of wisdom through the purification of the mind. They are right effort, right mindfulness and right concentration. These factors when practiced, enable a person to strengthen and again control over the mind, thereby ensuring that his actions will continue to be good and that his mind is being prepared to realize the truth, which will open the door to freedom, to enlightenment.[13]

Right effort means that we cultivate a positive attitude and have enthusiasm in the things we do, whether in our career or in our practice of the dharma. Moreover, as the mind cannot be kept empty, one should constantly endeavor to fill the mind with good ideas and retain such ideas in the mind. This rule points out that even the one who is at high up on the path cannot afford to take a moral holiday without running the risk of slipping down.

7. Right Mindfulness (*Samyaksmrti*)

The ultimate truth of *dhamma*, is not something mysterious and remote, but the truth of our own experience. What brings the field of experience into focus and makes it accessible to insight is mental faculty called mindfulness. Mindfulness, which is awareness, is a certain function of the mind. Right mindfulness or constant remembrance of the perishable nature of thing. One should constantly remember and contemplate the body as body, sensations as sensations, mind as mind, mental state as mental state. About any of these one should not think, 'This am I', or 'This is mine'.[14] The right mindfulness should be applied to each and everything we do. In all our movements we are expected to be mindful. Whether we walk, stand or sit, whether we speak, keep silent, eat, drink or answer the call of nature in all these and in all other activities we should be mindful and wide awake. "Mindfulness, monks, I declare, is essential in all things everywhere", says the Buddha.

8. Right Concentration (*Samyadsamadhi*)

The eighth factor of the path is 'Right concentration'. In Buddhist terminology, Samadhi literally means 'placing firmly together' or 'putting together' with reference to the state of mind and method formed to induce that state. Etymologically, it means 'one—pointedness' of mind upon a single object. By virtue of having quality of one pointedness, the English word 'concentration' is frequently used as synonymous with Samadhi.

This path gives rise to vision, knowledge, peace, higher wisdom, enlightenment or nibbana.[15] This should be understood that 'Samadhi', which comes under the name 'sammasamadhithi', is one of the original terms employed by the Buddha himself. Right concentration, in its widest sense, is a kind of mental concentration which is present in every wholesome state of mind and hence is accompanied by the least right though, right effort and right mindfulness wrong concentration is present in wholesome state of mind, and hence is only possible in the sensuous, not in higher sphere. 'Samadhi' used alone always stands in the sutta for 'Sammasamadhi'.

Thus there is a need to practice the above eight-fold path in day-today life. Since Buddhism allows equal status to all classes of people there will be no scope for group clashes among various castes. No importance is given to caste in Buddhism. As a result of which inter-caste marriages are held bringing Harmony among the people belonging to that religion in the modern society. Further, we observe that, on the occasion of the marriage, the Hindus follow the custom of taking an oath (agni sakshi wedding) in the presence of a burning fire. Whereas the followers of Buddhism take their oath in the marriage ceremony considering one's own Soul as a witness (manassakshi). Also the Buddhists celebrate the marriages without any pomp and luxury, just in the presence of their kith and kin with a limited number of their friends and well wishers thus avoiding unnecessary expenditure on the part of marriages. This will naturally encourage the youth in shaping their future. This is one of the reasons why Buddhism is still very popular in far-east countries.

Thus, Goutama's method was not mythical but a combination of rational, empirical, ethical and spiritual. In Buddhism we discover a ray of hope and light for all communities. The teachings of Buddha's *Astangamargas,* thus respect human values and make humanity live as human beings keeping away their inhuman ways of living.

If we practice *Astangmarga,* we can create an ideal society.

Notes and References

1. Sivananda, B.S., Srimad Bhagavad Geeta, IVth Chapt. p. 159.
2. Rhys Davids, *Dialogues of Buddha*, pp. 187-88.
3. Barathelemy Saint-Hilaire, *The Buddha and His Religion*, pp. 90-91.
4. Edward J. Thomas, *The History of Buddhist Thought*, pp. 189-194.

5. Vide Rhys Davids, *Dialogues*, I. pp. 62-63.
6. Sastri, M.N., *The History of Buddhism*, p. 164.
7. Jatva D.R., *Philosophy of Buddhism and Marx*, p. 39.
8. David, *Buddhism and Religion, International Encyclopedia of Buddhism* Ed., Nagendra Kumar Singh, Vol. 32, p. 3610.
9. Lord Chalmers, *Buddha's Teaching*, Delhi, p. 78.
10. Herman Oldenberg, *Buddha, His Life, His Doctrine*, p. 305.
11. *Ibid.*, p. 297.
12. Rhyas David, *Dialogues of the Buddha*, p. 61.
13. *Ibid.*, p. 62.
14. Jafae Mahammad, *Buddhism, Religion and Meditation*, p. 49.
15. The word Nibbana or Nirvana is a state of nothingness it is a matter of self-realization. Nibbanam paramam sukham (Nibbana is bliss supreme).

17

Theravadic Buddhism and Modern World

Ven M. Ratanjothy Thero

1. What is Buddhism?

Sabba Pappasa Akaranam, Kusalassa Upasampada, Sacitta Pariyodapanam, Etana Buddhanu Sasanam:

> "Refain from evil, Do good, purify your mind, these are the teachings of Lord Buddha."

2. The Noble Triple Gem

Lord Buddha—Theravada tradition admits human nature of the Buddha. He is considered to be the supreme human being; not because he was born differently than others, his body was also subjected to human bodily pain and decay; but because he cultivated great qualities such as 'Araham' (not doing sinful actions even secretly), 'SammaSamBuddha' (fully enlightened one), 'Vijjacaranasampanno' etc.

Dhamma/Dharma—Lord Buddha founded 'Dhamma Vinaya' the "doctrine and discipline." Dhamma is the ultimate truth or reality. We describe Dhamma through words such as 'Sanditthiko' (here-and-now), 'Akalika (timeless), 'Ehipassika' (come and see, not come and believe) etc.

What attracts in the modern world is this open-minded quality, illustrated in Kalama Sutta in Anguttara Nikaya. "Do not believe in anything (simply) because you have heard it. Do not believe in traditions because they have been handed down for many generations. Do not believe in anything because it is spoken and rumored by many. Do not believe in anything (simply) because it is found written in your religious books. Do not believe in anything merely on the authority of your teachers and elders. But after observation and analysis when you find that anything agrees with reason and is conductive to the good and benefit of one and all then accept it and live up to it."

Further, Buddha's preaching shows no attachment to any almighty God or to oneself. According to the first stanza of 'Dhammapada', 'manopubbanga ma dhamma' which says that one is responsible for one's good and bad deeds, and one will be rewarded for his meritorious deeds, vice versa; the neo- logic and scientific base of Buddhism is clearly seen in this modern era.

Sangha—To provide a social structure supportive of the practice of Dhamma, and to preserve teachings of posterity, the Buddha established the order of 'Sangha'—'Bhikkus' (monks) and 'Bhikkunis' (nuns). The teachings were passed down orally within the monastic community. In keeping with an oral tradition that long predated Lord Buddha (250 B.C.).

3. Theravadic Buddhism, How it Began

Within two centuries after the Buddha's passing, as the Dharma spread out of India, several different interpretations of some of Buddha's original doctrine arose leading to schools of many traditions. One of these sects, the 'Mahasanghika' eventually gave arise to a reform movement that called itself 'Mahayana', (the greater vehicle), that referred to the other schools disparagingly as 'Hinayana/Theravada' (the lesser vehicle). Theravada, the "doctrine of the Elders" is one of the schools of Buddhism that draws its scriptural inspiration from the texts of the pali Tipitaka, which scholars generally accept as containing the earliest surviving record of the Buddha's teachings. For many centuries, Theravada had been predominant religion of South- East Asia. In recent decades Theravada has begun to take root in the West. The West has begun to take notice of Theravada's unique and spiritual legacy and teachings of awakening.

4. What is in Theravadic Buddhism?

Lord Buddha laid out essential framework upon which all his later teachings were based. This framework consists of the four noble truths, four fundamental principles of nature of life. These truths are not statements of belief. Rather, they are categories by which we can frame our direct experience in a way that is conducive to Awakening.

These are 'Dukkha' (Suffering), 'Samudaya' (Cause of Suffering), 'Nirodha' (Cessation of Suffering) and 'Magga' (The path leading to the Cessation of Suffering).

The pali word 'Dhukka', means 'incapable of satisfying' or 'not able to bear or withstand anything': always changing—impermanence or 'Anicca', incapable of truly fulfilling us or making us happy. Suffering is something we usually do not want to know. We just want to get rid of it or suppress it. One can see why modern society is so caught up in seeking pleasures and delights in what is new, exciting and romantic. We tend to emphasize the beauties of youth whilst the ugly side of life—old age, sickness, death, boredom etc. are pushed aside. I encourage you to try to understand Dukkha: to really look at it, stand under and accept your suffering. The second noble truth states that there is origin of suffering and that the origin of suffering is attachment to the three kinds of desire: 'Kama Tanha' (for sensual pleasure), 'Bhava Tanha' (desire to become) and 'Vibhava Tanha' (desire to get rid of). If we contemplate desires and listen to them we are actually no longer attaching to them allowing them to be the way they are.

Then we come to the relization that the origin of suffering, the desire, can be laid aside and let go off.

The third noble truth with its three aspects is: there is the cessation of suffering, of 'Dukkha'. The cessation should be realized. The whole aim of the Buddhist teaching is to develop the reflective mind in order to let go of delusions. Cessation is easy to understand on an intellectual level, but to realize it may be quite difficult because this entails abiding what we think we cannot bare.

The fourth noble truth has three aspects: there is the eightfold path, the 'Attangika magga'—the way out of suffering; the second aspect is: 'this path should be developed'; the final insight into arahantship is: the path has been fully developed. The elements of the eightfold path, grouped into three sections, 'sila' (morality or virtue).

'Samadhi' (concentration) and 'panna' (wisdom). Meditation is the only way to develop wisdom. It is being practiced by many Easterners and Westerners in the modern world.

5. Meditation

In Buddhism, the word meditation designates two kinds: one is called "Samatha', the other 'Vipassana'. Samatha meditation is one of concentrating the mind on an object such as sensation of breathing, rather that letting it wanders off to other things. The other practice is 'Viapassana' or 'insight meditation'. With insight meditation, you are opening the mind up to everything. You are not choosing any particular object to concentrate on or absorb into, but watching in order to understand the way things are, is that all sensory experiences impermanent. Everything you see, hear, smell, touch or taste; all mental conditions your feelings, memories and thoughts—are changing conditions of the mind, which arise and pass away.

6. How we can Use Theravadic Buddhism in the Modern World?

Making Peace with Despair

Human beings have a reflective quality that steps back from experience and say 'I don't like this. It shouldn't be this way. Stop it.' The aim of the spiritual path is to fully understand that the main problem of life is not that the government is unfair, that one is not getting enough money, that there is hunger, violence, pain or sickness, not even that one isn't loved—but the feeling in the reflective mind of being bound down by these circumstances. Once we have clearly understood the mind, we can experience patience, equanimity, and release—even in predicaments that can be difficult or unpleasant.

Reflections on Metta

Metta is unattached love with no limits: first it is directed towards oneself, and then it radiates towards all beings, not to wish harm upon another, even in anger or ill will. Metta is not binding, it means that you are willing to admit weakness, faults within your experience of life, without making that into anything i.e. not getting angry or depressed out of it. Its clarity: the mind is clear, radiant, bright and reflective, rather than just a pink cloud that we blot out every ugly thing with. Once one radiates Metta, one's heart become full of peaceful. The qualities such as anxiety, guilt, remorse etc fade away.

Self-forgiveness and Compassion

When we begin to appreciate that we have in common with those around us, and then we realize that there are basically no boundaries, no ultimate separation. There is an interconnection, which we can all be sensitive to and through which we can come in contact with each other. We can begin to see things just as they are, to have the willingness and the courage to let the past be. Let the fear and delusion go. When we look around, what we're seeing is our minds: our perception of the world is a reflection of our own mental state. If we're at peace and fearless, we help to project into the world a state of peacefulness. We can make the world more peaceful, benevolent and compassionate. When the judgment comes from compassion, one see one's life clearly, accept that one is human and allow the past to go.

> "Yesterday is a memory. Tomorrow is the unknown. Now is the knowing".
>
> May you all be Happy and peaceful! May the Devas protect you!

May the blessings of the noble triple gem be with you forever!!!!

References

1. Narada, Mirror of the Dhamma (2001), Sri Lanka: Buddhist Cultural Centre.
2. Sumedho, The Four Noble Truths (1992), U.K.: Amaravathi.
3. Sumedho, *et al*, peace and Kindness (2002), U.K.: Amaravathi.
4. Sumedho, Now is the Knowing (1992), U.K.
5. Bapat, V.P., 2500 Years of Buddhism (1956), India: Govn. Publication.
6. www.accesstosnsight. org/theravada. html.

18

Transference of Merit—Punya Parinama Dana in Buddhism

Dr. M.V. Ramankumar Ratnam and L. Udaya Kumar

Punya (merit) in Indian thought has two connotations viz., religious and moral. Religious merit were in it refers to the merit arising from the performance of a religious act. Moral merit is the resultant arising from the performance of an ethical righteous act. It is the prospective result of karma, after the karma performed in the present life becomes purva karma **purva karma** in later life, and matures resulting in the production of merit-punya. Hence, karma is the substrate, and punya is a derivative potential.

In fact the Philosophy of dana is pivoted around the generation of punya[1] karma or moral merit. In the **Payasi sutta**[2] the Buddha contents that 'We give Dana to gain merit in the next world'. Punya is in the nature of a 'beneficial potential' of an ethical act, which fructifies in future, in the subsequent rebirths of the donor, who thus becomes the would-be beneficiary of the 'donation' generated by himself. In other words, while the immediate beneficiary of a Dana is the donee, the donor, in accordance with the doctrine of karma, is the eventual beneficiary of his own Dana, he reaps the benefits in the form of punya.

Punya dana is the transfer, by way of gift, of the potential religious or moral merit, which will accrue when the karma will fructify in future. It is not a dana of an intangible service but merely a conceptual gift, a samkalpa, a resolve, a commitment to transfer the potential of one's good karmas to another. It is dana-punya dana, wherein, the transfer as a gift of the punya, moral or spiritual merit, the time of maturation (karma vipaka) of the potential of an act, in particular of its merit, is wholly uncertain, which takes place in a future life or lives.

In fact, the donor of punya himself does not know when he could possibly experience the punya of his karmas, much less he or the donee forsees the time when it will bear fruit after transfer. Scholars opine that in this kind of Dana, nothing passes. They also rise the queries such as when and whether the recipient will be able to enjoy the gifts is indeterminate. In this sense, punya dańa is a gift of something like a transfer transaction in futures with an uncertain time of maturity. It can be referred to as transfer of adrsta.

Canonical Buddhism

The Buddhist canonical texts do not support the transfer of punya Dana. The **Anguttara nikaya**[3] rejects the concept of another person enjoying the resultants of one's karmas. It says that no one can be as surely, or more precisely a substitute (patibhoga),[4] in four things: decay, disease, death and 'the fruit of those evil deeds (papa) that defile and lead again to becoming deeds unhappy whose fruits in future time is pain, rebirth, decay and death.

The Buddhist contend that all karmas, including ethically punya karmas, are 'evil' (papa), as they are the cause of rebirth and the concomitant aging and suffering. The **Khuddakapatha**[5] **of the Khuddaka nikaya** states that the treasure (nidhi) created through Dana (gifts) cannot be shared with anyone.

The **Kathavatthu**[6] discussing the question; can one bestow happiness on another? It puts forth that the explanation does not centre on the proposition that one can transfer one's own happiness to another or another's happiness or one's happiness to another (third party). In other words, it is confirmed that one cannot transfer one's own or another's happiness. To remove all ambiguity, it is denied that one can act for another or that one's good and ill are caused by another's acts. It proclaims that an enlightened being like the Buddha can remove unhappiness and confer happiness on others through his teachings. It is in this sense that the statement that one can bestow or transfer happiness on or to another is to be understood.

Post-Canonical Buddhism

The Post-Canonical literature does speak of transfer of merit, punyadana. The **Milindapanha**[7] emphasizes that a good deed can be shared but not an evil one. In the **Silanisamsa jataka,**[8] the bodhisattva saves his companion, a barber from shipwreck at sea. While the boatman had taken the bodhisattva on his boat, he was opposed to doing so in the case of the barber, as he was not a man of holy life'. The bodhisattva overcomes the resistance of the boatman by proclaiming I give him (dammi), the fruit (pattim) of the gifts I have given (dinnadana).

Aryasura in his **Pranidhanasaptatinamagatha**[9] speaks of sharing the virtues the bodhisattva has collected with all beings. Santideva[10] in **Bodhicaryavatara** vows to use the merits he has accumulated to liberate all beings from eveil forms of existence. Further, Santideva[11] in **Siksasamuccaya** speaks of renouncing one's merit for the sake of humanity. In the **Dhammapada Atthakatha**[12] (Dh.A)., we have numerous references about transfer of Punya. To quote: I have to make over to you the merit obtained by this action transfer of Punya. Pratyekabuddha (Dh.A.II.1); the reward of this alms-giving has been made over by me to my master; I transfer to my parents the merit contained in this act of preaching or intoning of the sacred word (Dh.A, XXIII.5).

There is also the mention of the purchase of punya from the

doer of the meritorious act in this text. The rich man Sumana says. 'I will give him (annabhara) a suitable price for his gift and make this portion of alms my own'[13]. Further the instance of Jotika gifting the sap of sugarcane belonging to him to the Pratyekabuddha. The sugarcane gifted actually belongs to his brother, which was also gifted conditionally: 'I will give my elder brother either the price of the sugarcane or the merit thereof'.[14]

Further in the post-canonical literature, punya dana was believed to multiply the accumulation of merit. The donee is the beneficiary of punya dana, the donor adds to his punya by the very act of such a donation. At the same time, he is not deprived of the merit originally acquired by him. By anumodana[#], rejoicing in the 'joy of rapport' on the part of the recipient, he also becomes a participant in the original deed. Thus the beneficiary is getting even greater merit then the original does the rationale for the concept of punya dana[15] is two-fold:

(i) To root out the idea of self-hood, an expression of total renunciation;
(ii) To promote the practise of the Dana paramita, maitri and karuna. It paved the way for nekkhamma paramita (renunciation), maitri and karuna. It was an effective means to support and maintain bhiksus, sadhus and brahmanas. Thereby, punya dana is purposeful for promoting selflessness and altruism. The concept of merit transfer is essential to motivate action (karma).

There is also a distinction of carya (conduct) within the framework of the theory of karma for the laymen as distinct from Bhikkus. The concept of merit transfer resolves this conflict between the carya of laymen and Bhikkus. The Sangha is the field of merit for laymen. By joining the sangha through ordination, a layman not only accumulates merit for himself, but also expands the field of merit and the opportunity for earning merit. The offerings to the sangha including sponsorship of laymen to ordination for joining the sangha constitute the supreme moral acts and hence the means of acquiring or transferring merit. The transference of merit strengthens specific social bonds such as between the children who transfer merit, and their parents, who are the transferees of such merit. Thereby, it can be said that 'without the idea of merit transference there would be an irresistible conflict between the demands of the society and the demands following the path of the Buddha according to the Vinaya'.[16] Essentially, there is no conflict between the goals of layman and monks. The former aim at attaining heaven (svarga), which is liable to death and rebirth and from which there is retrogression, whereas the latter seek to obtain nirvana i.e., total cessation of rebirth and death and no falling away.

The latter Buddhist especially Mahayana brought about a revolution, they have brought about a paradigm shift in the concept of Dana by introducing the aspect of punya 'parinama' Dana. To quote: there is something more precious than a bodhisattvas' health, limbs, wife and children, and that is his merit (punya).[17] He should give it for the good of all being, which is possible; by the addition of the term—Parinama. Herein, it refers to the bending round or towards, transfer or dedication of ones merit-punya for the benefit of others.

The Mahayanists presented a more socially oriented conceptualized 'quantitative' aspect of punya, which seems to shift their much-vaulted ethics into a system of **Social arithmetic.** They contend that 'every good deed produces a certain fixed amount of punya'. A certain quantity of punya confers a particular kind of happiness on earth or in a heaven only for a certain period of time, after which it is exhausted. This quantitative view of punya has culminated in the doctrine of parinama (transfer of merit).

The Mahayanist contends that merit protects motives of a person and can even work miracles in his favour. To quote: 'it can make trees bloom out of season and convert a fiery furnace into a lovely lotus-pond.[18] It can save mariners from shipwreck, and ward off the attacks of demons and hobgoblins. Even the cyclic evolution and dissolution of the Universe are due to Merit. The sun and the moon owe their entire splendor to it'.[19] In Mahayanists literature it has been glorified to such an extent that it is finally regarded almost as the equivalent of wisdom (prajna) and bodhi. In the early period of the Mahayana, punya was considered to be only the means of securing happy re-births, while Enlightenment was reserved for those who acquired jnana (knowledge) through the processes of sila and samadhi. It was with the increasing concern for the practise of active altruism in social life that the Mahayanists' gave rise to the evolved idea that punya by itself could lead to Enlightenment. Santideva [20] exalted its importance by substituting "transfer of punya" for the Perfection of Wisdom (prajna-paramita) as the final goal of a bodhisattava's career.

The Mahayanists evolved a more humane teaching that even a sinner was not destined to suffer in the states of woe, as the bodhisattvas could cancel his demerit by giving him some of their merit. Avalokitecvara was described as releasing the sufferers from the purgatories without paying any regard to the law of karma. Here, the Mahayanists reinterpreted the old law of karma and have introduced the dimension of karuna.

The later Mahayana doctrine speaks of the practice of two kinds of parinama. Firstly, a bodhisattva may "apply" the merit of a good deed for his own Enlightenment (bodhi). Secondly, a bodhisattava may also "apply" his merit for the welfare and spiritual progress of all creatures. The later kind of parinama is regarded as more commendable in the later Mahayana, which prefers altruistic activity even to the ideal of Enlightenment. In this case, a bodhisattva shares his "roots of merit" with all beings. He wishes to allay and appease their pain and misery, to save them from all fear, and to lead them to virtue, serene meditation and true knowledge. He desires that all beings should enjoy the blessings of health, strength, friendship, purity and unity, and also gain the knowledge of the Buddhas.

To conclude, post canonical Buddhism laid more stress on 'active altruistic service', for it recognised the universal interdependence of mankind. The doctrine of karma in its earlier form repudiated the bond of social solidarity and dissolved society into a vast number of isolated individuals. The early Buddhists opined that man existence was essentially a personalized existence, whereas the later Buddhist infused the concept of a 'social being', Mahayanists emphasis was towards the practice and cultivation of the values social sympathy and sacrifice. They realised that the Buddhavacanam in its final import meant that 'no one was born unto himself alone and no one died unto himself alone'.

Notes and References

1. It is necessary to clarify that punya is produced not only by dana, or what is known as danamayipunnakiriyavatthu but also by certain activities and practices, viz., sila (good conduct) and bhayana (concentration). We are, however, concerned with punya producing dana only. Such punya producing actions are altruistic karmas involving gifts to monks, the samgha or to the community in general such as works of public welfare: construction tanks and wells for providing drinking water welfare of handicapped and disabled persons construction of hospitals, bhesajja dana (gift of healing), establishment of schools and temples, etc. R.C. Childers says in Dictionary that the word patti is sometimes used for the merit, gain advantage or prospective reward of a good action, and that this merit may be transferred by superegoration to another by an exercise of the will. Patti is the Pali equivalent of Sanskrit prapti (gain, attainment, profit), the result of the action done in a former life (Apte *ibid*). As such it cannot be equated to punya-transfer concurrently which is really the transfer of gain or merit that will accrue in future life; it will become and that can happen only in the next life. In other words, apttidana cannot be equated to punyadana.
   This will find support from the fact that punya is produced in three ways:
   1. Danamayampunna kiriyavatthu punya produced by dana;
   2. Silamayampunnakiriyavatthu, punya produced by good conduct;
   3. Bhayavanamayam punnakiriyavatthu, punya produced by concentration.
2. Digha nikaya (11.23) punna-tthika danass' eva phalam.
3. Anguttara nikaya (II, 182) (ponabhavikani sadarani dukkavipakaniayatam jatijara maranikani tesam vipako ma nibbattitin' atthi koc patibhogo.
4. The word patibhoga means a surety, a guarantor. Rhys Davis and Stede in Dictionary explain it to mean 'one who has to be made use of in place of someone else'.
5. Khuddakapatha of the Khuddaka nikaya (1.8.9) V. Trenckner in A Critical

Pali Dictionary (Copenhagen, 1924-45) explains it as 'not shared with others'. See also Childers in Dictionary; Nanamoli in The Minor Readings (London, P.T.S. 1960) which is the English translation of the Khuddakapatha, also adopts the same meaning.

6. Kathavatthu (XVI, 3) It may be noted that Buddhaghosa in his commentary the Kathavathuppakarna Atthakatha emphasizes that 'we are not able to hand over our happiness or other's happiness to another' and explains that producing happiness in another does not mean handing over his own happiness. The Debates Commentary (tr. Of Kathavatthuppakarana Atthakatha by B.C. Law (London, P.T.S. 1940). Prof. Bechert (*ibid.*, p. 16) points out that The Theravadins arrived at negation of the possibility of transfer of merit'. Prof. H. Bechert (*ibid.*, p. 15) also takes transfer of merit in the sense of the Buddha's teaching leading to nirvana of his followers. He states that as a result of a Buddha's teaching, numerous beings attain nirvana without having to observe the long and arduous discipline to a bodhisattva, that he shows the way to salvation to beings who are not mature of salvation by means of their own karma. But we must point out that teaching the doctrine and the consequential benefit to the taught do not involve transfer of merit (punyadan). Dharma dana and Vidya dana are not channels for transfer of karma but of knowledge. Teaching the way to emancipation is not transfer of religious merit of the teacher to the disciple.
7. Milindapanha 295-96.
8. Silanisamsa jataka (190): adam attana dinnadana rakkhitasile bhaveta bhavanaya et assa pattim dammiti nahapito anumodani samiti.
9. Pranidhanasaptatinamagatha (Aspirational Prayer in Seventy Stanzas) (70).
10. Bodhicaryavatara (X,31).
11. Siksasamuccaya (26).
12. Dhammapada Atthakatha (Dh.A) Aham te ito pattim dammi . . . Imamin me pinda pati samina patti dinna . . . matupitunam imasmin bhanne pattim dammi.
13. Dh.A XXVI. 10.12a.
14. DH.A.XXVI, 33.
15. G.P. Malasekhara in his Transference of Merit in Ceylonese Buddhism (Philosophy East and West; Honolulu, 1967, p. 86) explains the rationale of the concept of merit transfer: human beings have numerous opportunities of doing good deeds and there by earning merit, whereas such opportunities are few and far between for the denizens of the other world, viz. devas, animals and plants. In fact, he emphasizes that the devas are in need of constantly supplementing their stock of merit, so that they can continue to exist in the deva world. Human beings can earn considerable merit by transferring the merit of their meritorious actions to the deves. This explanation is inconsistent with the concept of karma bhumi

and bhoga bhumi which are essential features of the doctrine karma. According to the karma doctrine, human beings alone belong to karma bhumi where in they have opportunity of doing karma and earning merit and demerit (punya and papa). In the bhoga bhumi, a being only experiences the results of his past accumulated karmas, and he there by exhausts them. There is no fresh accumulation of karmas for such beings. It is, perhaps, because of this concept that the janussoni Sutta of the Anguttaranikaya (V, 177) explains that beings other than human beings, viz. deves, animals, plants or those born in purgatory (nirayam) cannot receive the sraddha, gifts, because they subsist on food proper to their states existence. But, if he is born as a peta, he subsists on the offerings of fellow kinsmen and beloved relations (natisalohitanam). Thus, dana for the benefit of deceased beings can be effective only in the case of pretas. In fact, such dana is considered essential for redeeming pretas, disembodied souls awaiting reincamation.

16. G.P. Malasekhara in his Transference of Merit in Ceylonese Buddhism' (Philosophy East and West, Honolulu, 1967).
17. Ciksa., 32.
18. Ava-Ca., I, 221. Ksemendra, ii, 645.II, 735.16, 797.97.
19. Fa.Ma., 28.22.
20. Ciksa., 31.19, Ksemendra, I, 1089.3.

    # Anumodana, (expression of) thanks by the donee to the donor, is interpreted by R. Gombrich. See "Merit Transference in Sinhalese Buddhism' in History of Religious (Vol. 1, To me this appears far-fetched. The word anumodana in Skt. means approval, assent, seconding acceptance, thanks, especially after a meal of after receiving gifts; pleasing, causing pleasure, applauding sympathetic joy. 11, 1971, p. 206) as implying acceptance of a gift.

19

Emancipation of Women, A Buddhist Path

Dr. (Smt.) Nanda Parekar

Women in general and Buddhist women in particular is one of the most neglected subject in Indian history. There are scholarly works on the position of women in ancient India. But most of these works are confined to the dominant Hindu community. The exclusion of the other religious communities and marginalized groups is the serious limitations of these works.[1]

It is well known that the status of woman in India was on a whole low in pre-Buddhist age. Her rights to pursue religious life and move freely in society were considerably restricted.[2] But with the rise of Buddhism, the position of women began to improve. Women enjoyed more equality and greater respect and authority which was denied to them in pre-Buddhist age. Buddhism rejected any kind of distinction on the basis of caste or gender.[3] In fact it was a humanist force. It tried to uplift the position of women in society. It needs to be examined whether Buddhism tried to offer an equal status to women on a humanitarian ground or in terms of a radical approach. In present context too it is very significant to understand the Buddhist attitude towards women. Present paper is a modest attempt to throw light on the emancipation of women under Buddhism and to trace the extent to which Buddhism acted as catalytic factor in transforming the existing social conditions.

Buddhist literature in general throws a flood of light on the attitude towards women. But Therigatha—a self expression of Buddhist women is more useful to understand the prevailing social structure and the experience of women from different backgrounds. Instead of concentrating on factual details, it is necessary to identify the change and reformative element of Buddhist comparing to pre-Buddhist age. Therigatha in fact is a reflection of the existing social realities and the opportunities offered by Buddhism to women.

Patriarchy seems to be the main characteristics of pre-Buddhist or Vedic society. Therefore women were kept at a secondary status. Birth of a girl-child was looked upon as a curse or catastrophe. A daughter was regarded as a source of misery according to Aitareya Brahmana.[5] Similarly a desire to have more and more sons in Vedic literature too reflects a typical patriarchal approach in pre-Buddhist days.[6] But under Buddhism there occurred a change in the attitude. Buddha's views regarding the birth of a girl-child were progressive and path-making. Kosala King Pasendi was disappointed when his Buddhist queen Mallika gave birth to a daughter. At that time Buddha said, "A girl may prove even a better offspring." This remark of Buddha[7] stands exactly in contrast to that of Vedic tradition. It is very clear that birth of girl-child was not considered as a curse under Buddhism. Another reference to Mahasuvanna's desire to get a son or a daughter as he was childless is very important. Birth of a son or a daughter makes no difference for Mahasuvanna.[8] This is really a progressive approach. When pre-Buddhist tradition was openly welcoming the birth of male-child, Buddhist tradition welcomed the birth of a girl-child. A reference to adoption of Samavati[9] by householder Mitta was a revolutionary step. Adopting a daughter and not a son was definitely a step forward. Of course a gender bias of earlier epoch was not totally disappeared. Kisa-Gotami was disdainfully treated by her neighbours until she bore a son. It means being a mother of a son was honoured. But in spite of the dominant patriarchal bias in society what Buddha tried to introduce is very significant. Bringing complete change in the existing social condition and subordinate status of women was a difficult task. But at least Buddha started this process by welcoming a birth of girl child.

The progressive approach of Buddhism is evident in its stand against child-marriage. Samavati's father refused to give her to the king. He said, "We the householders do not give young girls for fear that people will say that they are male maltreated and ill-used."[10] When the pre-Buddhist tradition was propagating a child marriage, Buddhist tradition stood against this custom.

Marriage as an institution was not challenged under Buddhism. But to be unmarried was not regarded as a disgrace. In case of married women too, a traditional approach was not totally attacked by Buddha. There are examples of wifely servitude[11] of women in Therigatha. A reference to Sujata, a daughter-in-law, of Anathapindaka Sresthi and explaining ten categories of wives by Buddha to her and a sentiment that 'slave-type' wife as an ideal wife definitely reflects a subordination of women.[12] Isidasi tried to serve her husband by following various roles of wife such as mother, sister, friend and slave too. But her husband could not get over his dislike for her.[13] This indicates that Vedic notion of male dominance had not completely disappeared. But it should be remembered that Buddha's path was a middle path. The traditional values and customs did not come to an end immediately. Wifely devotion was one of these notions. Buddha's way out to this situation was the explanation of the duties of a husband towards a wife. It was a matured and balanced view towards women. A sentiment that a husband should take care of his wife and should give respect to her suggests an equal treatment. In fact a husband-wife relationship under Buddhism was based on moral values. In the Buddhist Dhamma the emphasis is on chastity. Buddha spoke openly to Dhammika, one of his followers at the Jetavana, about the householders life.[14] His advice to a householder about self taming is very significant. The ideal is that a man should so tame his own mind that with reference to chastity, he should have the mother mind, the sister mind and the daughter mind towards all women who were not his wife, regarding them as his mothers, sisters or daughters (according to their age). This is not merely a humanitarian approach towards women. Buddha's emphasis on chastity stands against the practice of polygamy. It may be regarded as an indirect attack on the injustices against women in the marriage institution. The concept of sharing equal responsibilities by a husband and a wife is also remarkable. A story of Nanda who decided to secede from the Sangha due to the remembrance of his noble wife Janapadakalyani,[15] indicates an intimacy of love between husband and wife. There are few records of grief at a wife's death too. It may be concluded that though Buddhism does not challenge the marriage institution as a whole, the one-sided wifely devotion was definitely challenged by Buddhism. This was a change in earlier approach.

Similar approach has been reflected in case of widows. Widowhood in pre-Buddhist days was terrible. But under Buddhism, a widow was treated as a human being. A tradition of widowhood full of hardships in pre-Buddhist days was not totally forgotten as a woman in the Vessantara Jataka[16] fears about widowhood. But the widow was not considered as a dreaded creature or ill omen under Buddhism. There are records of widows[17] who joined the sangha. Joining a Sangha opened up a new kind of life for them.

Caste, marital status, age or economic status was not at all a barrier for entering a Sangha. Buddha gave equal treatment to all women. Ambapali—a courtesan paid a visit to Buddha and invited him for meals. Shortly afterwards Buddha received an invitation for meals for the same day from the princely family of the Licchavis. But he refused them and kept his promise to Ambapali.[18] Licchavis were powerful in every sense but keeping the promise given to Ambapali was more important. This indicates a progressive approach.

In the field of religion too, Buddhism gave equal access to women. It is true that Buddha was reluctant to admit women in sangha. It was only when Ananda, Buddha's favourite disciple, made a strong plea that Buddha sanctioned the admission of women in sangha.[19] This reflects a work pattern of Buddhism. Ananda's convincing capacity played a vital role in changing Buddha's views. It is indeed remarkable that Buddha changed his opinion about women after an appeal from a disciple. We do have the examples scattered in the vast mass of Vedic literature bearing on the prejudiced attitude towards women. The so called debate[20] between Gargi and Yajnavalkya in the court of Janaka reflects the existing male dominace and the imposed silence on women. Gargi was forced to remain silent.[21] But Buddha never dictated his views on his disciples. Listening to others and accepting it openly the most democratic feature of Buddhism. Regarding the entry of women in Sangha it seems that Buddha changed his earlier views. His earlier reluctance should not be misinterpreted. Similarly the eight chief rules[22] for nuns are often interpreted as an absolute subordination of women. Especially a rule that a Bhikkuni, even if of a hundred years standing shall make salutation to and bow down before a Bhikkhu, if only just initiated, clearly indicates the secondary status of women. But it seems to be an addition to the original Buddhist text.[23] Buddha's comment about the survival of Sangha after admission of women is also interpreted as a humiliation of women. But here too a reading between the lines is required. Buddha was well aware of the nature of man. He might have visualized the problems in future regarding the nuns and the monks. He was very much careful about the safety of the weaker sex.[24] After Uppalvanna's rape incident[25] the treatment given by Buddha to her was very practical, sober and rational. She was never condemned as guilty. If such was the approach of Buddhism towards women, there is very less possibility of imposing humiliating rules for nuns at the time of the establishment of their order. In fact the order of nuns opened up new avenues of spiritual growth for women. Among Buddha's famous disciples, there were thirteen ladies whose merit was appreciated by Buddha.[26] Dhammadinna, for example was the most distinguished one who became a teacher of the doctrine and taught her husband.[27] The entrants like Khema, Mahapujapati Gotami belonged to royal class. Bhadda Kundalekesha or Uppalavanna belonged to merchant families. Bhadda of the Kapilas belonged to a Brahmin family. There are references to some low-caste entrants from a poor strawplaiter and basket-maker family.[28] The courtesans like Vimala or Ambapali, too were the leading figures in Sangha.[29] This is a very remarkable feature. Bhikkuni Sangha was a training ground for these women in their journey towards salvation.[30] These women from different social backgrounds not only shared their experiences in sangha but also attained the highest spiritual positions. They came from traditional patriarchal and discriminatory society. But after renouncing the world out of unhappiness with life, they followed the Buddhist path of kindness, humanity and equality. In their own writings like Therigatha, the existing notions about women are reflected. But at the same time their struggles and accomplishment along the road to arhatship has also been described. Buddhism tried to bring change in the existing approach towards women. Giving equal opportunities to women in the religious field and trying to shake the age old notions about women was definitely a step forward.

Notes and References

1. Kumkum Sangari and Sudesh Vaid, Recasting Women (An Introduction), Reprint 1999), Delhi, p. 4.
2. Meena V. Talim, *Female Reformers of the Buddhist Period* (600 to 100 BC) in "Buddhism in India and Abroad", ed. By Kallpakam Sankrityayan, Motohiro Yorotomi and Shubhada Joshi, Mumbai, 1996, p. 361.
3. C.V. Rajwade, *Dighanikaya* (Marathi Translation) Second Edition, Aurangabad, 1999, pp. 122-123.
4. P.V. Bapat, 2500 years of Buddhism, Delhi, 1956, p. 1.
5. Bharatiya Vidya Bhavan, *The Vedic Age*, Vol. I, Bomday 1988, p. 458.
6. A.S. Altekar, The Position of Women in Hindu Civillzation, Reprint 1983, Delhi, p. 3.
7. Dharmanand Kosambi, *Buddhaleela Sarsangriha* (in Marathi), Mumbai,

1977, (2nd edition), p. 282.

8. I.B. Horner, *Women under Primitive Buddhism*, Delhi, 1975, (first reprint), p. 21.
9. Dhammapada, Commentary on verses 21-23 qutoted in I.B. Horner, *op. cit.*, p. 23.
10. I.B. Horner, *op. cit.*, p. 29.
11. Vasant Moon, *Women's life in Buddhism* (in Marathi), Poona, 1989, p. 23.
12. Dharmanand Kosambi, *op. cit.*, p. 214.
13. Rhys Davids, *Therigatha: Psalms of the early Buddhists*, Pali Text Society, London, 1909, Verse LXXII, pp. 158-159.
14. *Sacred Books on the East*, Vol. X, Suttanipata, p. 395.
15. *Dhammapada Commentary Series* 13-14 quoted in I.B. Horner, *op. cit.*, p. 59.
16. Durga Bhagwat, *Siddhartha Jataka* (in Marathi), Vol. VI, Poona 1978, pp. 444-445.
17. I.B. Horner, *op. cit.*, p. 76.
18. Rhys Davids, *op. cit.*, Verse LXVI, p. 120.
19. *Sacred Book of the East*, Vol. XX, The Chullavagga, pp. 320-321.
20. *Brihadaranyaka Upanishad* III 6 and 8.
21. Sharmistha Adhya, "Evolution of Women's Educational System in Ancient India" in *Quarterly Review of Historical Studies*, Vol. XL, p. 44.
22. *Sacred Books of the* East, Vol. XX, The Chullavagga, pp. 322-324.
23. Dharmanand Kosambi, '*Bhagwan Buddha: Jeevan Aur Darshan*' (in Hindi) Allahabad, 1993, pp. 153-155.
24. I.B. Horner, *op. cit.*, p. 156.
25. Rhys Davids, *op. cit.*, Verse LXIV, pp. 155-156.
26. R.K. Mukharjee, *Ancient Indian Education*, Third Edition, Delhi, 1960, p. 464.
27. *Ibid.*
28. C.V. Rajwade, *op. cit.*, p. 123.
29. *Ibid.*
30. I.B. Horner, *op. cit.*, pp. 171-172.

20

Benefactresses of Buddhism in Early Andhradesa

Dr. E. Sivanagi Reddy-Sithapati and
Dr. P. Chenna Reddy

Like the other parts of India, Andhradesa also witnessed a tremendous spread of the Dhamma since the time of the Buddha. Soon after the down fall of the Mauryan Kingdom, Satavahanas, the immediate successors continued to lend their support for the propagation of the Dhamma, as a result, hundreds of Buddhist aramas rose in Andhradesa. Not only kings and queens but all sections of the society were influenced by Buddhism. Even during the rule of Ikshavakus the same fervor prevailed. Particularly noteworthy is the fact that unlike the male members of the ruling family, women from the harem extended enormous patronage to Buddhism. It was the same case with other upasikas from the trading and other communities. Copious references to the contribution of women for the cause of Buddhism can be seen from the early Brahmi inscriptions of Andhradesa datable to the period between the 1st and 4th centuries A.D.

The inscriptions from Dhanyakataka (Amaravati) and

Sriparvata—Vijayapuri (Nagarjunakonda) reveal that women out number men in making liberal donations in the form of structural members of the Mahachetiyas such as ayaka pillars, parts of the railings, toranas Buddhapadas and the images of the Buddha. The Amaravati inscriptions contain maximum number of women benefactors mostly house wives belonging to the families of the agriculturists (Gajhapatis) and merchants whereas the Nagarjunakonda inscriptions refer to the ladies of royal families, and rich sections of the society.

A close look at the inscriptions of Amaravati datable to the 1st and 2nd centuries A.D., reveal that along with the nuns, upasikas enthusiastically volunteered in donating various salved slabs to the Mahachetiya. Bhagi[1] wife of a Gahapati; Hamghi[2] daughter of Bodhi; Buddha,[3] a house wife; Tuka[4] wife of Buddhi, Nagabuddha[5] another housewife; Kaliga,[6] another lady from the family of gahapatis and Dhanamjana,[7] another housewife are the female donors who gifted casing slabs, cross bars, coping stones and railings to the Mahachetiya. A solitary example of a cowherd making donations is noteworthy. According to an inscription, a lady (name lost) daughter of a mahagovaka (chief of the cowherds) offered certain gifts to the chetiya.[8] The next set of the female donors come from the merchant community. Nagachampaki,[9] wife of a merchant, Chandasiri[10] wife of a Caravan leader Buddhila and Siddhi,[11] wife of a merchant residing at Vijayapuri were said to have come forward to donate certain coping stones to the railing of the stupa with great devotion. Siddhi made a long journey from Vijayapuri (Nagarjunakonda) to Dhanyakataka lying at a distance of 150 kms., with an exclusive purpose of making donation.

Among the Upasikas who made certain donations that facilitated the structural activity at Dhanyakataka, include Kama,[12] Utara[13] and Sivala.[14] Bhikkunis, samaṁikas and antevasins also joined for the promotion of Buddhism. Buddharakkhita,[15] a female disciple of Vidika, donated a carved slab at the northern gate of the Maha Chetiya along with her grand daughter Chula Buddarakkhita. In another instance, a meritorious gift of an upright slab was made by a nun (Pavajika) called Sangharakhita[16] along with her daughter and grand daughter. Another Bhikkuni by name Buddharakhita,[17] a female disciple of Bhadanta Buddharakhita, the overseer of the repairing works of the railing of the great stupa, made certain gifts along with her daughter. Samanika[18] Samghamitra, and her brothers and sisters offered carved slabs to the Mahachetiya at the time of its renovation. Almost all the women made their gifts in the presence of their family members particularly, daughters, indicating their liberality, devotion, freedom to participate in Dhamma activities, which were open to all people without discrimination.

It is very interesting to note that several women of the Ikshvaku family patronized Buddhism and caused the erection of a number of Buddhist structures including the Mahachetiya, in the Nagarjunakonda valley.[19] A good number of inscriptions of the 3rd century A.D., reveal that the most prominent lady who contributed her mite was Chantisiri, sister of Chantamula-1, the founder of the Ikshvaku dynasty.[20] An inscription[21] from the apsidal Chaityagriha located on the eastern side of the Mahachetiya, records the construction of a Silamandapa, surrounded by a Chatusala (quadrangular building probably a vihara having four wings) provided with all facilities for the acceptance of the teachers of the Apara Mahavinaseliya sect, for the longevity and victory of her son-in-law, for her own welfare and happiness in both the worlds and for her liberation.

Similarly, all the four wives of the King Virapurisadata, viz. Bapisirinika, Chhatisiri, Bhatideva and Rudradhara Bhattarika had also donated pillars (ayaka khambhas) to the Mahachetiya and caused the construction of certain Viharas for the residence of the Buddhist monks. Queen Bapisirinika, according to an inscription, set up an ayaka khambha, with due regard and for the sake of attainment of the bliss of nibbana for herself.[22] Chhatisiri was said to have set up an ayaka khambha with due regard for her mother Hammasirinika and for attaining the bliss of nibbana.[23] A decorated stone pillar recovered from the north-west side of the Mahachetiya, records that Mahadevi Bhatideva erected a vihara, which was provided with all essentials for the benefit of the achariyas of the Bahusrutiya sect.[24] She was also credited with the construction of another vihara, called Devi-vihara provided with all necessary things for the monks of the same sect.[25] This is the earliest record that informs us about naming the viharas after the donors, particularly ladies in Andhra. Another inscription reveals that Rudradhara Bhattarika, princess of Ujjain, set up a stone pillar and donated one hundred and seventy dinar mashakas to the Mahachetiya which was under construction with the munificent grants made available by the Mahatalavaris of the Ikshvaku family including Chatisiri.[26]

Inscriptions of Nagarjunakonda also reveal that women from the same royal family but belonging to the next generation had also evinced keen interest in making donations for the construction of Buddhist structures at Sriparvata—Vijayapuri. Kodabalisiri, the daughter of Maharajan Madhariputa Virapurisadata and the wife (Mahadevi) of Maharajan of Vanavasi, set up a pillar and a vihara for the acceptance of the achariyas of the Mahisasakas and in the name of the sangha of the four quarters and for the welfare and happiness of all sentient beings.[27] Another inscription found carved on another ayaka pillar commences with an adoration to the Buddha and records that the Mahatalavari (name lost), who was the wife of the Mahasenapati, Mahakamdasiri and mother of Vinhusiri set up the selakhambha, with due regard to both the families of her, and for the welfare and happiness in both the worlds and nibbana.[28] Atavi Chatisiri daughter of Chatamula and wife of Mahatalavara, Mahasenapati, Mahadandanayaka Skandhavisakha of the Dhanaka family erected a stone pillar at the Mahachetiys.[29] Similarly, Mahasenapatini Chula Chatisiri, wife of Mahasenapati Skandasitakirana, erected another pillar at the Mahachetiya.[30]

Not only the royal ladies, but also ladies from the families of the nobility took keen interest in making donations to the Buddhist establishments at Vijayapuri. In this connection one can cite an inscription carved on the pedestal of the broken image of Buddha, which records the installation (patithavita) of the image (padima) by Mangala, wife of Kodabuddhi.[31] Similarly one lady by name Buddhi, who was said to be the sister of certain Moda, belonging to the saka clan gifted a Buddhapada slab.[32]

There are also references to single individuals, that too women from merchant community donating much more than the royal ladies. One such example comes from an inscription carved on the floor of Chula Dhammagiri Vihara also known as Sihala vihara.[31] According to it, Upasika Bodhisiri, belonging to a trading family and married into a wealthy family of Govagama was a staunch believer and follower of Buddhism. The inscription further provides information on her interest in construction of variety of Buddhist structures at various places. It records the construction of a chetiyaghara, with flooring of stone slabs and a Chetiya with all amenities at Siripavata, on the eastern side of Vijayapuri, at the vihara on the Chula Dhammagiri for the sake of her own husband, Buddhimnaka, her father-in-law Gahapati Revata, her mother-in-law Budhamnika, the brothers of her husband Chamdamukhana, Karum-Budhima and Hamghamna, his sister Reevatimnika, his brother's son Chamdamukha, the elder Maha Chandamukha , the elder Maha Chandamukha and Chamdamukha, the younger Chula Chamdamukha, his sister's sons, Mula, the elder Maha Mula, and Mula, the Younger Chula Mula, his grand mother Buddha, of her maternal uncles, the treasurer Bada, Bodhisamma, Chanda and Bodhika, of her own maternal grand mother Bhadila and Bodhi, her own father Buddhi, a merchant, of her own mother Mula, of her sisters Budhamnika, Mulamnika, Nagabodhinika, of her daughter Viramnika, her sons Nagamna, and Viramna and her daughter in law Bhadasiri and Misi. Mentioning of all her relatives shows how strong were family bonds. It also shows that the names of all persons mentioned were all Buddhistic.

It further records that she also built a Chetiyaghara at the Kulaha vihara, Bodhirukka pasada (a shrine for Bodhi tree) at Sihala vihara (Cylonese monastery) and cells for the residence of the monks, one cell at Mahadhammagiri, she had also donated a pillar for the mandapa of the Mahavihara, the central hall at Devagiri. She got excavated a tank and constructed a varanda and a mandapa at Purvasaila. Her donation also helped in the construction of a silamandapa (stone pillared hall) at the eastern gate of the Mahachetiya at Kantakasela (Ghantasala) and Puphagiri. She also built viharas for the benefit of the Buddhist monks at Hirumuttuva, Papila and Dhanyakataka. Thus she offered donations for construction of varieties of structures witch include Chetiyaghara, shrine for Bodhi tree, silamandapas, viharas and a tank. She had not limited her activities at a single site. As seen from the above, she might have traveled widely on pilgrimage to various Buddhist places like Dhanyakataka, Nagarjunakonda, Ghantasala, Puphagiri, Purvasaila, Papila and Hirumuttuva and got inspired by the dhamma activities which led her to offer munificent grants for raising different types of structures. It is also mentioned in the inscription that she had built all these, for the endless welfare and happiness of her relatives and of all the world.

Bodhisiri made all the above donations for the merit of members of her own and her husband's families who had harmonious relations, mutual understanding sharing the same values. Wealthy learned with great vision believed and practiced the principle of dana (liberality) and built all the above, structures for the benefit of the monks who in turn educated the local masses by their teachings.

As seen from the above details, the benefactors made offerings for their own merit, for the benefit of their family members and for the happiness of all living beings.

One or two instances are recorded of making donations to the Buddhist establishments during the Post-Ikshvaku period. The only example is from the Vishnukundin inscription datable to the 4th century A.D. The Tummalagudem copper plates of the Vishnukundin King Vikramendra Bhattaraka Varma refer to donations made by his wife Parama Bhattaraka Mahadevi of Vakataka family. She built a vihara for the benefit of the Buddhist monks at Indrapalanagara (identified with the present day Tummalagudem in Nalgonda district) and named it as Mahadevi vihara.[32]

All these donations were made by the devotees to share the merit that may accrue, with all members of their families and all living beings. Such sharing is made by the donor of the good deeds resolving that so and so may partake the 'merit' of his/her good deeds. As most Buddhists believe that sharing becomes effective when the recipient becomes aware of the good deed and rejoices therein which is called anumodana.[33]

It seems that the benefactresses referred above also practiced the Paramita of giving, as the Buddha taught that wealth, wisdom and long life are all karmic results as giving of wealth results in obtaining wealth, the giving of teaching results in attaining wisdom and giving of fearlessness results in obtaining health and long life.[34] Thus all the women donors irrespective of their social status might have wished to have wealth, wisdom and long and healthy lives by practising dana and sharing their merit with others.

Notes and References

1. C. Sivaramamurthy, *Amaravati Sculpture in Madras Government Museum*, Madras, 1942, Ins. No. 90.
2. *Ibid.*, Ins. No. 100, p. 297.
3. *Ibid.*, Ins. No. 85, p. 294.
4. *Ibid.*, Ins. No. 104, p. 299.
5. *Ibid.*, Ins. No. 117, p. 301.
6. *Ibid.*, Ins. No. 73, p. 291.
7. *Ibid.*, Ins. No. 151, p. 284.
8. *Ibid.*, Ins. No. 91, p. 295.
9. *Ibid.* Ins. No. 108, p. 299.
10. *Ibid.*
11. *Ibid.*, Ins. No. 111, p. 300.
12. *Ibid.*, Ins. No. 83, p. 294.
13. *Ibid.*, Ins. No. 53, p. 284.
14. *Ibid.*, Ins. No. 7, p. 274.
15. *Ibid.*, Ins. No. 99, p. 297.
16. *Ibid.*, Ins. No. 31, pp. 277-278.
17. *Ibid.*

18. *Ibid.*, Ins. No. 78, p. 293.
19. P.R. Srinivasan, S. Sankaranarayan, *Inscription of the Ikshvaku Period,* Hyderabad, 1979, p. 4.
20. *Ibid.*, p. 4 and also see, *Epigraphia Indica,* (henceforth E.I.), Vol. XX, Ins. Nos. A4, C3, D4.
21. E.I. Vol. XXI, Ins. No. E.
22. *Ibid.*, Vol. XX, p. 19, Ins. No. C. 2.
23. *Ibid.*, p. 20, Ins. No. C. 4, and *Ibid.*, Vol. XXI, p. 62, Ins. G.2.
24. *Ibid.*, p. 23, Ins. No. G; and *Ibid.*, Vol. XXI, p. 62, Ins. G.2.
25. *Ibid.*, Vol. XXI, p. 62, Ins. No. G.3.
26. *Ibid.*, Vol. XX, p. 19, Ins. No.B. 5.
27. *Ibid.*, Vol. XX, p. 24, Ins. No. H.
28. *Ibid.*, p. 20, Ins. No. C. 5.
29. *Ibid.*, p. 18, Ins. No. B. 2.
30. *Ibid.*, Ins. No. B.5.
31. *Ibid.*, p. 22, Ins. No. F; Also see, S. Veeranarayana Reddy 'Upasika Bodhisiri'.
32. B.S.L. Hanumantha Rao, N.S. Rama Chandra Murthy, B. Subrahmanyam and E. Sivanagi Reddy, *Buddhist Inscriptions of Andhradesa,* Hyderabad, 1998, pp. 197-207.
33. For more details on sharing of merit see, G.P. Malala Sekhara in *Gems of Buddhist Wisdom Taipei,* 1997 (3rd Edn.), pp. 70-71.
34. Ven. Master Chin King, Buddhism: *The Wisdom of Compassion* and *Awakening,* Taipie, p. 105.

21

Buddha's Attitude Towards Women—An Overview

Koppula Saidi Reddy and Mohammed Osman Pasha

It is generally argued that the Buddha was anti-Vedic and that he discouraged women from joining Sangha. But being a rationalist and reformer, he had discarded only the ritual part of the Veda and admitted women to Sangha obliging the convincing argument based on reason and logic put forth by his foster mother. He advocated freedom for women exhibiting himself a great respect for them.

In the later Vedic period, women are discouraged from practicing certain rites and rituals and were also prohibited from reading the scriptures. Corporal punishments were suggested in the Law Codes for any transgressions.[1] This demarcation between man and woman is manifested in the social and domestic sphere where woman is seen as comparatively inferior in course of time.[2]

The equal and respectable position which women once enjoyed in the spiritual and religious spheres was later denied to them.[4] The Buddha allowed women to have equal and unfettered opportunities in the field of spiritual development and to enjoy the bliss of Nibbana on a par with their male counterparts.

The Anguttara Nikaya[5] contains valuable advice which the Buddha had given to young girls who were at the threshold of marital life. Foreseeing the difficulties that will arise with the new in-laws, the Buddha advised the girls to give due respect to their parents- in-law, serving them as lovingly as they were their own parents. They were also requested to honour and respect their husband's relatives and friends so that a congenial and happy atmosphere would be created in their new homes. They were advised to study and understand their husbands' nature, ascertain their husbands' activities, character and temperament, and to be useful and co-operative at all times in their new homes. They should be polite kind and watchful in their relationship with the servants. They should also safeguard their husbands' earnings and ascertain that all household expenditure was economically maintained. Such is the timeless quality of the Buddha's advice.

The Buddha appreciated that peace and harmony; in a home is to a great extent ensured by a woman. Thus, His adviced women on their role in their married life was which is realistic and practical. On different occasions, the Buddha advised that a wife[6]:

1. should not harbor evil thoughts against her husband;
2. should not be cruel, harsh or domineering;
3. should not be a spendthrift but should be economical and live within her means;
4. should zealously guard and save her husband's property and hard-earned wealth;
5. should always be virtuous and chaste in mind and action;
6. should be faithful and harbor no thoughts of any adulterous acts;
7. should be refined in speech and polite in action;
8. should be kind, industrious and hard-working;

9. should be thoughtful and compassionate towards her husband and her attitude should equate that of a mother loving and protecting her son;
10. should be modest and respectful;
11. should be cool, calm and understanding—serving not only as a wife but also as a friend and adviser to her husband when the need arises.

The Buddha's teachings on the real nature of life and death of karma and the worldly living influenced the contemporary social attitudes towards women. This is especially so with regard to the greater importance attached to the birth of a son in the Brahminical religion. Buddhism did not teach that a son was essential for the father's passage to heaven. The Buddha taught that according to the Law of Karma, one is responsible for one's own action and its consequence. The well-being of a father or grandfather does not depend upon the action of the son or the grandson. Each individual is responsible for its own actions. Therefore, there was no cause for the married women to be anxious just because they could not beget sons just for the sake of performing the 'rites of the ancestors' and so daughters need not suffer any ignomy.[7]

On one occasion when King Kosala was with the Buddha, news was brought to the King of the birth of a daughter to him. Expecting a son, the King was displeased. Noticing this, the Buddha paid a glowing tribute to women, delineating their virtues so that the King could welcome the birth of a daughter.

The Buddha opened the gates for the full participation of women in the field of religion by making them eligible for admission into the Bhikkhuni Sangha—the Order of Nuns which he had set up in the fifth year of the Buddha's ministry. This opened new avenues of culture, social services and opportunities for public life to women and in doing so enhanced the status of women.

The Buddha clearly showed that women were capable of understanding His teachings and also practice them to some degree of spiritual attainment. This is clearly indicated by the advice that the Buddha gave different women on different occasions.[8]

The nuns were not restricted by the Buddha where the teaching and preaching of the Dhamma was concerned. The Bhikkhuni Order produced a remarkable number of brilliant preachers and exponents of the Dhamma like Sukha, Patacara, Khema, Dhammadinna and Maha Prajapati.[9] By granting women an active share in the religious life, the Buddha raised their status in secular life of women and brought them to a realization of their importance to society. He opined that the women were weaker than men only in respect of physical strength but that factor alone could not hinder their spiritual progress. He saw the innate good of both men and women and assigned to them their due place in His teachings. Sex is no obstacle to attaining Sainthood.[10]

The Arahants Khema and Uppalavanna were made the two chief female disciples in the Order of Nuns. Women were placed under unfavourable circumstances before the advent of the Buddha, and this new Order was certainly a great Blessing. In this Order queens, princesses, daughters of noble families, widows, bereaved mothers, helpless women, courtesans—all despite their caste or rank—met on a common platform, enjoyed perfect consolation and peace, and breathed that free atmosphere which is denied to those confined in cottages and palatial mansions. Many who otherwise would have fallen into oblivion distinguished themselves in various ways and gained their emancipation by seeking refuge in the Order.[11]

Real freedom in the Buddhist Sense is that of being free from all forms of bondage. It can be achieved only through the proper spiritual development and purification of one's own mind—of cleansing oneself from all taints of greed, hatred and delusion. No amount of public debates, demonstrations and universal charters can bring full freedom. These can only be achieved through one's own diligence and heedfulness through regular practice of meditation as taught by the Buddha.[12]

The Buddha, in promoting the cause of women was considered

to be the first emancipator of women and was the promoter of a democratic way of life. It is in the Buddha-Dhamma that women were not despised and looked down upon but were given equal status with men in their spiritual endeavour to gain wisdom and liberation.

References

1. Dhammananda , Ven. Dr. K. Sri *'Status of Women in Buddhism' in Gems of Buddhist Wisdom,* Buddhist Missionary Society, Kaula Lumpur, 1996 (2nd Edn.), p. 419.
2. *Ibid.,* p. 419.
3. Narada, *The Buddha and His Teachings,* Kaula Lumpur, 1998, p. 312.
4. Narada, *A Manual of Buddhism,* Kaula Lumpur, 1995, pp. 83-84.
5. Dhammananda, *op. cit.,* 1996, p. 424.
6. *Ibid.,* p. 425.
7. *Ibid.,* p. 427.
8. Narada, *op. cit.,* 1995, pp. 83-84.
9. Ambedkar, Dr. B.R., *The Buddha and his Dhamma,* Taipei, 1997, pp. 193-200.
10. Phinga Cham, Ven. Dr. C., *Buddism for Young Students Wat Dhammaran Sunday School Michian,* United States of America 1990, p. 74.
11. Rameshan, N., *Glimpses of Buddhism,* Government of Andhra Pradesh 1961, p. 29.
12. Dhammananda, *op. cit.,* 1996, p. 420.

22

VALID INFERENCE IN BUDDHIST LOGIC

DR. R.T. INGALALLI

In Indian intellectual tradition Nyāya, as Logic, has occupied an important place, because it has been considered as 'the lamp of all sciences, the technique of good actions and the resource of all virtues'. Buddhist Logic, also as a branch of Indian Logic focuses its positive analysis on the structure and function of human reason for the realization of values (purusārthas). The aim of the present paper is to analyse the theory of valid inference in Buddhist Logic. I have mainly considered the views of Dharmakīrti (700 A.D.) in his work entitled: Nyāya-bindu-tika (N.B.T.) by Nyāya—(N.B.) along with an important commentary namely Dharmottara (9th century A.D.), a Buddhist logicisn. In this context the views of modern writers like Stcherbatsky (1950) and R.S.Y. Chi (1977) are critically considered. In the sequel the nature of knowledge (samyag-jnana), types of valid inference (anumana pramana), and its application to moral discourse have been analysed.

Since anumana-pramana as sound inference yields knowledge (prāma), it is necessary to understand the nature of knowledge (samyak-jnānam) in general according to Nyāya-bindu and Nyāya-bindu-tika. There is a close relationship between knowledge and right action, because all successful human action is preceded by knowledge (samyag jnanam). The concept of knowledge is defined as that true congnition (knowledge) which is not contradicted by experience (N.B.T.:1.1). Dharmottara's elucidation of the definition of knowledge implies that in common life, a man has spoken truth if his words direct or suggest us to obtain or avoid an object or fact. A person is reliable if he utters a true sentence and a sentence is true if it corresponds to a fact. Neither true cognition generates its object nor it brings it to the knower. However, it directs us to obtain or avoid it through appropriate purposive action: Indeed knowledge had the power to initiate a man into action in accordance with his will. Thus the proper function of knowledge as true cognition is to establish a relation between a knower and a known fact.

There are two types of true cognition, viz; direct perception (experience) and inference (valid reason). The function of sense-perception is that it makes us feel its presence. However, in case of valid inference an indirect true cognition as inferential knowledge also points out its fact and initiates into purposive action. Knowledge or true cognition differs from error or false cognition as water seen in mirage. A cognition is false if it does not correspond to any object and it does not lead to fruitful activity. In case of an erroneous cognition, a form of fact or object is not properly represented. A cognition is also false when it wrongly represents the place of an object, e.g. the radiance of a jewel seen through the chink in a door when mistaken for jewel itself which is behind the door. Similarly, a cognition is also false if it represents an object as existing at a time when we really do not perceive it e.g. seeing an object in dream at midnight which was seen at noon cannot be right cognition.

According to Dharmakirti, right knowledge is the cause of successful action; it is two fold namely perceptual and inferential, knowledge. Human action has an aim in the form of desired object. There are two types of objects namely the objects to be attained and the objects to be avoided. However, an indifferent object is undesirable. Accordingly an action is successful if one succeeds in obtaining an object or avoiding some other object. And such a successful activity is called production of a cognitive behaviour where as form of action directed by knowledge is called right behaviour which consists in avoiding the avoidable and attaining the attainable. It is made clear that successful action is possible when cognition has rightly constructed the corresponding fact whose existence has been pointed out; however false cognition cannot function in that direction.

Valid inference as a source of mediate knowledge: Valid inference is two fold, namely inference for one self and inference for others. Inference for one self is also called an internal inference in which we cognize something internally for ourselves and its verbal formulation is inference for ourselves and its verbal formulation is inference for others; following is the definition.

"An inferential cognition is produced through a mark that has a mark that has a three fold aspect and which refers to an object (not perceived but) inferred". (N.B.T. II)

There are three kinds of reason namely negation, identity and causation, (i) An inference containing negation may be analyzed as follows:

Thesis: There is no jar on some particular place.

Reason: Because it is not perceived, although the conditions of perception are fulfilled.

Following is a logical formulation of the above example.

Premises

1. If a thing is not perceived in a particular place under normal conditions, then it is absent in that place.
2. A jar is not perceived in a particular place.

Conclusion: Therefore it is absent in that place. In this inference the reason is in negative form-because of non-x i.e. non-perceptibility of a certain object.

Application to Moral Situation

1. If a vice is not observed in a person then it is absent in that person.
2. A vice is not observed in that person.
3. That person does not possess a vice.

(ii) *Identity Inference:* Identity is a reason for deducing a proposition when the subject alone is sufficient for that deduction. (N.B.T.16). According to N.B.T. the essence of a thing can be a valid logical reason. A predicate whose presence is dependent upon no other condition besides the mere existence of the fact constituting the reason a predicate can be analytically deduced.

Following is an Example

Thesis : This is a tree
Reason : Because it is an Asoka (N.B.2)

Logical formulation may be given as:

1. All Asokas are trees.
2. This is an Asoka.
3. This is a true

In this argument, the conclusion does not imply a mediate knowledge; it is like a perceptual judgement. However, there is a clarification in Nyāya-bindu-tika if a person does not know the proper use of the word 'Asoka' and some person would point out to him a tall Asoka and also a small Asoka tree. Actually above inference is analytic, because the sentence 'every Asoka is a true' is an analytic sentence in which predicate 'tree' is contained in subject.

6. The sentence all Asoka trees are trees is analytic sentence. Following are other examples.

(i) All stars are self-luminous
Sun is a star
∴ Sun is self luminous

(ii) Every even number is divisible by two.

Eight is an even number.
∴ Eight is also divisible by two.

Above analytical inference is based on a principle of essential identity.

7. A valid reason based on the relation of causality is stated below:

Thesis	:	There is fire.
Reaso	:	Because there is smoke (N.B.)

Corresponding complete inference is as follows:

1. All cases of smoke are the cases of fire.
2. That place has smoke.
3. Therefore there is fire.

The causal relation is familiar in common life and is derived from repeated experience of existence of effect and its cause.

8. Next, the structure and function of inference for others is elucidated below. It is usually defined as that valid inference which consists in communicating the three aspects of the logical mark to others (N.B.T.: III.1).

Valid inferences are based on method of agreement and method of difference (N.B.T.—III.5.)

Premise-1	:	All products are impermanent, e.g. Jar.
Premise-2	:	The sounds of speech are products.
Conclusion	:	They are impermanent.

Following inference is based on method of difference:

P1 : All eternal entities are not products.
P2 : But the sounds of speech are products.

∴ C : They are impermanent.

There is also a formulation of analytical inference in which method of agreement is used.

P1 : Everything that exists is momentary.
P2 : The sound exists.
∴ C : It is momentary.

Syllogism of causality in the method of agreement is explicated below.

P1 : Wherever there is smoke, there is fire.
P2 : There is smoke.
∴ C : There is fire.

Modern analysis: Fundamental concepts of Buddhist Logic have been interpreted by modern thinkers like Stcherbatsky, R.S.Y. Chi etc. Here mainly the interpretations of Stcherbotsky and R.S.Y. Chi have been considered. Stcherbatsky in his books entitled **'Buddhist Logic'** volume one and two has analyzed the Original texts:

Nyāya-bindu by Dharma-kirti and Nyāya-bindu-tīka by Dharmottara. He deserve thanks for his scholarly work. He tried to in interpret Buddhist theory of inference in terms of Aristotalean ideas of formal logic as syllogistic theory. For example the traditional inference in terms formulated in Nyāya-bindu have been formalized as shown below.

1. All the cases of smoke are the cases of fire.

2. That place is a case of smoke.

∴ 3. That place is also a case of fire.

Following is the form of syllogism, with modern symbolic form.

1. All M is P	1. (x) $(Mx \supset Px)$
2. All S is M	2. (x) $(Sx \supset Mx)$
3. All S is P	3. (x) $(Sx \supset Px)$
	(Modern form)

Above form of syllogism is valid, because it comforms to the rules of valid syllogism namely: R1 The middle term M should be distributed at least in one of the premises. R2. A term (S) which is distributed in the conclusion should be distributed in the corresponding minor or second promises.

Similarly, another traditional inference based of essential identity is formalized according to Aristotalean Logic as given below with corresponding modern form.

1. All Asokas are trees	1. $(x)(Ax \supset Tx)$
2. That is a Asoka	2. $(Ex) \supset (Ax)$
∴ 3. That is also a tree	∴ 3. $(Ex) \supset (Tx)$

Above inference is valid, because it has the same valid form as explained above.

However, in case of contra-positive inference the form is slightly different.

1. All the places of non-fire are the places of non-smoke.
2. That place is a case of smoke.

∴ 3. That place is a case of fire.

Following is a syllogistic form of the argument, along with modern form:

1. All Non-P is non-M		1.	(x)	$(Px \supset Mx)$
2. All S is	M	2.	(x)	$(Sx \supset Mx)$
∴ 3. All S is	P	∴ 3.	(x)	$(Sx \supset Px)$

(Modern form)

The form of this argument is valid if "All M is P" is treated or equivalent to "All non-P is non-M".

Eventhough the types of inferences formulated by Dharmakirti in his Nyāya-bindu are formally valid, it is necessary to consider the truth of the elements of inference. According to Western formal logic including Aristotalean Logic, the formal validity is an important aspect of Logical analysis. However, for Indian Logicians, both the formal validity and truth of the elements of inference are necessary to produce inferential knowledge. Anumana-pramana is a source of inferential knowledge. Accordingly anumana-pramana is formally valid and also its elements are true in order to produce mediate knowledge. It is necessary to formalize epistemic inferences according to the standers of epistemic logic in which elements of valid inferences are considered as knowledge claims.

A knower S claims to know that P as true if he has good or adequate reasons in the form of known propositions. One of the traditional examples may be formulated as given below:

1. S knows that there is fire in that place.
2. Because he knows that there is fire in that place.
3. He also knows that wherever there is smoke there is also fire.

Following is a valid epistemic inference.

1. S knows that 'all the case of smoke are the case of fire'.
2. He knows that there is smoke in some place.

∴ 3. He knows that there is fire in that place.

This inference is formally valid and elements are true propositions.

10. Application of Buddhist Logic for Moral discourse. Even though, the theory of valid inference satisfies the criteria of sound inference in the domain of factual discourse, it is possible to extend its scope to moral discourse, containing value judgements. Consider some of the following moral precepts given by Buddha.

1. Take the precept to observe non-violence.
2. Take the precept to abstain from stealing.
3. Take the precept to abstain from lying.

Above sentences imply moral imperatives which are universalizable. Accordingly following are the correct inference in moral discourse.

1. All human beings ought to be non-violent.
2. All Indians are human beings.

∴ 3. Indians ought do be non-violent.

It may be expressed in Buddhist inference.

(i) 1. Devadatta is virtuous.
2. Because he is non-violent.
3. All non-violent persons are virtuous.

Or

(ii) 1. That act is good.
2. Because it is a non-violent act.
3. All non-violent acts are good.

There are also negative formulations of inference.

(iii) 1. No human ought to tell lies.
2. Politicians are humans.
3. They ought not tell lies.

Corresponding affirmative formulation is this:

(iv) 1. All humans ought to tell truth.
2. Scientists are human beings.
3. They ought to tell truth.

(v) 1. That speaker is virtuous.
2. Because he is truthful.
3. All truthful persons are virtuous.

It may be expressed in five membered inference as shown below.

1. That speaker is a virtuous man.
2. Because he is trustworthly.
3. All trustworthy persons are virtuous.
4. That person is trustworthy.

∴ 5. That persos is virtuous.

Above arguments are valid and also informative.

CONCLUSION

Modern researches in Buddhist Logic are fruitful. However, formal aspects of Buddhist logic are necessary but not sufficient. Accordingly epistemological analysis of inference is relevant for understanding Buddhist theory of inference in realistic framework.

Notes and References

1. Acharya Chandrashekhara Shastri (1954): The Nyāya-bindu of Sri Dharma-kirti with (Nyāya-bindu-tike) a Sanskrit Commentary by Sri Dharmottaracharyá, edited with Notes, Introduction and Hindi translations Kashi Sanskrit series 22 (Buddhist Nyāya, section No.1 chaukhambha Sanskrit Sansthan Varanasi.
2. Chi, R.S.Y. (Reprint, 1984): *Buddhist Formal Logic* (First Published: The Royal Asiatic Society of Great Britain, 1969); Motilal Banarsidass, New Delhi.

3. Copi, I.M. (1971): Symbolic Logic, Prentice Hall, India.
4. Ingalalli, R.I. (2000): "Bauddha dharmada svarupa" (in Kannada), published in Gurudeva, pp. 101-107, Shri Shivayogeeshwara Math, Inchal.
5. Ingalalli, R.I. (2000): Modern Symbolic Logic, Sachchidananda Prakashana, Dharwad.
6. Ingalalli, R.I. (2003): "Scientific Law as Subjunctive Generalization" in Journal: Bihar Philosophical Research, Parts I & II, pp. 77-82, Patna.
7. Ingalalli, R.I. (2003): "Mind in Navya-nyaya" in Human Mind and Machine, Edited by Prof. V.N. Jha, Indian Books Centre, New Delhi.
8. Madhvacharya (1961): *Sarvadarsana Samgrah*: Translated by Cowell G.B. and A.G. Gough Chankhamba Sanskrit Series, Varanasi.
9. Radhakrishanan, S. (1972): *Indian Philosophy*, Vol. I, Blacki & Sons, Mumbai.
10. Stcherbatsky, Th. (1962): *Buddhist Logic*, Vol. I, Dover Publications Inc. New York.
11. Stcherbatsky Th. (1962): *Buddhist Logic*, Vol. II, Dover Publications Inc. New York.
12. Vidyabhusana, S. (1971): *A History of Indian Logic*, Motilal Banarsidas, New Delhi.

23

BUDDHIST CONCEPT OF ENVIRONMENTAL CONSERVATION

DR. RAHUL RAJ

During the past many years, there have been fundamental changes in the attitude of man towards environment. There was a time when environment meant only sanitation and public-health. Today, the environment is conceived in its totality, and a holistic approach is made while planning for better quality of life stressing the sustainable development.[1]

The two components of nature, '*organism*' and '*environment*' are not only much complex and dynamic, but also interdependent, mutually reactive and interrelated. The ecosystem is capable of self-maintenance. However, the equilibrium is very sensitive to external stimuli, such as human activities promoted by socio-economic goals.[2] The human beings impose changes on natural ecosystem and increasing control of his environment often creates conflict between his goals and natural processes.

On the occasion of the 'First International Conference' on 'Environmental Education' held at New Delhi in 1987, the late Mrs. Indira Gandhi observed that Environmental Education is to help arouse social consciousness and make community aware of the fact that the good of the individual and the community are both harmed by ecological disruptions.[3]

Tathagat Buddha viewed humanity as part of nature, and if nature is encroached upon or destroyed, humanity cannot exist, and by making an effort to disrupt the ecological balance, human beings harm themselves. Being an integral part of nature, trees and animals can live without man, but man cannot live without them.[4]

Although the teachings of the Buddha are more focused over the spiritual emancipation of human being, he ultimately does not differentiate between all living beings and Nature around him.

It is also important to note that nature and forests are very much associated with the four major events of his life, which are:

(i) Birth in '*Lumbīnivan*',
(ii) Enlightenment in '*Uruvelavan*' under '*Bodhī Tree*',
(iii) First Sermon (Dhammachakkapavattan) in '*Mrigdayavān*', and
(iv) Mahapārinibbān in '*Salvan*'.

Various types of animals are associated with Budha's life such as elephant, ox (*Vrish*), horse, lion, nagas etc. His birth is symbolised by elephant, Rashi is symbolised with ox (*Vrish*) and renunciation with horse.

In the Digha Nikaya, it is said that 'Whereas some recluses and Brahmanas while living on food provided by the devotees continue to injure the seedlings and growing plants whether propagated from the roots or cuttings joints or budding or seeds, Gotama the recluse hold aloof from such injury to seedlings and growing plants.[5]

The Buddha's concept of environmental conservation is beautifully revealed in his statement that 'As a bee, without harming the flower, It's colour or scent, flies away collecting only the honey, ever so should the sage wander in the village.

To make this world a better place to live and prosper, Buddha emphasised in Karaniyametha sutta[7], that all the living beings whether small or big, medium or tiny, small like a molecule, seen or unseen (with eyes), far or near, born or yet to be born, all the beings should live happily by neither saying ill nor insulting each-other. Man should keep a compassionate attitude towards other living beings and strive for their prosperity just as a mother does for his only son.

Buddha's teachings cover respect for life of both the flora and the fauna. Buddha knew very well that there is life in plants and trees. Foolish are they who cut them.[8] People used to cut green palm trees and make shoes by it's leaves. Buddha stopped this act and proclaimed it as a sinful act (dukkat) because violence over living being is committed by cutting green trees.[9]

Buddha befriends animals, tends plants and enjoins his followers (monks) to observe a period of retreat during rainy season (varshavasa) so that they could avoid trampling on insects abounding in the rainy season.

It is clearly evident form the geographical as well as architectural characteristic of Buddhist Monasteries that Buddha stressed the sanctity of environment form the very beginning. They were properly broomed and cleared by novice monks every morning.[10] Toilets were built at a distance from the main building. Their commodes (Vacchakup) were fitted with covers (apidhan) to stop the air pollution. Wastewater was drained out by underground or covered outlets to check the growth of insects and worms. In the same way, urinal (Passavkumbhi[11] or Passavdoni)[12] were also covered to avoid foul odour in the monastery.

Special stress was given on the purity of water. Separate arrangements were made for drinking water (paniya) and non-drinking water (uparpaniya).[13] A particular place in the monastery was specified for the storage of water (udakshala) to maintain cleanliness.

Underlining the importance of environment to mankind, the monasteries were constructed neither too close nor too far from the cities. Generally, they were situated in the midst of a forest or garden. In such case they were termed as Aramas e.g. Jetvanaram and Purvaram in Savatthi, Ghoshitaram in Koshambi, Venuvanaram in Rajgriha etc. Those monasteries which were not situated in a garden were simply termed as 'Viharas'.

Ashoka 'The Great', was one of the notable followers of Buddhism. His attitude towards the conservation of environment and ecology was highlighted by his Second Rock Edict, in which he emphasised to grow more medicinal herbs and plants not only in his own empire but in other neighbouring states also.

He arranged for the medical treatment of not only humans, but also animals. He also ordered for tree plantation especially fruit-bearing and shady trees all along the roadside. In order to provide clean and cool water to passengers he ordered to dig up wells all along the highways. He also constructed the Rest-Houses for the comfort of travelers.[14]

In Ashoka's First Rock Edict, we get a glimpse of his compassionate and Buddhist tendencies. In the beginning he prohibited killing of peacocks and deer except for one deer and two peacocks for the royal kitchen. But later on he even prohibited killing of them.[15] He specially stressed not to kill any birds, animals and aquatic animals during their breeding period. We can rightly say that the Buddha initiated the sense of environmental conservation and ecological ethics, and Ashoka implemented and propagated it.

According to Prof. Angaraj Chaudhary, if we follow the social ethics preached by the Buddha and even if we observe the first precept of abstaining from killing in both its negative and positive aspects [not killing beings is the negative aspect (Virata Sila); developing kindness and compassion for them is the positive aspect (Charitta Sila)]. We will reduce our craving and aversion which will enable us to save our environment and ecology.[16]

Today, the whole world, particularly the developing countries face a near-crisis situation, both economic and environmental. It is interesting to note that both the words (economics and ecology) have the same root 'olkos' meaning 'house'. While economics deals with financial house-keeping, ecology deals with environmental house-keeping. Time has come when sustainability in development has to enter our planning process.[17] To materialise this, we must once again remind ourselves about Buddha's concept towards environmental conservation, then only the modern society can live in perfect harmony with its surroundings on this planet.

Notes and References

1. Sharma, P.D., '*Ecology and Environment*', Preface, p. vii.
2. *Ibid.*, p. 285.
3. *Ibid.*, p. 467.
4. Angane Lal, '*Ecological Ethics and Buddhism*', Proceedings of XXIVth I.B.C., Bodh Gaya—1999, p. 2.
5. 'Digha Nikaya', Vol. I, Sutta No. 1.
6. Maha Thera, Ven. Narada (ed. & tr.), 'Dhammapada', Puppha Vagga' Verse-6.
7. Karaniyametha Sutta' (Pali), Gatha Nos. 4-7, 'Chatubhanavar Pali'.
8. Kashyap, Bhikkhu Jagdish (ed.), 'Mahavagga' (Pali), pp. 209/27, 28.
9. *Ibid.*, pp. 209/5.
10. Sankrityayan, Rahul (ed. & tr.), 'Vinaya Pitaka' (Hindi), p. 1.
11. Kashyap, *Bhikkhu Jagdish* (ed.), 'Chullavagga' (Pali), pp. 231/1.
12. *Ibid.*, pp. 231/17.
13. *Ibid.*, pp. 321/21.
14. Second Rock Edict of Ashoka.
15. First Rock Edict of Ashoka.
16. Chaudhary, Prof. Angaraj, '*Buddha's Ecological Ethics*', proceeding of XXIVth I.B.C., *Bodhgaya*, 1999, p. 13.
17. Sharma, P.D., *op. cit.*, p. 286

24

THE INFLUENCE OF PALI LANGUAGE AND LITERATURE ON TELUGU

Y. RAMAYYA

INTRODUCTION

It is a misnomer to call Pali a dead language (Mrita Basha). On the contrary, it is an Amrita Basha for two good reasons. One is, its canonical part Tripalkas are recorded in the exact language the Master spoke, and two, it has a very vast literature both canonical and non-canonical, dating back from the 5th century B.C. It is a language embellished with regular grammar, its poetical works like the Dhammapada, Pali Prosody, Alankara Sastra, Atta Kathas, by highly learned persons, like Buddha Ghosha not to speak of the non-canonical literature 'Jataka Tales' about the Master's previous births. Few other faiths have as large literature as Pali. Its stages of evolution from the local Kosalan language with the Vedic Sanskrit called Ardha Magadhhi, later known by the name 'Pali', gradually gave rise to prakrit languages including Sauraseni, Paisachi etc. and evolved into more modern Indian languages. Sanskrit, (samskruta). As its name itself suggests, was a reformation of some other regional dialect contemporary with Magadhi and spoken by people around Benares. It, therefore, could not have been derived from Sanskrit, which is a later formation.

CANONICAL LITERATURE

This consists in the three Pitakas, Nipathas etc. These are Buddhists' sacred texts. The Pali of the canonical works was based on the standard Kosala (at that time the paramount power in Northern India), the vernacular as spoken in the 6th and 7th centuries B.C. As it was not in written characters, it cannot be called the literary form or a modification of that vernacular. It was the mother tongue of the Buddha. In one of the earliest Pali documents, he is represented as calling himself a Kosalan.

After the Sinhalese Bhikkus resorted to writing the canon in their own tongue, some peculiarities of their vernacular as well as, may be, some other niceties and nuances of the Dravidianisms (Kalingese?) might have crept into Simhalese, changing its form a little. There is no good evidence that the Simhalese Bhikkus at that time knew Sanskrit.

The purpose of this paper is to trace and sketch, in broad outline, the use of idioms and proverbs and the influence of the Pali on Telugu as a member of the Dravidian family of languages.

ON THE LANGUAGE

(1) Both the main schools of Buddhism viz., Theravada & Mahayana held sway over the lower Kalinga country (the present-day north Andhra) for well over ten centuries during which period the Pali non-canonical literature, by its interaction with whatever language was prevailing at the time imported good many Pali terms into the common man's Telugu which imported a good many Pali terms into it.

(2) The influence of Pali Cannon itself, so far as the Telugu language is concerned was little.

(3) This influence was on the form of the Kalingans' language by making it a vowel-ending one, which the other members of the Dravidian family of languages are not.

(4) The reader of this paper has collected 3036 Pali words which crept into the Telugu language by direct entry due to modification (Tatsama) by adding only case endings (Du, mu, Vu & lu) from a Pali vocabulary of about 12,060 words in common use in Pali. Of the above, 325 are direct adoptions from pali 924 are tatsamas 1718 tatbhavas and 151are ardha viparinamas. The modification of the Pali roots was as below: (only 10 examples under each head of classification are given).

(a) By direct absorption into the Telugu language as Aggi, Atavi, Ati, Abala, Abhinandana, Abhivadana, Abhiruchi, Abhisarika, Ambu, Ayya, etc.

(b) Examples of entrance of Pali words as Tatsamas: Anjanamu, Adika, Agadha, aghamu, Ankura, Anga, Angara, Anganaa (woman), Akkaramu, Ankura etc.

(c) Examples as Tadbhavas:
Acchara (P): Acchara (T):, Anguta (P): Angulamu (T)
Anguli (P); Anguli (T); Atchasanna (P)
Atyasanna; Ajjapaka (P); Adhyapakudu (T)
Attha (P); Asta (T); Addharatta (P);
Ardharatra (T); Ati Luddha; Ati lubhdha (T)
Anavesaka (P); Anveshakudu (T)

(d) Examples as Ardhaviparimamas (not many); Abbuta (P); Adhbuta (without fear). Ayomaya (P) (made of iron); Ayomaya (confused) (T) Atanka (P) disease; obstacle (T); Vinaya (P) (discipline); Humility (T) Apanna (P) (Quick with child); uncared for (T) Upanayana (P): (bringing near): sacred-thread ceremony (T) Kana (P) fine powder between husk and grain of rice: atom (T).

II. In the matter of idioms, and proverbs it is found there are close parallels, which by inference, is possible only when there could have been good interaction between the two languages. This point requires an in depth study.

The paper on this subject is essentially preliminary and must perforce be stated in broad outline only, as Telugu works prior to poet Nannaya are not now available. The categories of literary work are the Mahabharata, Prabhandas, Chatus, Yakshaganas, Satakams (centuries of verses). Of these, whichever contain Accha Telugu words in plenty are to be studied diligently in detail for etymological origins with a view to finding their nearness to Pali vocabulary. The search will doubtless be rewarding to establish the Pali—Telugu connection more significantly. For the kind information of the scholars present, the origin of following are niceties in Telugu good many of which are traceable to the Pali sources.

The following are some idioms which reveal the close relationship of the Pali and Telugu expressions.

No detailed explanation is necessary.

Baha-bahi; Potapoti; Balaa Bala; Atalakutala.

Halahali; Amee—Tumi; Musta musti; Khanda—Khandikam; Akula pakula (confusion).

Pubba-para (P) purvaa Para; Phalaa-phala (Various kinds of fruit).

Familiar expressions in Pali smacking of Telugu idiom:

Kalam karoti He dies.

Rajyam Karoti. He rules.

Hastagatam Karoti . Got into his hand.

Itareetara: whatsoever.

Example of dwanyanukuranam (Sound eching sense) Murumurayati: to

Cause sound like Murumura.

Accukatku to erecting bunds on land for wet cultivation

This is a purely Telugu word which entered Pali

Ama: Dravidian word meaning "Yes" at in Pali

Aramasma aramam from garden to garden

Gamagamam: from village to village

Seegha seegha = Quickly, quickly

Mande Mande: slowly slowly, little by little

Matupakka = on mother's side

Pithupakka = on father's side

Hikka (P) = (Hiccoughs) Yekkilly (T)

Hora hori: Horaa Hori

Palapana = Pelapana (chaff, useless talk)

III. Pali prosody or Vuthodaya (exposition of metres as its Sanskrit counterpart; containing 106 stanzas. The stanzas are vuttas whose metre is governed by the arrangement of syllables in each verse or quarter (charanams).

Due to constraint on space and time, it is not possible to describe at length the Akkaras (syllables), Jati (Stanza), Ganas (groups of syllables eight of them) or their respective notations.

During a study of the above meters what attracted my significant attention was the metre of Ariya giti under 'geeti' classification. The first and third quarters contain 12 matras (syllabic instants) and the second and fourth contain 20 matras. A close study of this metre and of the 'Kanda" metre in Telugu and 'Kannada' will reveal a perceptible identity in the arrangement of syllabic instants.

The following are the examples:

Pali: Ariya pubbhaddham yadi
Garunekhenadhikenanidhaneyuttam

Yadi Pubbhadhasamanam
Daramitaram chodita Yamariya geeti

Except for the stipulation of 'prasa' and 'yati' as in Telugu Desi prosody they sound like 'Kanda Padya'. There can be no doubt that this metre is, with slight variation, a Pali import into Telugu and Kannada which are identical in metres. This shows the strong influence of Pali prosody on Telugu long before the latter was embellished with Sanskrit metres. Of Telugu metres the surviving 'desi' metres are kandam, seesam Tatageetham, Ata veladi. Dwipada, Manjari Dwipada, etc. How many desimetres having Pali influence became extinct thro' efflux of time, it is well high impossible to state now; until painstaking research and incisive thinking brings the precious little information out. Universities of A.P., with financial help from the U.G.C. may encourage scholars in this field to take up this work which will establish beyond a shadow of doubt the strong literary connection between the two languages.

Bhawatu Sabba Mangalam
May All People Be Happy

Notes and References

1. Geiger, Introduction to Pali Literature and Language, , page 1, para 2, Munshiram Manoharlal.
2. Ramayya, Y., "Telugu, Pali Connection", 'Suhrullekha' (April-June 1994), Ananda Buddha Vihara, Secunderabad, p. 38.
3. Rhys David, Pali-English Dictionary, Para 2, p. 1, Motilal Banarsidass.
4. Moggallana's (Sangarakkita Thera) Vuthodaya, 12th Century A.D.
5. Jinananda, B., The Vuthodaya (The Pali Prosody), Nava Nalanda Mahavihara Research Publication, Nalanda, Patna, Vol. 11.
6. Manohara Gupta, K., "Linguistics in Pali", Sundeep Prakashan, Dev Nagar, Karol Bagh, New Delhi.

25

Buddhist Tribes of the N.E. Region Rich in Cultural-Heritage But Poor in Modern Amenities

Dr. P. Vijayaraghav Reddy

It is rightly said that the North Eastern Region of our country is a paradise for Anthropologists and Linguists and a treasure house for Folklorists. I would like to extend this statement to Buddhist-theologists/scholars and put forward that this is the only region of India where about 30% of the population is tribal, whereas the national average percentage of tribal population is only seven. Though bulk of the tribal population has adopted Christianity, among the others there is good percentage of followers of Buddhism. As Sikkim is included in the North Eastern Region, at present the region consists of 8 states i.e., Arunachal Pradesh, Assam, Manipur, Meghalaya, Mizoram, Nagaland, Sikkim and Tripura covering the area of 2,62,123 sq. k.m. and having 3,90,35,578 population (2001 Census). State-wise break-up figures including the percentage of literacy in brackets are as follows: Arunachal Pradesh: 10,91,117 (54.74%). Assam: 2,66,38,407 (64.28%). Manipur: 23,88,634 (68.87%). Meghalaya: 23,06,669 (63.31%).

Mizoram: 8,91,054 (88.49%). Nagaland: 19,88,636 (67.11%), Sikkim: 5,40,493 (69.68%). Tripura 31,91,168 (73.66%). If we turn towards the demography pertaining to various religions. We notice a quite different picture than the mainland. Chart showing Religion-wise figures (1971) along with the tribal population figures is appended. Form the chart it can be seen that four states viz., Mizoram (94.26%). Nagaland (88.61%). Meghalaya (80.48%) and Arunachal Pradesh (79.02%) are predominantly settled by the tribal population and in these states with exception to Arunachal Pradesh. Christianity is the prominent religion with 86.08% in Mizoram, 66.76% in Nagaland and 46.98% in Meghalaya.

As for as Buddhism is concerned 30% of the population of Sikkim and 13.13% of the population of Arunachal Pradesh are Buddhists. In Arunachal Pradesh more than 63% of the population follow Adim Dharma, which is known as DONIYOPOLO, where Sun (Doniya) and Moon (Polo) are worshipped. It is worth mentioning here that Buddhist number exceeds Hindus in Mizoram. (Buddhists=22,647 and Hindus=21,229). In no other State in India Buddhist population exceeds Hindus. Such multiplicity races, religions and languages of the region pose a challenge not only to the social scientists but also to the politicians and administrators.

I had a rare privilege to work among the tribal people of the region for about 4 years as a head of the N.E. Regional Center of the Central Institute of Hindi (Government of India). During my tenure I had an opportunity to travel and stay in remote places for about three weeks in every programme, conducting short-term reorientation programmes for the in-service Hindi teachers of the religion and meet administrative heads and interview some of the religious leaders and publish articles and books about the socio, cultural and linguistic situation of the region.

We can divide all Buddhist tribes of the region into three categories. They are:

1. Tribes who follow Lamaism of Mahayana School,

2. Tribes who are followers of Theravada of Hinyana School, and
3. Semi-Buddhist tribes.

Lepchas, Monpas, Sherdukpens, Bhotiyas and Memba-Khambas are termed as Mahayana Buddhists. These Tribes are live in Sikkim and three Western Districts: Tawang, West Kameng and East Kameng of Arunachal Pradesh. These Districts have borders with Tibet. Tibeten language is used as lingua-franca among the various tribes of the districts and Buddhist scriptures of Monpa language is written in Tibetan Script. Tawang is the place where 350 years old famous Buddhist Gompha (Monastery) is situated at 3,048 meter altitude in which 500 lamas can perform rituals at one time. In Tawang district there is a 700 years old historical Buddhist Stupa. In the folk-tales of the tribes one can find such Mantras and Folk beliefs regarding deification of Buddha, female counter parts of Bodhisatva, terrible demonical Buddhas, esoteric methods of meditation and ritual practices for the realization of the supreme goal are depicted. Religious scrolls. Prayer-flags, prayer-wheels are the main items, which are occasionally mentioned in the tales. Besides these MANI, and MANI PADMA probably symbolized forms for PADMASAMBAHAVA and a Mantra OM MANI PEME HUM are found in the tales.

Tribal-lore can be taken as a testimony of the Tribal culture and their heritage. As already said Lapchas of Sikkim and Sherdukpens of Arunachal Pradesh are followers of Mahayana cult. Let us refer two tales.[1]

1. *The Lotus that Scatters Golden Rays*. Which is a Lapcha folk tale and
2. *Be Merceful to the Beings*. Which is a Sherdukpen folk tale.

Identically in both the tales Buddha's teachings are depicted in such a way as if the tales are from one tribe. In these tales sons of two widows are heroes. Both were able to obtain the MANI PADMA and surmount all the dangerous, ghosts and evil-spirits and attain eternal peace with the help of small creatures like pigeons, rats and dogs. In both the tales the sacred mantra OM-MA-NI-PAD-ME-HUM and the patron god: Avalokiteswar are mentioned occasionally. This is credited with bringing to an end of the cycle of rebirth and thereby giving entrance to Nirvana. Mani is symbolized as avalokiteswara and the mantra is said to be essence of all happiness and prosperity and knowledge and great means of liberation. It is also said that the OM closes the door of rebirth among the gods. MA among the ASURAS. NI among the Mankind and PAD among the sub-human creatures. ME among PRETAS and HUM among the inhabitants of hell.[2]

Chakmas (Mizoram and Tripura State and Tirap Dt. of Arunachal Pradesh) Mugs, (Tripura) Khamtis, Tai Pakels, Singpos, Turangs and Kemengs of Assam are followers of Hinayana. Large settlements of khamtis and Singpos are found in Lohit and Changlong Districts of Arunachal Pradesh. In the tales of these tribes one will come across Bhikkus and their performing rituals in Buddha Purnima (Paya Puthikam). Robe offering ceremony (Kathing/Civara Dana) their beliefs: that the world is full of ghosts (Fi) evil spirits (Pikta) and demons (fi-fai) and that Buddha serves as a general protector against all the dangers: and the generic condition of suffering can be alleviated, renouncing the world in favour of Buddha (Fala). Dharma (Tala) and Sangha (Sangkha) are found in their tales. Symbolic creatures: as black tiger with white spot on its forehead, a tree with silver branches and golden flowers with frangrance are also described in the tales.

In a chakma fable, RADHAMAN AND DHANAPATI. Radhaman, the hero after performing puja to Metiya, the goddess who guards against the attacks of the black tiger, and with her help could able to reach the tree with silver branches and golden flowers with sweet fragrance. And from there he killed the black tiger with white spot on forehead. After performing some rituals he could be able to rescue his four friends who were killed by the black tiger earlier. These four noble friends of Radhaman are symbols of the four noble truths of Buddhist doctrine.

The other Major tribe KHAMTI who follows Hinayana cult of Buddhism is said be a race of warriors. They have a glorious past history. Ahoms of Tai race ruled Assam for 6 centauries beginning from 13th century. Khamtis are believed the off shoots of the Ahoms. There is an historical evidence[3] that Ahom king Rajeswar (1751-69) allowed the Khamtis to settle on the banks of river Tengapani—which is called namsoon by Khmatis. Their immigration and consequent expansion in Assam continued over a hundred years. Later Ahom king appointed one Khamti chief 'Chau-mu-mgan-lung' as Sadiya Khowa Gohain (Subedhar or Jageerdar of Sadiya province) Khamtis speak a language of the Tai group and have a script and literature of their own. Khamti literature is quite rich consisting of Pitakas. Ramayana, Maha Bharata, historical chronicles, works on law, social and political conditions, tantrika mantras etc. They are fine craftsmen, good traders and skillful farmers. They also played a distinct role in the history of Assam. As far as khamti Ramayana is concerned in their language it is called as 'LIK-CHAU-LAMANG' i.e., the epic of Rama and/ or 'CHAU-ALANG-LAMNG' i.e., story of Rama Avatara. It is in 35 chapters and 7 Kandas in 12,678 lines in Tai Script. In the prologue it is said that at the age of 80 Lord Buddha when he was taking rest at Kushinagar in the shalivana, Ananda asked Buddha to tell Ramayana story. On the request of his disciple. Buddha told the story. In the epic it is said that Buddha said that after him 10 Bodhisatvas will come and they propogate Buddhism in the world. After the tenth Bodhisatva eleventh Bodhisatva will be born at Jamboodweepa and he is the CHAU-LAMANG, i.e. Sri Rama.

Khamti versions of Jataka stories are very popular in their society. Angulimala story is told with an intensity and significant twist. In another tale Buddha's mother in heaven with a pre-recognition that her son would discard his royal garments on the very next day in order to become monk. She sits whole night without sleep and weaves a robe on her loom and send it through a messenger to present it to her son.

Buddhist stupa has been discovered in the excavation of Archaeological Survey of India at the barks of Naodihing River in Changlong District of Arunachal Pradesh. Near by the site many metal images of Buddha also found. All these prove the most significant cultural and religious heritages of Khamtis and Singpos of Hinayana cult of Buddhism of the N.E. Region.

Tribes like Remos, Bokars and Aitoniyas of Arunachal Pradesh are termed as Semi Buddhist tribes. They are called Semi-Buddhist tribes because in the legends and tales of the tribes we can find the inter woven beliefs of Buddhism and animistic beliefs.

I conclude the paper with my findings from my personal visits and information gathered from the interview with Chakma MLA of Mizoram state Assembly. Though Khamtis have glorious past and rich cultural and religions heritage, as for as modern amenities are concerned they are in lack of proper educational, medical and transport facilities. Khamtis constructed Buddhist Stupa in 18th century in a place previously known as Jah Natu. Which is now a day called Vijayanagar in Changlong District of Arunachal Pradesh. When we find that there is no road even to this place from the Main settlement of Khamtis of Assam, no doubt they are very poor in modern amenities.

I had an opportunity to interview with Sri Harikisto Chakma. The MLA of the Mizoram Assembly. Full text of the interview in Hindi has been published in my book entitled SANSKRITI SANGAMUTTAR POORVANCHAL (Cultural Synthesis of North East Region). Some important points of the interview, which through light on the situation of the Chakmas in Mizoram are given here under. In Sri Hari Kisto chakma words:

> We are of Anakanese origin speaking a language of Tibeto-Burmese sub family. Our forefathers immigrated to Chittagong hill tract in 16th century where they inter married largely with the Bengalees. With the fusion of Bengali language our language has been utterly changed and now the Chakma

languages is labeled as a dialect of Bengali. While at Chittagong, Chakmas embraced the Thervada cult of Buddhism, which was introduced by Buddha Glossa, the writer of Visuddha magga. Thervada cult reached Chittagong between 15-16th centuries travelling through Nagarjuna Konda. Dravidadesha: Kanchipuram, Srilanka. Thai Desha and Kambodia. Our first chief was Raja Bijoygiri who ruled a big portion of Chittagong hill track. In the regime of Kalindi Rani (1855-1873) Sanghraj Saramit Mahasthivar came to Chittagong from Anakam in the year 1864 on the invitation of Kalindi Rani to reform the Buddhism. With his efforts religious loyalty has increased among the followers of Buddhism. Mr. Chakma further said firmly that due to this loyalty Christian missionaries could not able to attract our people for conversion: where as other tribes have embraced Christianity. During the Kalindi Rani's regime since 1871 hundreds of Chakma coolies were sent to Lushai hills (Now known as Mizo hills) along with the British Military expedition to help the Military personnel. Many Chakmas who went in the expeditions were given shelter in the hills and they settled their and now they are bonafied citizens of Mizoram.

After presenting the Glorious history he deplored the present situation of the tribe. According to him all the Chakmas are Buddhists. Who are settled in 3 countries. Bulk of the population about 3 lacs is in Bangladesh (Chittagong) 50,000 in Tripura, about 50,000 in Mizoram and 40,000 are settled at Arunachal Pradesh as refuses and others are in Arakan. Though under the provision of 6th shedule of the constitution. Chakmas got an autonomous District Council of their own. But their religious centre demagiri (Dhammagiri) is outside of the District. The fertile land of the Karnafuli river belt is not included in our district. We ae backward in all respects. Literacy percentage is very low where as it is very high in Mizos. There are thousands of graduates and hundreds of post-graduates in Mizo population. Where as in Chakmas the figure is only in a dozen. The head quarters of our District council is very far away from the Minland. It will take 3 days to come to this place from silchar the nearest rail station for Mizoram. As Mizos have united and joined with the international presbitarian church society. We chakmas of the thervada school of Buddhism scattered in different places also want to form an organization and want to make links with the worldwide Thervada population and develop our society in a Modern way. Lord Buddha may help us in this respect. Tathastu.

Notes and References

1. Full texts of the two tales in Hindi version presented by me and entitled as Sunhari Kirane Bikhernewala Kamal and Prani Matra Per Daya Karo have been published in Folklore. Feb. 1981 and in my book entitled Uttar Poorvanchal Ki Lokkathayen (1984) respectively.
2. Sarkar (1977), Minor religious structures of the Monpas and Sherdukpens. Resarun. Vol. 3, No. 3, Dept. of Research, Government of Arunachal Pradesh.
3. Gogai, Lila (1971), The Tai Kamtis. Chowkhan.

Chart Showing Religion-wise Figures of the N.E. States (1971 Census)

State	*Tribal Population*		*Hindus*		*Muslims*		*Christians*		*Buddhists*		*Followers of Adimaa Dharma*	
	No	*%*	*No*	*%*	*No*	*%*	*No*	*%*	*No*	*%*	*No*	*%*
1	2	3	4	5	6	7						
Arunachal	3,69,408	79.02	1,02,832	21.99	842	0.18	3,684	0.78	61,400	13.13	2,96,674	63.45
Assam	16,67,657	11.15	1,06,25,847	71.04	35,94,006	24.03	6,67,151	4.46	45,212	0.30	62	—
Manipur	3,34,466	31.18	6,32,597	59.96	70,969	6.61	2,79,243	26.03	495	—	83,167	7.75
Meghalaya	8,14,230	80.48	1,87,140	18.50	26,347	2.60	4,75,267	46.98	1,878	0.18	3,18,168	31.41
Mizoram	3,13,299	94.26	21,229	6.38	1,882	0.56	2,86,141	86.08	22,647	6.81		
Nagaland	4,57,602	88.61	59,031	11.43	2,966	0.58	3,44,798	66.76	179	—	1,08,161	20.94
Sikkim	61,428	30.0	1,43,332	70.0	—	—	—	—	61,428	30.0	—	—
Tripura	4,50,544	20.95	13,93,689	89.55	1,03,962	6.68	15,713	1	42,285	2.71	—	—
Total	55,68,634	27.67	1,31,65,697	65.43	38,00,974	19.08	14,04,846	7.05	2,35,524	1.17	8,36,293	5.20

26

Conversion of Alavaka Yaksha in Nagarjunakonda Sculptures

J. Krishna Kumari

Gautama Buddha converted several kings, tribes (Yakshas, Nagas etc.), and commoners to his faith by his discourses after his enlightenment. There are a number of anecdotes relating to his success in this mission. The story of Alavaka Yaksha is one such.

Gautama Buddha was practical in his approach. He never compelled people to adopt his doctrines. He had the necessary perseverance and skill to bring the people to his path of righteousness by gentle persuasion. He is used to illustrate his lectures with simple tales to enable people to comprehend them easily. Alvaka Yaksha was converted by such discourse with simple illustrations.

The Yakshas, as a tribe, are difficult to identify. They may be an aboriginal tribe with belief in life after death. They believed that the spirit of the deceased would dwell in trees. As a result people believed Yaksha as superhuman beings living in trees. They figure in the mythologies of all religions of India. They were shown as uncivilized in some sections of literature and as civilized in some. It is presumed that they are below Devas but above spirits or goblins.

According to Hillebrant: "Yaksha is magician, uncouth— being unseen spiritual enemy etc." Later, they are recongnised as super natural beings of exalted character. The earliest inscriptional evidence for the Yakshas is from Amaravati: *"Yakho Cadamukho Vakulanivas"*. (Yaksha Cadamukha residing in vakula) and the chaitya must have been erected there in his honour.

The Suttanipata contains the story of Alavak Yaksha's conversion by Buddha. He was a resident of the village Alavi and was described as a cannibal. But, according to the story, he possessed an advanced state of thinking. His questions to Buddha were intricate and thought-provoking. He possessed the wisdom to appreciate and accept the answers of Buddha. In the sculptures of Nagarjunakonda he is depicted in normal proportions but not in ugly deformities.

Alavala Yaksha was the leader of a primitive tribe-Yakshas. He lived in a banyan tree in Alavi. He ate all those who came within its shadow. When the Buddha was staying at Jetavana, during the 13th year of his enlightenment, he heard about Alavaka and decided to convert him to civilised way of life. When Alavaka Yaksha saw the Buddha, he tried all his cruel methods of coercion against him. But, the Buddha remained resolute. Then, Alavak decided to put Buddha's knowledge to test. If he failed, Alavaka threatened to put the Buddha to a cruel death. The Buddha accepted the challenge. The Alavaka put a number of intricate questions about securing real happiness, acquisition of wealth and fame and conquering the pain of death. The Buddha answered them to the Yaksha's satisfaction. Then Buddha asked the Yaksha to refer to any sage if there could be any virtue greater than truth, self-restraint, liberality and forbearance.

As a practical teacher, the Buddha narrated the story of Madhubindu in his discourse with Alavaka.

The story reads as follows: A man, hotly chased by a wild elephant, hid himself in a well. He held the rots of a tree, hanging into the well. But, to his misfortune. There was a deadly snake ready to strike him if he came within its reach. From a beehive drops of honey trickled down and fell into his mouth. He sustained himself on those drops of honey. But soon, the bees began to sting him all over his body. Meanwhile, a rat started biting away the rots form which he was hanging. The story illustrates that the life is so fragile and transient. It is full of misery and agony. Death follows everyone closely like his own shadow, and may strike at any time. Only faith in the virtues of Dharma makes taster the sweetness of truth and to understand the real nature of life.

Alvaka was perfectly satisfied. He became a disciple of the Buddha and became the torch-bearer of his Noble message of peace and fraternity.

The conversion of Alavaka alongwith the story of Madhubindu was exquisitely carved in two panels (Nos. 18 and 44 of Nagarjunakonda).

In one of the panels, Buddha is on the left side, seated in Sukhasana on an elevation. His hands are in Vyakhyanamudra. His left shoulder is covered by Sanghati and the right shoulder remains uncovered. He is looking at a person who is approaching him with a spear in his hand in a mood to attack. He may be identified as the Alavaka Yaksha. He is followed by an armed person. A woman stands on the right side of Alavaka, with an expression of anxiety. She may be the wife of Alavaka. She is trying to resist him from attacking Buddha. Two persons stand behind the woman. At the top, on the left side of the Buddha, there is an inset depicting the story of Madhubindu. The **vyakhyanamudra** and the inset suggest that the Buddha is narrating the story to Alavaka Yaksha. The inset contains, a person hanging from the roots of a tree in a well, where there is a serpant or a crocodile with its mouth wide open. A rat is biting the roots of the tree. The elephant is not shown in this panel. There are two persons squatting close to Buddha's elevated seat. They are looking at Buddha with folded hands. They may be Alavaka and his wife after his conversion. Alavaka's folded hands suggest his submission to the Buddha.

In the second panel, Buddha is on throne at the extreme left. He is in **arthaparyankaasana** and **vyakhyanamudra.** Alavaka is approaching him from the right side, holding a spear. His wife is on his right side, trying to prevent him form attacking Buddha. Alavaka's right hand is in raised posture, suggesting that he is challenging the Buddha. He appears confident while his wife looks anxious. The story of **'Madhubindu'** is dipicted in an inset on the right side of Buddha.

In this sculpture of **'Madhubindu Vrittanta'**, the rat is absent but the elephant is shown shaking the tree.

From the depiction, we can infer that Acc. 18 is earlier than Acc. 44. In the first one, men are tall and slim. Their ornaments are also exquisite. The ornaments and apparel bear a similarity to those found in Amaravati Sculpture. This style may be assigned to the last phase of Amaravati School. The persons in the second panel are comparatively short and rough. Their facial expressions are dull. Their ornaments, hair style, and apparel broadly look like those worn by the aborigins of the region. Alavaka's ornaments appear to be made of beads. The women have heavy bangles.

Though the sculptors of Nagarjunakonda have generally followed the Amaravati Traditions, they seem to have been influenced by the physical features, hair styles, ornaments and apparels of the local inhabitants.

Thus, the story of 'Alavakayaksha' depicted in the Sculpture of Nagarjunakonda—gives us an insight into the Philosophy and Dharma of Buddha-in a simple way.

References

Ananda, K. Coomaraswamy, Yakshas, New Delhi, 1971.

Sacred Books of the East (Sutta nipata).

G. Sivaramamurthy, 'Amaravati Sculptures in the Madras Government Museum'.

K.V. Ramachandra Rao, Nagarjunakonda Sculptures.

Edward J. Thomas, The Life of Buddha as a Legend and History.

27

Recent Discoveries of Buddhist Site at Phanigiri (Nalgonda District of A.P.)

Dr. G. Chandra Reddy and B. Padmalatha

There are nearly 150 Buddhist sites, which have been identified in Andhradesa so far. These Buddhist settlements range in the periods between 3rd century B.C. and 12th century A.D. Phanigiri is one of most important Buddhist sites of Andhra Pradesh. This Buddhist center flourished during the second-third century A.D.

IMPACT OF ANDHRA BUDDHISM

Buddhism played a significant role in the transformation of cultural evolution of Andhra people. Even today these remains remind us the origin and development of Indian fine arts in general, art and architecture in particular. Buddhism pulled down the differences among the castes and preached the principle of social equality. It also contributed for the development of Indian medicine, philosophy, literature and languages. The Andhra

Buddhism influenced the paintings at Ajanta and Srigiria (Ceylon).

The *recent excavations* of Phanigiri revealed many stupas, viharas, chaityas, sculptures, coins and inscriptions. Many carvings of Buddhist panels and roundels including life events of Siddharta, Jataka stories and human figures. We hope this Buddhist site will become a major destination in the Buddhist circuit of Tourism, which attracts domestic and international tourists if we develop properly.

LOCATION

This Buddhist complex is located on a hillock (Latitude: 17°.25.3 North: Longitude: 79°.28.4 East) about 200 ft high adjacent to Phanigiri village, which is about 35 km. Away from Janagaon railway station of Warangal District, Andhra Pradesh. It is just 4 km from Thirumalagiri, a mandal headquarters in Nalgonda district of Andhra Pradesh.

ETIMOLOGY OF PHANIGIRI

The word **'Phani'** means a snake and '**Giri**' means a hillock. The name of the village 'Phanigiri' appears to have been derived due to the appearance of the hillock like a snake.

CLUSTER OF BUDDHIST SITES

There is a cluster of Buddhist sites in the close proximity of this site, namely Gajulabanda, Vardhamanakota, Thirumalagiri, Arvapalli, Yeleswaram and Thummalagudem.

PATRONS OF BUDDHISM

During the period of Satavahana and Ikshvaku Rule, Buddhism became the popular and mass religion. It received the support of the peasantry, artisan and merchants and the women of royal family as well as common folk.[1] There was development of communication and trade routes,[2] connecting the Buddhist centers. All classes and sections of people belonging to different professions embraced Buddhism and they were responsible for the rise and growth of Buddhist establishments. Buddhism was able to build-up much wider social base.

TRIAL EXCAVATIONS

In the year 1942-43, excavations were conducted at Phanigiri by the Director of Archaeology, the Nizam's government of erstwhile Hyderabad state, which unearthed coins (Satavahana, Ikshvaku and (eastern kshatrapas), brick structures of stupas, viharas, chaityas, sculptured pieces, of Buddhist, panels, Jataka stories, Yaksha, Yakshi (Mithuna) and others. Pieces of early historic pottery and other cultural materials datable to first century A.D. were also found.[3]

RECENT EXCAVATIONS

In the year 2002-03, the Department of Archaeology and Museums, Government of Andhra Pradesh discovered a large number of Buddhist remains at Phanigiri. The excavations brought to light a mahastupa, a stone-pillared congregation hall, three viharas, two apsidal chaitya-grihas, many Buddhist sculptured panels, Brahmi inscriptions, coins[4] etc. belonging to the Satavahana and Ikshvaku period, besides historic and cultural materials datable to first century B.C. to third century A.D.

The purpose of the paper is to study the significance of the Buddhist site in general by briefing the recent unearthed remains and highlight the Architecture, Sculpture and Inscriptions in particular.

ARCHITECTURE

Stupas

There were ruins of thirty stupas at Phanigiri, most of them were circular in plan and were raised over rectangular stone basements. They were constructed with different tiers and hemispherically built, but not in the spoked-wheel pattern.

Mahastupa

The fresh excavations brought to light a Mahastupa located on the southern-most part of the complex, built on tiered and wheel-shaped plan having four ayaka platforms on four cardinal directions. The wheel shaped plan was followed probably to give a structural stability to the stupa and to save the material and to introduce the sacred wheel, which is one of the great symbols of *Buddhist Dhamma*. The Andhra Buddhists are believed to have developed this typical stupa architecture. At present only the remains of limestone ayaka pillars are seen on the western and northern ayaka platforms. The diameter of the stupa is approximately twenty meters. The stupa has a drum and dome. The occurance of limestone panels at the base of the drum suggests that the entire drum and ayaka platforms might have embellished with plain and carved limestone panels depicting the pilastar motifs. This stupa is built with brick mason veneered with limestone panels. The measurement of the brick is 60″28′8 centimeters.

Apsidal-stupa Chaitya

On the southern side of the maha stupa, two apsidal chaityas were unearthed. One of the chaityagrihas, which was fully exposed, has brought to light a stupa built in brick masonry veneered with limestone panels depicting the pilaster motifs at regular intervals. This chaityagriha is connected with a *pillared hall* for the purpose of conference of devotees.

Viharas

In the northern and southern side of the monastic complex existed three viharas. Each vihara consists of six to nine cells having a common verandah. Each cell measures 2.70 m, which might have accommodated two monks easily. The walls, the floor of the cells and the verandah are well plastered with lime. The occurrence of several floral art pieces moulded in stucco suggests that the external walls of the viharas were decorated with floral designs of various sizes and shapes. The *material* of the complex used was brick, limestone (might have brought from Jaggayyapeta area), lime plaster, stucco and concrete.

SCULPTURE

Among the recent finds of the sculpture at the site are medallions and fragments of railings, sculptures of Buddha, Jataka Stories, Mithunas, Dharmachakra Pillars, Buddha-padas and human figures etc. Previous excavations unearthed the beautiful sculptures depicting Yaksha, Kubera-Yaksha and few panels representing bull chased by an elephant and by man.[6]

Buddha-padas

In the early phase of Buddhism, Lord Buddha was represented through symbols like *throne, Dharmachakra, Bodhi Tree, Chaitya, Triratna, Swastika and Feet of Buddha.*[7] On the eastern side at the base of the stupa on an elevated platform, a beautiful limestone slab with Buddhapadas in low relief was found. The slab consisting of the Buddhapadas is intact and the figures are very clear. The Buddhapadas are shown with ashtamangala symbols. A Brahmi label inscriptions showing the characters of first century A.D. is noticed on the slab at the toes of the padas. This reads as "*Sidham baya (vaka . . .) sata kasa buda kasa caya dhamma padasa.*"

Life Events of Siddharatha before the Enlightenment

The important sculptural panels describe (i) One piece depicts the scene of the descent of White Elephant from Tushita heaven. The future Buddha was conceived by his mother in a dream, in which she saw him descending from the Tushita heaven in the form of a white elephant. (ii) Prince Siddhartha takes his jewel hilted sharp sword from Channa's hands, cuts away his crown and head dress and tossed in air. The Indra or Shakra (Sakka) received the jewel casket crown and placed it in Trayastrimsa heaven and

Gods adored it. This is the scene of carrying the headgear (jewellery) of the Buddha to heaven. This pulsating sculpture is paralleled in its composition of dancing gods and goddesses clustering around a transporting central figure by a well-known relief of the translation of the alms-bowl of Buddha to heaven in a railing medallion of Phanigiri. (iii) The scene of Mahabinishkramana from Kapilavastu. On his horse Kanthaka, Siddhartha rides forth at night from Kapilavasthu [the great departure] in the 'Great Renunciation',, escorted by the gods who silence the neighing of the steed [horse] and hold up its hoofs, lest the city by awakened. There is witness of flying Devas, Yakshas, Nagas and servants with flywhisks, one servant with Royal Chatra and one servant with chamara riding on elephant. The Chatra, sign of royalty, denotes the rank of the possessor Siddhartha. (iv) The scene of Siddhartha's Great departure from Kapilavastu.[8] (v) Siddhartha is seen along chatra with his charioteer or Chenna drove in the streets of city Kapilavastu and came across the four great scenes, i.e., an old man, a patient, a dead body and an ascetic.[9] These events are beautifully carved in low relief.

Head of Bodhisattva, Mithunas are seen in anjali posture and flanking either side of the pedestal of Dharmachakra. Some of them have Roman headgears, mutilated images of Buddha, Bodhisattvas are found in excavations. Few fragments of limestone are depicting the Jataka stories. One of the roundels shows the portrayal of 'Mandhatha Jataka'.[10] This Sculpture depicts main episode and one of the most favourite Jataka Story with moral, of the rocketing rise to partnership of the heaven of the thirty-three (trayastrimsa) gods and abysmal fall to earth, due to overweening pride and avarice, of cakravartin Mandhatha. He is seen here in the boastful act of causing a shower of gold, surrounded by the seven jewels of sovereignty—the wheel, the elephant, the steed, the pearl, the wife, the general and the minister.[11]

Yakshis

On pilasters of thoranakudya, the scene portrays worship of

Dharmachakra by female standing figures with folded hands on either side of the Dharmachakra pillar. There are many representations of the worship of Dharmachakra which mounted on pillars in various sizes. On these slabs, Dharmachakra is depicted beautifully placed on a pillar and flanked by lady worshippers on either side called as Yakshinis or Mithunas.

Yaksha Figures

Depicting Yakshas and Yakshinis were the favourite themes in early Buddhist art. They were considered as auspicious and popularly worshipped as semi-divine beings in ancient India. Yakshas carry heavy garlands to worship the stupa and Yakshas associated as minor deities in the Buddhist pantheon. They are also considered as the guardian deities of gateways of Buddhist establishments. Buddhist literature describes them as efficient builders. It is believed that theYakshas possessed great might and wealth.

At Phanigiri on a limestone, a figure of **Dwarf Yaksha** (probably Kubera) with a belly is represented in low relief. He is decorated with chakra-kundalas, a round tarque, (Tape-shaped), broad wristlets and a turban with a middle knot. He is holding a long staff in his left hand. Its artistic features and styles are comparable to South-Indian characters. His smiling facial expressions and the movements of limbs are suitable to the space and time. The ear lobes and other ornaments are carefully depicted.

Another sculpture is representing the upper part of the body of a beautiful **Yaksha.** He appears with bulbous eyes and an aquiline (eagle-like) nose. In the center part of his elongated ear lobes, few beautiful ring typed ornaments are arranged. He wore a turban around his head. He is lively looking with chubby cheeks. A small branch of leaves is arranged on his head indicates his victory on others. It reveals the Greek tradition. This piece of art leads us to establish that there might have been either **Greek influence** or the Greeks themselves were in royal service in Andhradesa. It is also an opinion of the few scholars that the South Indian sculptors were influenced by Western traditions and styles through Northern India and the East and West sea coasts.

Lid-cum-Spout

In one of the viharas, we found a red-ware pot luted with lid-cum-spout. The external surface of the spout is meticulously moulded with human bodies, each holding the hand of others, forming a human chain—a "*maanava haaram*," with the vegetation in the background. This perhaps symbolizes the **unity, harmony** and **prosperity** of the people in those days.

It is interesting to note that the 'logo' of the "Janmabhoomi" Programme in Andhra Pradesh being implemented in the State also consists of "*maanava haaram*" and vegetation in it.

Inscriptions

Apart from it, several fragments of inscriptions were carved on limestone in Brahmi script reading "**Chantamula Maharaja**".

"Jambhudweepa Mulavayumyam," (Ancient Andhradesa was called as Jambhudweepa) "Mahatalvarisa" (husband of **Chantisiri**) and "Twaraa Purakiya" etc., were also found near the congregation hall.

One inscription describes about **Mahatalvari Chantisiri,** the sister of Vasistaputra Chamtamula, gave his daughter to Virapurushadatta. She and other royal ladies donated gifts for the victory, health and longevity of King Virapurushadatta. Many Buddhist structures were enlarged, decorated and richly endowed with.

On the basis of the paleographical and other cultural evidences so far unearthed at this site, it can be said that the Buddhism at Phanigiri had its origination during the **Satavahana Dynasty,** but it flourished and prospered during the rule of the founder of the **'Ikshvaku' Dynasty,** Chantamula Maharaja and Virapurushadatta who ruled from Nagarjunakonda. There is enough evidence to say that the Buddhist monastic complex at Phanigiri has started during first century A.D. Thus the Buddhism flourished here and its surrounding areas for about 500 years.

CONCLUSION

In view of the discovery of the Buddhapadas, other symbols and figures of Lord Buddha, it can be said that both schools, i.e. Theravada and Mahasanghika were existed here. Basing on maturity in form and workmanship, these sculptures are very similar and may be compared with Amaravati and Nagarjunakonda schools. After Ikshvakus, the later dynasties such as Pallavas, Chalukyas and Vishnukundins became the staunch followers of brahmanical Hindu religion. They patronized and raised Hindu temples on the top of the Buddhist stupa. At present, we can witness the temples of Rama, Hanuman and Goddess Durga on this Buddhist site. This was a final deathblow to this Buddhist center. This was the period of unrest in the religious life and caused for the damage of Buddhist centers of culture and heritage. The message of Buddhism and its ideals were reflected in the art and architecture discovered at Phanigiri.

Notes and References

1. M. Kamala Devi, *Andhra Women in Inscriptions,* pp. 8, 9.
   S.N.G. Prasad Rao, *Salivahana* (Telugu), p. 57.
2. S.N.G. Prasad Rao, *op.cit.,* p. 18.
3. P.V. Parabrahma Sastry, *Satavahana Epoch—A New Light,* pp. 29-30.
4. *Report of Excavations at Phanigiri,* 2002 & 03, Dept. of Archaeology & Museums, Government of A.P., Hyderabad.
5. Kwhaja Mohammed Ahmed, *Phanigiri Bouddharama Sidhilalu* (Telugu), Dept. of Archaeology and Museums, Government of Andhra Pradesh, Hyderabad, pp. 1-3.
6. G. Chandra Reddy, *Buddhist Remains in Telangana,* (unpublished Ph.D. thesis), p. 115.
7. Veeranarayana Reddy (Ed.), *Suhrullekha,* April-June 2003, Quarterly, pp. 53-55.
8. *Ibid.*
9. Veeranarayana Reddy (Ed.), *Suhrullekha,* April-June 1999, Quarterly, pp. 8-9.
10. P.R. Ramachandra Rao, *The Art of Nagarjunikonda,* Department of Tourism, Governent of A.P., Plates XIV, XVIII.
11. *Ibid.,* Plate XXXVI, and T.N. Ramachandrani, Nagarjuna Konda, p. 32.

28

Buddhist Philosophical Foundations

Dommeti Satyanarayana Bodhi

Buddhism originated in the 6th century B.C. Buddhism is the direct result of the most intensive research voluntarily conducted over a long period of time by a kind hearted Noble Prince SIDDHARTHA GOUTAMA imbued with infinite love and deep Compassion for suffering humanity. The aim of Buddhism is to release human beings from worldly sufferings, from the cycle of birth and death and guide them towards achieving liberation without becoming slaves to certain beliefs and practices that people uphold in the name of religion.

Buddhism has not only stimulated the intelligentsia and philosophers of the world but has been a noble religion. It is an uncontested fact, that Buddhism has played a very prominent role in finding the most convincing reasons and remedies for all types of human sufferings, from the first teachings of Buddha till today and perhaps even into the future also. Buddhism has been the originator and promoter of philosophy, psychology, Socio-economics and political thoughts etc. Buddhism recognises man as a source of all actions. It teaches to love fellow human beings only and not any divine powers or beings. It does not lead to the attainment of divinity as the final goal, but it aims at leading the man to become perfect human being. Lord Buddha was against war and violence. He was a man who dedicated his time and life for perfect peace. He prohibited his disciples from following the profession of a soldier. Ambition, hatred, and lack of compassion lead people to war, this was one of the main objectives of Buddha's teachings.

No individual can make a claim of survival, unless he is in harmony with Nature. He should have proper response in him to the Nature's pulses. He does not live merely because there is life in him, but there is life in one's surroundings.

Example: If a man has to live in an atmosphere of poor supply of oxygen, he shall cease to exist. The fire that burns, the water that flows and the air that blows (these are the natural substances as we know) prove that their existence not merely for themselves alone, but for others also.

The primary need of the hour is to uphold the validity of religion and work effectively for establishing the inter-religious harmony and understanding. Mere academic study of comparative religion cannot help to achieve the desirable objective. There must be inter-religious understanding for the harmony.

Mankind is prone to be influenced by a large number of materials that give him, temporary pleasures. This has led him to develop greed, hatred, jealousy, delusion and selfishness. Greed, ignorance and hatred are the main causes of regional conflicts, National apprehensions, inter-state misgivings, family disputes, marital discords and racial and or ethnic or religious misunderstandings.

Buddhism offers an effective but simple solution to these crucial problems through its teachings, like Trisarana or 'Triple Gem' . 'Pancha Seela', four 'Noble Truths', The Noble Eight Fold Path, and the three characteristics of existence. Any person who follows and practices these teachings will acquire good behaviour which turn him to be wise. Without cultivation of these Noble qualities, there can be no social harmony, no peace or no

Inter-National understandings. Those who do not practice these noble qualities, ignorance, mental agitation and sorrow will persist and conflicts will remain unsolved. Dr. B.R Ambedkar said "Morality is the essence of DHAMMA. Morality in Dhamma arises from the direct necessity for man to love his fellow men".

TRIPLE GEM

The true significance of the expression "**BUDDHAM SARANAM GACCHAMI**". Is that "I follow the Buddha" —that I tread the path trodden by BUDDHA.

The Buddha passed away in the Great Demise over 2500 years ago. How can we request assistance from a person who is not alive to-day? The only assistance, the only help and the only use one can get from Him who is not there to-day, is treading the path, he trod, and following his advice.

The true significance of the expression "DHAMMAM SARANAM GACCHAMI" is that I follow the "DOCTRINE". The Doctrine (Dhamma) is not a person. It is not a thing. The only use one can make use of, it is to follow it.

The true meaning of "SANGAM SARANAM GACCHAMI" is that "I will receive advice and guidance from the Sangha" it is in that way that one can take refuge in the Sangha.

THE PATH OF PURITY (PANCHA SILA)

The path of purity teach that a person who wises to be good must recognize some principles of life.

1. Not to injure or Kill.
2. Not to steal Abstain from taking things not given.
3. Not to speak untruth.
4. Not to indulge in lust.
5. Not to indulge in intoxicating Drinks.

The practice of Pancha sila (Five precepts) helps one to cultivate five ennobling virtues.

PHILOSOPHICAL FOUNDATIONS OF BUDDHISM

The four noble TRUTHS, which the BUDDHA Himself discovered and revealed to the world, are the chief characteristics and the unshakable foundations of Buddhism.

THE NOBLE TRUTH OF SUFFERING: (DUKKHA-ARIYA SACCA)

I. Birth is suffering, decay is suffering, disease is suffering, death is suffering, to be united with the unpleasant is suffering, to be separated from the pleasant is suffering, not to get what one desires is suffering. In brief the five aggregates (RUPA, VEDANA, SANNA, SAMKHARA and VINNANA) of attachment are suffering.

II. "The Noble TRUTH of the cause of suffering, (Dukkha samudaya Ariya Sacca). It is the craving which produces rebirth, accompanied by passionate clinging. It is the craving for sensual pleasures KAMATANHA, craving for becoming BHAVATANHA, and craving for annihilation Vibhavatanha".

III. This is the NOBLE TRUTH of the cessation of suffering; it is the complete separation from and destruction of this very craving, its forsaking, renunciation, liberation, detachment.

IV. The fourth noble TRUTH is the path leading to the cessation of suffering, which is embodied in the Noble Eight fold path, the via media—the golden mean path—of the Buddha.

The first three deal with the philosophy of the Buddha's Teachings and the fourth with the practice in accordance with that philosophy.

Buddhism as such is neither an ordinary philosophy nor an ordinary ethical system. It is a moral and philosophical teaching, founded on the bedrock of facts that can be tested and verified by personal experience.

Strictly speaking Buddhism cannot be called a religion either, because it is not a system of faith and worship which emphasises the existence of a Supernatural power. By religion if it is meant a teaching which distinguishes between right and wrong, and which furnishes men, with a guide to proper conduct, then it is a religion of religions.

THE PATH OF RIGHTEOUSNESS (THE NOBLE EIGHT FOLD PATH)

The Noble Eight fold path (ARIYA ATTHANGIKA MAGGA) discovered by the Buddha Himself, is the only way to NIBBANA. It avoids the extreme of self mortification that weakens one's intellect, and the extreme of self-indulgence that retards one's Spiritual progress.

The **Noble Eight** fold path consists of the following eight factors:

1. Samma Dithi	Prajna	Right View (Right understanding)
2. Sammasankappo		Right Thought
3. Samma Vacca	Sila	Right speech
4. Samma Kamanto		Right action
5. Samma Ajivo		Right Lively hood
6. Sama Vayamo	Samadhi	Right Effort
7. Sama Satti		Right Mindfulness
8. Sama Samadhi		Right Concentration

ASHTANGA MARGA—OR—THE PATH OF RIGHTEOUSNESS, SAMMADITTI— (RIGHT VIEWS)

The first and foremost element in the Asthanga Marga, is "To realize the importances of SAMMA DITTI" (Right Views) one must realize that the world is a dungeons and man is a prisoner in the dungeon.

Indeed, man has not only become blind by living too long in the darkness, but he very much doubts if any such strange thing as light is said to be, can ever exist at all.

Mind is the only instrument through which light can come to man.

• But the mind of these dungeon dwellers is by no means a perfect instrument for the purpose.

It lets through only a little light, just enough to show to those with sight that there is such a thing as darkness.

Thus defective in its nature, such understanding as this is.

Further explaining to the PARIVRAJAKAS, THE BUDDHA said, the case of the prisoner is not as hopeless as it appears.

For there is in man a thing called will. When the appropriate motives arise the will can be awakened and set in motion.

"With the coming of just enough light to see in what directions to guide the motions of the will, man may so guide them that they shall lead to liberty.

"Thus though man is bound, yet he may be free, he may at any moment begin to take the first steps that will ultimately bring him to freedom.

This is because it is possible to train the mind in whatever directions one chooses. It is mind that makes us to be prisoners in the house of life, and it is mind that keeps us so.

But what mind has done, that mind can undo. If it has brought man to thralldom, it can also, when rightly directed, bring him to liberty.

"This is what SAMMA DITTI can do".

Samma Ditti means is the destruction of AVIJJA. It is opposed to MICCHA DITTI.

"AVIJJA means the failure to understand the Noble truths, of the existence of suffering and the removal of suffering."

"SAMMA DITTI requires giving up of belief in the efficacy of rites and ceremonies, to have disbelief in the sanctity of the SHASTRAS".

"SAMMA DITTI" requires the abandonment of superstition and supernaturalism.

"SAMMA DITTI requires the abandonment of all doctrines which are mere speculations without any basis in fact or experience.

Finally SAMMA DITTI requires free mind and free thought.

1. Right thoughts serves the double purpose, eliminating evil though and developing pure thought (SAMMA SANKAPPA) are three fold. They are the thoughts of Renunciation 1. NEKKAHAMMA SANKAPPA, which are opposed to lustful desires. Benevolent thoughts. 2. AVYAPADA SANKAPPA, which are opposed to ill will and thoughts of harmlessness. 3. AVIHIMSA SANKAPPA which are opposed cruelty these tend to purify the mind.
2. (SAMMA VACHA) Right speech deals with refraining from falsehood, slandering, harsh words, and worthless talks.
3. (SAMMA KAMANTO) Right action deals with refraining from killing, stealing and unchastity.
4. (SAMMA AJIVO) Right lively hood deals with the five kinds of trades which should be avoided by a lay disciple. They are trading in 1. Arms, 2. Human beings flesh (that is, breeding animals for slaughter), 3. Intoxicating drinks, 4. Poison, and 5. Hypocritical conduct is cited as wrong lively hood for monks.
5. (SAMMA VAYAMO) RIGHT EFFORT IS FOURFOLD—Namely:
   I. The endeavour to discard evil that has already arisen.
   II. The endeavour to prevent the arising of unrisen evil.
   III. The endeavour to develop unrisen good, and

IV. The endeavour to promote that good which has already arisen.

6. (SAMMA SATI) Right Mindfulness, SAMMA SATI calls for mindfulness and thoughtfulness. It means constant wakefulness of the mind. Watch and ward by the mind over the evil passions is another Name for SAMMA SATI.
7. (SAMMA SAMADHI) Right concentration is the one pointedness of the mind. It gives a habit to the mind to think of good and always to think of good. SAMMA SAMADHI gives the mind the necessary motive power to do good.

THE THREE SALIENT TRUTHS

Anica

The Buddha said that all conditioned phenomena are impermanent. When we look around us we can see that death comes to all living things. We can see our friends and relatives die, we can see the death of animals and plants overtime. However, it is not only living things that are impermanent, even inanimate objects have a life span. We can see that in course of time, everything deteriorates and decomposes. In actual fact at every moment material form changes. So that what something was a moment ago is not the same as what it is a moment later. The perception, however, is that the form remains the same. Even objects that seen permanent such as granite rocks are eroded slowly by wind, sand, and rain. Our vision is limited to our life span; as such some things we know are impermanent because during our life span we can see that they change. Some others we know they have changed by applying scientific methods. For example we know that in course of time the earth has changed, lush green forest lands have turned into deserts and ice lands have melted.

Some things, however, may appear permanent because our vision is limited to a period of time.

Anatta

Not self, (Non ego) egolessness, impersonality; is one of the three characteristics of existence (TILAKKAHNNA). The ANATTA doctrine teaches that neither within the bodily and mental phenomena of existence, nor outside of them, can be found anything that in the ultimate sense could be regarded as a self-existing real ego-entity, soul or any other abiding substance. This is the central doctrine of Buddhism, without understanding of which a real knowledge of BUDDHISM, is all together impossible. It is the only really specific Buddhist doctrine, with which the entire structure of Buddhist teachings stands or falls, all the remaining Buddhist doctrines may, more or less, be found in other philosophic systems and religions, but the ANATTA—Doctrine has been clearly and unreservedly taught only by the BUDDHA. Therefore the BUDDHA is known as the ANNATA—VADI, or teacher of impersonality. Whosoever has not penetrated this impersonality of all existence, and does not comprehend that in reality there exists only this continually self consuming process of arising and passing bodily and mental phenomena, and that there is no separate Ego-entity within or without this process, he will not be able to understand BUDDHISM, i.e., the teachings of the 4 noble truths in the right light. He will think that, it is his ego, his personality, that experiences the sufferings, his personality that performs good and evil actions and will be reborn according to these actions, his personality that will enter into NIRVANA, his personality that walks on the Noble Eight Fold Path.

"Mere suffering exists, No sufferer is found.
The deeds are, but no doer of the deeds is there;
NIRVANA is, but not the man that enters it;
The path is, but no traveler on it is seen."

"whosoever is not clear with regard to the conditionally arisen phenomena, and does not comprehend that all the actions are conditioned through ignorance etc., he thinks that it is an ego that understands or does not understand, that acts or causes to act, that comes to existence at rebirth, that has the sense impression, that feels, desires, becomes attached, continues and at re-birth again enters a new existence."

Dukkha

"Birth is suffering, ageing is suffering, sickness is suffering, dissociation from the loved is suffering, not to get what one wants is suffering. In short, the five aggregates affected by clinging are suffering."

The BUDDHA said all conditioned phenomena is DUKKHA or full of suffering?

We know that life begins at birth, and birth is traumatic for the baby and possibly painful. We also know that old age, sickness, and death are sorrowful. Under normal circumstances, every living being faces these sorrows. In addition being separated from those we love is suffering, associating with those whom we do not like is suffering and not getting what we want is suffering. One of the main cause of suffering is CRAVING. There are also many who face the suffering of poverty, homelessness, torment, and abuse. All these are visible to us, and if we look around us at our lives of our loved ones, we will see that each and everyone of us has faced suffering at some point in life.

The truth is that happiness in this world is impermanent. This is why the truth that all conditioned phenomena are impermanent is so important in BUDDHIST Philosophy.

May all beings be happy.

REFERENCES

Ven: Weragoda Sarada Maha Thero:
"The greatest man who ever lived."
Ven: Narada Maha Thero,
"The Buddha and his teachings and a manual of Buddhism."
Dr. S.A. Ediriweera, "Essentials of Buddhism."
Nyanatiloka, "Buddhist Dictionary."
Dr. B.R. Ambedkar, "The Buddha and his Dhamma."

Radhika Abeysekera
(practicing the Dhamma with a view to Nibbana.)
The three characteristics of existence (tilakkhana)
explains magga vagga in dhammapada. :

1. *sabbe sankhara aniccati*
   yada pannya passti
   atha nibbindati dukkhe
   esa maggo visuddiya

Transient are all conditioned things: When this, with wisdom, one discerns, then is one disgusted with ill; this is the path to purity.

2. *sabbe sankhara dukhati*
   yada pannaya passati
   atha nibbindati dukkhe
   esa maggo visuddiya

"Sorrowful are all Conditioned things": When this, with Wisdom, one discerns, then is one disgusted with ill; this is the path to purity.

3. *sabbe dhamm anatta ti*
   yada pannaya passati
   atha nibbindati duddke
   esa maggo visuddhiya

"All Dhammas are without a soul: When this, with wisdom, one discerns, then is one disgusted with ill; this is the path to purity."

29

Buddhist Sites and Tourism Promotion in Andhra Pradesh

Dr. K. Vijaya Babu and Smt. S. Chandra Kala

India, the land of ancient cultures has experienced many a change in its socio-cultural life since times immemorial. The Vedic religion though it shaped the early cultural life of the people also has undergone several changes from time to time. Many socio-religious reformers emerged in different historical times and left indelible marks on the society. In 6th C. BC two religious reform movements were started. One by Lord Buddha whose teachings emphasized the equality of mankind and non-violence and condemned the rigid caste system and the Vedic rituals. The other one is Jainism propagated by Mahavira which stressed the importance of non-violence. Because of the simplicity of teachings and patronage of royal dynasties, the Buddhism became very popular not only in India but also in China and South-East Asian countries.

Asoka, the great, of Mauryan Empire (23rd Century BC), sent his religious missionaries to different parts of the Asian regions. Later, the Satavahana, rulers patronized Buddhism in the south.

Buddhism influenced art and architecture to a great extent. Many stupas, chaityas, viharas, were constructed throughout the length and breadth of India. Sanchi, Saranath, are the famous centers of Buddhist art and architecture in the north and, Amaravathi, Nagarjunakonda, Dhulikatta, Nelakondapally, Bavikonda, Phanigiri are very famous in our Andhra region.

The present paper is an attempt to focus light on the important Buddhist centres of Andhradesa which attracted Buddhist scholars, pilgrims from all over the world. These centres are also attracting tourists in modern times for their historical importance and grandeur of art and architecture. In this paper, some important centres of Buddhism located in Telangana, Andhra regions of Andhra Pradesh are presented with an emphasis on their tourism potentiality.

HISTORY OF BUDDHISM IN ANDHRADESA

Buddhism entered Andhradesa during the life time of Lord Buddha itself. One Brahmin named Bavari, who lived at Potali on the banks of the River Godavari between the Janapadas of Assaka and Mulaka sent his sixteen disciples to attend a sermon of Lord Buddha at Sravasthi. After the visit, one of the disciples named Pingiya alone returned to Potali. After the return of Pingiya to the south, several Andhra converts proceeded to north and settled there and were known as Andhakas.

The Hinayana Buddhism laid great stress on the worship of the 'stupa' in which the corporal remains of Buddha or the 'Arhats' were incorporated. The consecration of mortal remains in a 'tumulus' as practised by the Buddhists was not altogether a novelty in South India of the Pre-Christian times, since Megalithic burials were already in practice in South India. Buddhism was patronized initially by the commercial and well to do classes who built a series of 'aramas' or 'viharas'' which included monasteries, stupas, refectories according to a standardized plan. Though the human form of Buddha became popular only after the 1-2nd centuries

AD, his symbolic representations or the important episodes in his life and 'Jataka' tales pertaining to his previous births were profusely delineated on the walls and surfaces of the stupas and monasteries.

After the Kalinga War, a major part of Andhra came under the suzerainty of Asoka. The 13th Rock Edict of Asoka informs that the Andhras along with Daradas, Yavanas, Kambojas, Bhojas, Paithanikas, Pulindas were following the Dharma enunciated by Asoka. After the 3rd Buddhist Council, Asoka sent his missionaries to different parts of the Sub-Continent and one Mahadeva was dispatched to Mahisamandala the region between Godavari and Krishna rivers. While proceeding to their respective regions the religious missionaries sent by Asoka must have carried the sacred relics of Buddha for enshrining them in stupas. Mahadeva might have erected a stupa at Ghantasala or Amaravathi (Danyakataka). Later Hieun Tsang, the Chinese Buddhist scholar visited this Andhra region as part of his tour to South India. He made a detailed mention of the Buddhist Centres of the Andhra region in his writings.

After the decline of Mauryan Empire, the Satavahanas ruled the Andhra region. There was political stability and economic prosperity during their period. They patronised Buddhism and the rock-cut Buddhist caves at Nasik, Naineghat, Junar, Kude, Kanheri, Kondavite, Kondane, Karle, Mahad, Pithalakora, Bhaja, Bedsa were executed during this period. Similarly, the Brick-built Stupas at Amaravathi, Jaggayyapet, Ghantasala, Chandavaram, Bavikonda, Totlakonda and various other places were rebuilt or renovated and embellished with carved sculptures of great elegance. The artistic production was so prolific and magnificent that, it became popular as the Amaravathi style of art.

The Ikshvakus of Vijayapuri at Nagarjunakonda, the successors of the Satavahanas ruled the Coastal Andhra from Circa 220 to 290 A.D. They carried forward the great artistic tradition of the Satavahanas. During this period Nagarjunakonda became one of the greatest Buddhist centres of India. The end of the

Ikshvaku rule marked the beginning of the declension of Buddhism in Andhra.

Later rulers, Pallavas, Vishnukundins, Eastern Chalukyan and Kakatiyas patronised Vishnavism and Shivism, Jainism etc., Even though religious tolerance was maintained. Acharya Nagarjuna (140-200AD) who propounded and propagated the 'Madhyamika' School of Buddhist Philosophy must have spent the last part of his life at Nagarjunakonda after his retirement from Nalanda. Nagarjuna is said to have composed a work by name 'Suhrullekha' and 'Ratnavali' in the form of letters addressed to the Satavahana king Yagnasri Satakarni, who ruled from 172 to 201 AD.

In the 7th century AD, a Chinese traveller remarked that there were 50 monasteries with 4,500 monks in Andhra region which were declining and being gradually replaced by Jainism and Brahmanical order due to Royal patronage to these traditional religions.

Buddhist Sites in Andhra Pradesh: Buddhist sites in Andhra Pradesh are mostly found on the banks of the Godavari, and Krishna rivers in Telangana and Andhra regions.

TELANGANA REGION

1. Dhulikatta

This site is in a remote village in Karimnagar District. The Buddhist stupa and Vihara were constructed on a mound on the banks of two streams. The 'stupa' was constructed in the last quarter of 2nd century BC. It is a large and massive structure with Ayaka Platform, construction of the 'anda' with limestones, slabs carved with representations of stupa and Muchilindanaga. The first phase of the stupa was enclosed by a square platform to serve both to buttress the stupa as well as a circumbulatory path. The enlarged base of the stupa was bedecked with more than 50 carved slabs. One of the slabs the Muchilindanaga, a five headed cobra protecting the lord Buddha symbolically represented by his feet was exquisitely delineated. At the top of the Naga an inscription in early Brahmi script (2nd century BC) is found. The Department of Archaeology

(AP) has started restoration and conservation work at this site.

2. Gajula Banda (Gajula Bodu)

It means rocky mound of bangles on the bank of a big tank. It is situated near Phanigiri in Nalgonda District. A stupa vihara complex and a chaitya were found in the excavations. A rich collection of antiquities such as stucco figurines such as lion, lotus, creapers, animal figures were collected.

3. Gummadi Durru

Gummadi Durru a small village near Madhira in present Khammam District. The main stupa is wheel based with its drum veneered by a splendid array of sculptured slabs. Besides this there are a dozen small stupas. Most of the slabs depict scenes from the life of Buddha. Inside the Maha Stupa a silver casket was found containing a piece of bone.

4. Korukonda

Korukonda is a village near Aswaraopet in Khammam district. On the hill at Korukonda Buddhist remains of rock cut carvings and the remains of Monolithic stupas and two cave temples are found.

5. Kotilingala

It is 50 km from Karimnagar on the right bank of the Godavari river. A mud fortress of Satavahana times and two Buddhist stupas and several coins of Satavahana period were discovered.

6. Kondapur

It is a village in Medak district. Scholars belived that it was one of the thirty walled towns of Satavahana period. The remains of Stupa Chaitya and gold, silver and led coins were excavated.

7. Mudigonda

It is situated in Khammam District. An idol of standing Buddha and four panels of Buddhist sculptures in limestone were discovered here which shows important events in the life of Buddha.

8. Nagarjunakonda

It is about 150 km from Hyderabad situated on the right bank of the Krishna river in Guntur District. It is a mountain girt valley about 5 km in width. The place is named after the great Buddhist philosopher Acharya Nagarjuna. This place was also called Vijayapuri during 2nd and 3rd C. AD which was ruled by Ikshvaku dynasty. It was an important Buddhist centre and was known as Saranath of South India. It was also a seat of Buddhist learning and people from different parts of the Sub-Continent used to visit this place. Excavations had revealed remains of Stupas and Viharas and Chaityas and Mandapas, a Palace site etc. The constructions were made of burnt bricks. The sculptures were of grey lime stone. The slabs on the stupas were decorated with the scenes of important events of the life of Buddha and the stories from Jatakas. The Mahachaitya is with a diameter of 32 m. with a hight of 24 m. The ground plan of the stupa is that of a wheel with the hub and spokes.

The museum at Nagarjunakonda provides the visitors with evidence and information regarding pre-history, proto-history and history of the entire region. Magnificent limestone sculpture relics are in the museum as well as the colossal Buddha, moonstones and various minor objects.

9. Nelakondapally

It is a famous Buddhist site in Khammam District. A Mahastupa, two monasteries and other structures were unearthed here. Two large mounds at Viratraju gadda and Bairagi gutta exposed a monastic establishment and a workshop area, where Buddhist idols were carved.

10. Pashigaon

It is near Kotilingala in Karimnagar District. On a small hillock, there are traces of Buddhist settlements viz. a Chaityagriha and a Stupa. The Stupa Chaitya was built of brick and lime gravel.

11. Phanigiri

This site is near Suryapet in Nalgonda District with a large number of Buddhist remains. More than 25 Chaitya halls, Stupas and Viharas built of bricks have been found. Life size idols of Buddha were discovered.

12. Peddabankur

It is an unfortified non-monastic settlement located in Karimnagar District. Several secular brick buildings, wells, cisterns are discovered here. Satavahana and Roman coins were also unearthed.

13. Vardhamanukota

This site is near Suryapet in Nalgonda District. The mound is now known as Kotadibba and has yielded remains of Chaityas, Viharas, and Pillar Mandapas. An image of the Buddha was also found.

14. Yeleswaram

This site is near Devarakonda in Nalgonda District on the banks of the river Krishna. A chaitya, two stupas, a large bathing ghat leading to the river, a big mandapa with lime stone columns were discovered. Many Buddhist structures in brick terracotta figurines, human and animal figures, coins were also excavated.

ANDHRA REGION

1. Amaravathi

This site is near Vijayawada and is adjacent to the ancient Satavahana capital of Dhanyakataka. It was one of the four major Buddhist centres of worship in entire India. Two thousand years ago on the banks of the Krishna River, this largest Stupa in the country standing over 36 meters high, was built of kiln burnt bricks and faced with white limestone marble slabs. It was accurately called the Mahastupa and is still considered to be one of the most sacred Buddhist sites in South India. The Archaeological Museum at Amaravathi houses fine collection of sculptures, panels, posts standing Buddha and moonstones. There is also a very good model of the Mahastupa for interpretation purpose.

2. Bavikonda

This monument is located at Visakhapatanam. Archaeological excavations unearthed an extensive Buddhist settlement comprising a Mahachaitya containing sacred relic caskets of the Buddha, large monastic complex, circular chaityagriha. Silver coins belonging to Roman Empire, Satavahana coins and Buddhapaduka slabs decorated with Ashtamangala symbols were also found.

3. Bhatti Prolu

This site is 60 km from Guntur. It is one of the oldest stupas in Andhra. A few brick mounds and some marble pillers are found at the site. This stupa is a solid brick work with dome, Ayaka platforms, Ayaka pillars, pathway and railing.

4. Chandavaram

Chandavaram is a remote village situated in Prakasham district. Extensive excavations brought to light the Stupas, Chatyagrihas and Vihara complexes. There are a number of stone slabs with sculptures resembling those of Amaravathi.

5. Dantavarapukota

It is 32 kms from Srikakulam. The site is encompassed by an earthen rampart raised approximately to a height of 30 to 40 metres with 12 entrances. The mud fort comprises an area of about 800 acres. Recent excavations have brought to light two brick built votive stupas along with other findings like black polished ware, red ware, familiar knobbed ware beads and bangles. The excavations are likely to lead to the discovery of a Buddhist establishment.

6. Durgakonda

Situated north-west of the Gurubhaktakonda is a rocky hill known as Durgakonda. The name originated from a large slab image of the goddess Durga which stands in a natural cave there. In front of this cave and on the rock above it are some mounds which contained Buddhist remains similar to Gurubhakatakonda.

7. Ghantasala

Ghantasala is situated 24 km to the north-west of Machilipatnam in Krishna District. The mound known as Lanje-Dibba containing the ruins of the Mahachaitya was excavated in 1894. The internal construction of the dome is in the from of a wheel with concentric circular walls, connected to each other by sixteen radial walls, which is 34 meters in diameter. It is surrounded by a processional path paved with bricks. The stupa was once encased with lavishly decorated sculptural slabs, similar to that of the Amaravathi stupa. Ancient Ghantasala was a rich sea-port known for maritime trade. A number of Roman gold coins and hundreds of copper and lead coins of Satavahanas with ship motif found here are a testimony to the Indo-Roman trade that had once flourished. Ghantasala played an important role in the spread of Buddhism in the region.

8. Guntupally

Guntupally is 65 kms from Vijayawada. The Buddhist monuments of Guntupally consist of a rock cut circular chaitya griha, four rock cut monasteries, a ruined brick chaitya, remains of a large group of brick built votive stupas. Besides them other findings are early historic pottery and Buddha images, etc. Different stages in Buddhism in Andhradesh-Theravads Mahayana and Vajrayana systems appear to have flourished in Guntupally. A bronze image of Avalokitesvara is found on the hill.

9. Gurubhakta Konda

Gurubhakta Konda has on its north side the extensive ruins of a Buddhist monastery at a height of over 500 meters. At the west end of the monastery are the foundations of a large stupa 84 meters in diameter having pradakshina patha. There are also remnants of numerous viharas, chaityas etc., spread all over the hill.

10. Pavuralakonda

Pavuralakonda is situated about 45 kms from Visakhapatanam. Excavations have brought to light the structures of stupas, viharas, circular chaitya grihas, other important antiquities like Satavahana coins, Roman Silver coin, Brahimi inscriptions, polished black ware, red ware, red slipped ware and bowls of different varieties and storage pots in large quantity.

11. Salihundam

The site is 150 kms from Visakhapatnam, Salihundam was the seat of an ancient Buddhist Sangharama. A circular stupa-chaitya crowns the hill while the viharas are spread out on the slopes. Buddhist remains here reveal that Salihundam was a meeting place of thee northern and southern styles of Buddhist architecture. The majority of the stupas are of northern solid type. Numerous images of Vajrayana tantric Buddhism have also been noticed. A small museum has been set up at the site preserving the sculptures, important among them being Marichi, Tara and Majusri.

It was pointed out by ASI staff that some monks from Sri Lanka and Thailand visit the site during Karthik month. The number of domestic tourists at that time goes up substantially.

12. Sankaram

Sankaram is 45 km from Visakhapatnam. Sankaram site was excavated by Alexandar Rea in 1907-08 and numerous antiquities including a gold coin of Samudra Gupta were discovered. The remains of this old Sangarama consist of many monolithic stupas, rock-cut caves and other structural remains. A series of brick built viharas, chaityas are located on the eastern hill (Bojjanna Konda). The western hill (Lingale Konda) is studded with numerous rock-cut stupas in tiers dominated by a row of seven stupas on a common plat form. Some of the caves contain Buddha and Bodisatvas in relieves. The Vajrayana sect of Buddhism is evidenced by the image of Hariti.

13. Thotlakonda

Thotlakonda is 25 kms from Visakhapatnam. An extensive Buddhist settlement on hill top of Thotlakonda consists of Mahastupa, apsidal-chaityagriha, circular chaityagrihas, a large monastic complex, rockṣcut cisterns, a prayer hall, a refractory, retiring halls, votive stupas, Brahmi label inscriptions and stucco pieces. Satavahana and Roman coins were found during excavations.

14. Undavalli

The caves at Undavalli are 4 km from Vijayawada across the Krishna River. The hill contain fine specimens of architectural and sculptural models.

THE POLICIES AND PROGRAMMES OF THE STATE GOVERNMENT

The Government of Andhra Pradesh has been taking up a number of Tourism promotional projects in the State for the last ten years. The Tourism Promotion Councils of different districts under the Chairmanship of the District Collectors have taken up a number of tourism development projects in their respective districts. The aim of these projects is to generate employment opportunities to local youth in the field of tourism. The private agencies are invited to invest for the development of infrastructural facilities in different places which are potential with natural, and man made resources.

Buddhist Circuit

The Department of Tourism and the AP Tourism Development Corporation (APTDC) are developing popular Buddhist sites to attract tourists from India and abroad. It is estimated that Buddhist population in India is about seven million, while Andhra Pradesh has about 22000 of them. The Department of Tourism had published a booklet in 1997 entitled "Buddhist Heritage in Andhra Pradesh" in which 52 major Buddhist sites are identified. The APTDC Managing Director said that the cultural, religious and historical importance of the sites dating back to the 3rd and 5th centuries BC would be showcased for a panoramic view of Buddhist history. Fifty two major sites like Kalingapatnam, Ramatheertham, Pithapuram, Bavikonda, Ghantasala, Amaravathi and Nagarjunakonda had been identified. APTDC's focus is on Amaravathi and Nagarjunakonda and works are in progress. It will have an interpretation centre to display the Satavahana art and culture. The project cost is Rs. 4 crores. Nagarjuna Sagar will see "Sri Parvatha Arama" a Buddhist Theme Park being built at a cost of Rs. 8 corers. Work has started and the park will focus on the life and preachings of Gouthama Buddha, Acharya Nagarjuna etc.

The Department of Tourism has plans under way to develop Thotlakonda and Bavikonda near Visakhapatnam at a cost of Rs. 50 crores. The Andhra Pradesh State Museum is also planning to have a high security 'holy relics' gallery.

The year 2006 is a land mark for Buddhists in the state with His Holiness Dalai Lama's visit to Amaravathi for the "Kala Chakra" celebrations and International Buddhist Conference which held in the month of January, 2006.

OBSERVATIONS AND CONCLUSION

Buddhism entered into Andhradesa during the life time of Lord Buddha. His disciples introduced the new religion in different parts of South India and South East Asia during the reign of Asoka, and the same was patronized by their successors like Satavahana rulers and later by Ikshwaku kings. It is observed that the regional rulers and their family members, particularly women folk took keen interest in the philosophy of Buddhism and liberally patronized the new religion by giving donations for the construction of stupas, viharas, chaityas etc., in the length and breadth of Andhra Desa. These centres appear mostly on the banks of the rivers Godavari and Krishna and their tributaries. The river banks were centres of civilizations, where trade and commerce developed because of the trade carried out on the rivers in ancient times. The traders, and other rich sections of the people contributed a lot for the spread of the religion and also for the construction of the Buddhist settlements. These establishments are now in ruins at places like Dulikatta, Phanigiri, Peddabankuru, Gajulabanda, Gummidi Durra, Kotilingala, Nelakondapally, Yeleswaram, Amaravathi, Nagarjuna Konda, Ghantasala, Bavikonda, Undavalli, Bhattiprolu, Sankaram, Totlakonda, Guntupally, Pavuralakonda etc., The Buddhist sites in Andhra region were brought to light during the British period itself. But the sites in Telangana region are excavated during the post-independence period. Among all these sites, few sites like Dulikatta in Karimnagar district, Amaravathi in Guntur district, Nagarjuna Konda and Phanigiri in Nalgonda district are very important centres. They are treasures of Buddhist artifacts and were very famous centres of Buddhism in ancient times. The stupas, and other sculptures at these sites exhibit the socio-cultural life of the people of those times. The carvings and the sculptures also reflect the great skills of the then craftsmen. They not only spread the message of Buddhist Philosophy, but also attract the pilgrims and tourists as the heritage centres in modern times. They are truly the centres of our ancient culture.

The archaeologists tried their best to bring to light the great heritage of India by undertaking excavations at these sites. The Department of Archaeology and the Archaeological Survery of India have carried out excavations with the meager funds made available to them. In order to develop them as tourist centres, proper transport and communicational facilities are to be developed. Basic infrastructural facilities are also to be provided like approach roads, water facility, electricity, etc., Accommodation facilities, cafetarias, snack bars are to be set up for the visitors. Though the Department of Archaeology has taken up steps to protect the monuments, there is no proper security either to the monuments or to the visitors. At some sites, unauthorized quarrying and land grabbing is taking place causing destruction of the ancient settlements. Recently, it is reported that (*The Hindu*, dt.18-12-2005) the Real Estate Dealers have managed to change the survey numbers in the revenue records to grab the land at the Bavikoda Buddhist site in Visakhapatnam. At some sites the rural folk are carrying away the sculptures and other stones and bricks to build their own houses, and walls. The monuments are also being mutilated and defaced.

Inspite of all these problems, they are, no doubt our rich heritage sites and are having lot of potentiality to attract tourists. Among all these sites, Amaravathi and Nagarjuna Konda are developed to some extent to attract the tourists. These two sites are well connected by roads and are included in the Buddhist Circuit developed by AP Tourism Development Corporation. These sites are also important in the Indian Buddhist Circuits after Sanchi, Saranath and Buddha Gaya etc. All these are also part of the South Asian Buddhist Circuit. This circuit is attracting not only tourists from India but also visitors from foreign countries like China, Japan, Thailand, Nepal, Bhutan, Sri Lanka etc., The increase in the number of tourists from foreign countries is very much important in these days of globalization, as the foreign tourist arrivals help to improve the position of foreign reserves and strengthen our economy.

Andhra Pradesh can be promoted as an important tourist destination with all its heritage monuments particularly the Buddhist sites which attract not only the domestic but also foreign tourists. Through promotion of tourism, employment opportunities can be generated to a great extent. The Tourism Industry can be treated as an engine for economic growth of the region. It also helps to secure foreign reserves from the international tourists.

More over, the noble ideals of Buddhism like non-violence, love, truthfulness, humanism, tolerance, righteousness, spirit of sacrifice can be inculcated in the minds of the youth. These values are essential for international understanding in these days of globalization for co-existence and harmonious social life.

References

Administrative Reports, Field Survey Reports on the Excavations preserved in the Archaeological Museum—District Head Quarters, A.P.

Administrative Reports and Files Preserved in the Department of Archaeology and Museums, Government of Andhra Pradesh, Hyderabad.

Brochures, Pamphlets, Booklets on Tourist Sites, issued by the District Administration, Andhra Pradesh.

Brochures, Pamphlets, issued by the APTDC, Hyderabad.

Vision-2020, Document, Government of Andhra Pradesh.

National Action Plan for Tourism, May, 1992, Ministry of Civil Aviation, and Tourism Government of India.

Raj Gopal, M.V., District Gazetteers of Andhra Pradesh, Hyderabad, 1976.

S.C. Bhat, The Encyclopaedic District Gazetteer of India, Vol. II, New Delhi, 1997.

News Papers:

Telugu : Eenadu; Vaartha; Andhra Bhoomi; Andhra Prabha; Andhra Jyothi; Praja Shakti.

English : The Hindu; Indian Express; Deccan Chronicle.

Magazines:

The Week; India Today; Sunday; Analysis; Andhra Pradesh (Telugu); Yojana (Telugu); Supatha (Telugu); Destination India; Travel News; Indian Travel Guide; Business Traveler; Travel World; Travel Time; Travel Talk.

Journals and Proceedings:

Proceedings of the AP History Congress.

Proceedings of the South Indian History Congress.

Itihas, Journal of the State Archives, Hyderabad.

Books:

Rao, P.R., *Indian Heritage and Culture*, New Delhi, 1997.

Telugu University: *History and Culture of Andhras*, Hyd. 1995.

Chandraiah, K., *Hyderabad, 400 Glorious Years*, Hyd. 1996.

Radha Krishna Sharma, *Temples of Telangana*, Hyd. 1976.

Krishna Rao, Y.V., *Andhra Pradesh*, Hyd. 1996.

Mallampally Somashekara Sharma, *Vignana Sarvasvam*, Madras, 1961.

Ramaniah, J., *Temples of South India*, New Delhi, 1989.

Krishna Shastri, V.V., *The Proto—Early Historic Cultures of Andhra Pradesh.*

Venkateshwara Reddy, A., *Telugulo Boudham* (Tel.), Telugu Academy, Hyd. 2005.

Retrieving the Past: History and Culture of Telangana, Osmania University, Hyd., 2004.

Glimpses of Our Past—Historical Researches—In honour of Prof. Radha Krishna Sharma, Osmania University, Hyd., 2004.

Andhra Sangeetha, *Samskruthika Mahostva Vishesha Sanchika* (Tel).

Sanathana Dharma Charitable Trust, Hyd., 2001.

Satish Babu, *Tourism Development in India*, New Delhi, 1997.

Bhatia, A.K., *Tourism Development*, New Delhi, 1986.

Vasan, *India—A Tourist Guide*, New Delhi, 1997.

30

Towards an Integration of Buddhism and Psychoanalysis

Annapareddy Venkateswara Reddy

To an outsider and uninitiated Buddhism and psychoanalysis appear things fall apart, diametrically opposed to each other and with no hope of bridging the gulf, as the one is Oriental, born 2500 years ago, is a spirituai system and an ethical psychology, the other is Occidental, born only in the late 19th century, is a psycho-therapeutic system. The goal of the former is to realize the illusionaryness of the "the taken for granted self", whereas the later emphasizes the strengthening of the self and the ongoingness of existence. The one insists that we become 'nobody' in a spiritual sense before we become 'somebody' and the other that we become 'somebody' in a psychological sense before we become 'nobody'. The one employs *vipassanā Bhāvanā* which is moment-to-moment non-judgemental awareness of the ever changing objects of perception as its method, whereas the other, as its method free association, which is 'talking out' without censuring whatever that occurs in the mind.

This paper intends to show, despite the seeming differences, that on a closer examination the mist of opposition melts away. It intends further to prove that integration, a sort of cross-pollination, can be effected with a judicial consideration of the two systems.

Before an attempt is made at the integration of the two, we may have to take a little digression, in order to give a backdrop of Buddhism and psychoanalysis by pointing out to the juxtaposing of the two that has happened for the first time in history. This great event of linking the two has happened, when Romain Rolland, a French poet and author, a student of Hindu teachers Rāmakṛishana and Vivēkānanda, had written to Sigmund Freud to examine the meditative experience of the East from a psychoanalytic perspective in 1930.[1] Romain Rolland's description of eastern meditative experience inspired Freud to offer the famous analysis of the 'oceanic feeling' as 'limitless' and unbounded ego feeling of 'oneness with the universe' that seeks the restoration of 'limitless narcissism' and the 'resurrection' of the infantile helplessness."[2] His explanation, while catching the fusion of the meditator's mind with the object of meditation, did not take into account the analytical practices, most distinctive of Buddhism. The Freudian equation with pre-verbal, symbiotic, regressive oneness with the mother, for a time has gone virtually unchallenged.

Meditation as was understood by Romain Rolland is quite different from the *vipassanā Bhavanā* as was conceived by the Buddha, the ever-greatest psychologist. *Vipassanā*, the insight meditation, though includes the concentration meditation, the *samathā bhāvanā,* was invented by the Buddha himself that is unique to Buddhism. The avowed purpose of Buddha is to make the meditator realize through the practice of *vipassanā* that the world, including the *Nāma-Rūpa* i.e., the personality, is impermanent, a flux, a non-soul and suffering. These three distinct characteristics of the phenomena when expressed in *Pāli* in the words of Buddha are: (1) Sabbe sankhārā anicca. (all compounded things are impermanent) (2) Sabbe sankhārā dukkha. (all compounded things are suffering) (3) Sabbe dhammā anatta. (all dharmās are non-soul). It is Buddh's aim to transmit this knowledge of the three characteristics, not through intellect, but through experience. This experience is made possible only by means of vipassanā, the insight meditation.

Of course, the Buddhist *vipassanā* consists of two distinct attentional strategies, the first being concentration of mind on a single object with which the meditator fuses and becomes one with it. This state is always associated with pleasure feelings and relaxation and is called relaxation response which leads directly to what Freud termed 'oceanic feeling'.

The second attentional strategy of Buddhism is mindfulness, which is moment-to-moment attention to thoughts, feelings, images or sensations as they arise and pass away within the field of awareness. This mindfulness, which is unique to Buddhism, provides insights into the nature of the self i.e., the meditator will be able to experience the illusiveness of the self, which is the avowed aim of Buddhism.

This second strategy has not been taken up for study by psychoanalysts till recently. The first psychoanalyst to study the importance of mindfulness to psychoanalysis was Joseph Thomson (1924), who pointed out the similarities between meditation and psychoanalysis and described the Buddhist notions of the structure of the self as seen in the advanced stages of insight meditative practice.

What happens in advanced stages of mindfulness meditation? A therapeutic split is fostered in the ego taking itself as object and strengthening the observing ego to attend to moment to moment changes.[3] The development of mindfulness results in the synthetic capacity of ego that which coheres more complex levels differentiation and objectivation[4]. The synthetic function in Janet's terminology is 'pre-sentiation which means the capacity to attend to "the formation of the mind in the present moment"[5] that allows the reality to be grasped to the full. And in this much more advanced stages of mindful meditation a shift takes place from the intra-psychic content to an exclusive focus on to the intra-psychic process.

Thus "when thoughts occur only the generic process of thinking is attended to rather than the specific content of thought. Emphasis is on thoughts insubstantiality, their transience and the manner in which the meditator identifies with being the thinker."[6] This is what exactly happens in Buddhist meditation. Buddhist psychology studies mind in a minute way "precisely for the practical purpose of showing that there is nothing enduring and abiding, nothing we can call self or soul or spirit in the sense self-existent independent entity."[7] This drives home the Buddhist concept of "thinking without thinker," "action without actor."

After having discussed the meditative practice of Vipassanā, its goals and achievements now we arrive at the confrontation of the two—Buddhism and psychoanalysis. A cross-fertilization can be effected by recognizing the developmental stages in the images or representations of the self. While the western tradition traced the earlier stages of the development of the self by analysing how it is formed out of the schemas of who we are and what are our relations with others—this is the initial formation of the self with ego centrism—the Buddhist tradition identified the later or more developed stages in which decentring culminates in altruism. The two traditions are not talking about two separate things but about the same continuum of development, about the two segments of the same.

In each moment of experience the representation of myself and the representations of the objects of the self are constructed anew in our minds. This has always been the Buddhists' stand and now the modern psychodynamic theory falls in line. This world, including the inner world, is ever changing, lasting not more than a millisecond. This Buddhist truth is now confirmed by the physicists and psycho-physicists as the fundamental nature of 'reality'. Now psychologists say that observing and absorbing in this sort of reality does not lead to psychoanalytic regression but paves way for the attainment of new levels of psychological integration and well-being.

The stimulus-response connection of 'pleasure-approach',

'pain-avoid' which is believed to be natural and innate by the western psychologists, was unlinked long ago by the Buddha himself and he said it was volitional and learned. This Buddha's insight, in the last one or two decades made inroads into western psychology.

How Buddhist meditation can help a psychoanalyst has been the centre of attention of many today. Karen Horney speaks of 'whole-hearted attention fostered by meditation'.[8] Freud identified this kind of attention as essential to psychoanalytic listening,[9] but he did not offer any positive recommendations.

J.B. Rubin says, "meditation reduces self-criticism, aids psychoanalysts and patients to tolerate greater affect . . . fosters capacity to relate to self and other with greater openness and fluidity."[10] Psychoanalysts who meditate have more tolerance to listen to their patients more calmly, deeply and attentively with less narcissistic relationship to their theories. Meditative practices foster the cultivation of self-introspective abilities, which are useful to analysand. The attending to of experience non-judgementally self-critical stance develops the capacity to accept others.

Psychoanalysis can help us in getting more mileage from inner experiences made available to us so wonderfully by meditation. "So after becoming aware of our inner experience through meditation we need to utilize psychoanalytical methods to investigate what we have become aware of Psychoanalysis teaches Buddhists that it is crucial for self-formation that explores areas in our lives that meditation neglects, such as the shaping role of one's past, unconscious and character, our views of self and others, our strategies of self-protection and the nature and quality of our relationships."[11]

After having examined the inter-relationship and integration of Oriental Buddhism and Occidental psychoanalysis can we still join hands with Rudyard Kipling and say, that "east is east west is west and never shall the twin meet". Salmon Rusdie, in a recent collection of his stories expressed an opposite view: "I too have ropes around my neck, I have them to this day pulling me this way and that, east and west, commanding to choose . . . ropes I do not choose between you . . . I choose neither you nor both. Do you hear? I refuse to choose."[12]

"East may be East" and "west may be west" but in my experience if you are open to what psychoanalysis and meditation might teach us and allow the twin to meet, then our lives and the lives of the other with whom we work might well be transformed and greatly enriched."[13]

In conclusion it may be said whether east or west the fundamental human nature is the same.

Notes and References

1. As stated by Epstein in his article 'Beyond Oceanic Feeling', The Couch and the Tree, Ed. Anthoni Molino, North Point Press: New York, 1999, p. 119.
2. Freud, Sigmund, *Civilization and its Discontents*, The Penguin Freud Library, Vol. 12, Penguin, pp. 255-60.
3. Engler, J.H., Vicissitudes of the Self: According to Psychoanalysis and Buddhism'. In Psychoanalysis and Contemporary Thought, Vol. 6, 1983, pp. 29-72.
4. Epstein, Mark, 'The Deconstruction of the Self: Ego and Egolessness in Buddhist Insight Meditation', *Journal of Transpersonal Psychology*, Vol. 20, 1988, pp. 61-69.
5. Ellen Berger, H.F., *The Discovery of the Unconscious*, Allen Lane: London, 1970, p. 376.
6. Epstein, Mark, 'Beyond Oceanic Feeling: Psychoanlytic Study of Buddhist Meditation' in from The Couch and the Tree, Ed. Anthoni Molino, Northpoint Press: New York, 1999, p. 124.
7. *Ibid.*, p. 112.
8. Horney, K., *Final Lectures*, International University Press: New York, 1987, p. 18.
9. Freud, S., *Recommendations to Physicians Practicing Psychoanalysis.* Standard Edition, Vol. 12, Hogrth Press: London,1912, pp. 216-226.
10. Rubin, J.B., *Psychotherapy and Buddhism: Toward an Integration*, Plenum Press: New York, 1996, as quoted in *American Journal of Psychoanalysis*, Vol. 59, 1999, p. 8.
11. *Ibid.*, p. 22.
12. *Ibid.*, p. 22.
13. *Ibid.*, p. 22.

31

Buddha: The Greatest Social Reformer of all Times

J. Amar Jyothi

The Buddha, who was born in a royal family, made a very high sacrifice and had discarded selfishness fully. He presented himself as a great ascetic who was symbol of compassion and loving kindness. He was considered as the most active missionary in the world. He wandered from place to place for 45 years preaching his Dhamma not only to the general mass but also to the intelligentsia. Till his last moment, he served humanity both by example and by precept.

According to Narada Mahathera, the Buddha was a unique human being, the profoundest of thinkers, the most persuasive of speakers, the most energetic of workers, the most successful of reformers, the most compassionate and tolerant of teachers, the most efficient of administrators, and above all the Holiest of Holies.

Buddha protested against the caste system as part of his programme in order to eradicate social evils prevailed at that time. According to the Buddha, caste or colour does not preclude one from becoming a Buddhist or entering the order. The Buddha did not approve of the caste system which was like a wall that separated man from man. For that matter, fishermen, scavengers, courtesans together with the privileged were equally given positions of rank. Upali, the barber was made the chief in matters pertaining to the Vinaya, in preference to all others. Similarly, Sunita, the scavenger, was admitted by the Buddha Himself into the order. Ambapali, the courtesan entered the order and attained Arahantship, Sati, the monk, was the son of a fisherman. Saba was the daughter of a Smith, Purna was a slave girl. Capa was the daughter of a deerș stalker. There are many such examples to show that the portals of Buddhism were wide open to all without any distinction. It was also the Buddha, who attempted to abolish slavery for the first time in the known history of the world.

It was also the Buddha, who raised the status of women and brought them to the forefront of the society. He did not see any different in sex to attain Arhanthood. He saw the image good of both men and women and assigned to them their due place in His teachings.

It was only order certainly a great blessing to women and women belonging to different professionals joined the sangha irrespective of caste, creed and status. He liberated women who did not have even human freedom. Buddha asked 'what it wrong in being a female, if that person is wise' when King Kosala was in conversation with Buddha and the King was in distress at hearing the news that his queen Mallika gave birth to a girl.

Buddha, profounded loving-kindness and Mahakaruna, the great compassion to all living beings, i.e. men, women, and animals irrespective of their size. He strongly denied the animal sacrifice and one of the five precepts of the Buddha was to abstain from killing.

He was the great man who insisted upon discipline in the sangha of both Bhikkus and Bhikkunis.

He also advised people to earn money in right way and legitimately acquiring wealth by strength of arrow is lower than gaining by sweat which is a great blessing. He was the first man to advocate to channelise the wealth for the needy. He introduced Dana, giving in charity, as one of Shatparamita.

He also prescribed Vinaya (code of conduct for householder, children, pupil, husband and wife, master and servant and for girls). The Vinaya for householders is embodied in his discourse with Sigala, called the Sigalo-Vadasutta. He advised Sigala to avoid the four vices of conduct viz., the destruction of life, the taking of what is not given, licentiousness and lying speech. A man should also be free from addicted to intoxicating liquors, frequenting the streets at unseemingly hours, haunting fairs, being infatuated by gambling associating with evil companions, the habit of illness. At the same time a man should be away from six dangers and six perils. He also advised to know who is a good friend. One should respect and revere his parents, teachers, wife and children, friends and companions, servants workmen and his religious teachers.

According to Buddha, a child should minister to his parents saying: 'Once supported by them I will now be their support, I will perform duties incumbent on them; I will keep up the lineage and tradition of my family, I will myself worthy of my heritage'.

The parents should show their love for him, they restrain him from vice, they exhaust him to virtue they train him to a profession, they contract a suitable marriage for him, and is due to me they handover his inheritance.

Similarly, the Buddha advised the pupil, that a pupil should minister to his teachers by rising from his seat, in salutation by waiting upon them, by eagerness to learn, by personal service, and by attention when receiving their teaching.

For teachers the Vinay prescribed us, to love their pupil, to train him, to make him hold fast that which is well held, they thoroughly instruct him in the love of every art; they should speak well of him among his friends and companions.

Buddha also prescribed code of conduct of husband and wife. According to him, a husband should minister to his wife by showing respect, by courtesy, by faithfulness, by handing over authority to her, by providing her with adornment. A wife should love her husband, her duties are well performed, by hospitality to the Him of both, by faithfulness, by watching over the goods he brings, and by skill and industry in discharging all her business.

His Vinaya for the Master and Servant is praise worthy, 'A master should minister to his servants and employees by assigning them work according to their strength, by supplying them with food and wages, by tending them in sickness, by sharing with them unusual delicacies, by granting leave at times.

For servants and employees his Vinaya is unbiased. They should love their master, they rise before him, they lie down to rest after him, they are content with what is given to them, they do their work well, and they carry about his praise and good fame.

Similarly the Buddha also advised that 'a clansman should minister to religious teachers by affection in act and speech and mind, by keeping open house to them, by supplying their temporal needs. For religious teachers restrain him from evil, they exhaust him to good, they love him with kindly thoughts, they teach him what he had not heard they correct and purify what he has heard'.

The Buddha also prescribed Vinaya for the girls to train themselves to rise up early, and to be the last to retire, be willing workers, order all things sweetly and be gentle voiced. To honour, rever, esteem and respect all who are the husbands' relatives, whether mother or father, recluse or godly man, and on their arrival will offer them a seat and water. To be deft and nimble at husband's home-crafts, to know the work of each of the messengers and workfolk, by what has been done, their remissness, by what has not been done, to know the strength and the weakness of the sick; to divide the hard and soft food, each according to his share. To keep the money, corn, silver and gold that the husbands bring home, which and ward over it, and act no robber, thief carouser, wastrel therein.

Buddha was a man of great compassion and advocated the people to wish, may all beings be happy and secure may their hearts be wholesome let no one receive, harm another. He also told the people love their enemies.

He is also known for his generosity he was a consummate healer of Sorrow. He consoled Visaka, he comforted Kisagotami he took care of the suffering sick people. He was tolerant of the intolerant. His sense of equality and equal treatment was superb.

It should be reminded here that no political philosopher has uttered, to-date, so noble, so wide-ranging in implication, so great so democratic and so socialist who gave the slogan "may all beings be free of suffering", "may all beings be healthy", and "may all beings be happy". He wished the well-being of all beings with the expression "may all beings be happy", "Sabbe Satta bhavantu sukhitatta".

Hence, H.G.Wells, the distinguished thinker assigned to Him the first place amongst the seven great men in the world. Poet Tagore calls Him the greatest man ever born. His teachings, though 2500 years old, are ageless and relevent to the modern world.

32

The Aesthetics of Pali Literature

Professor Angraj Chaudhary

Aesthetics is the philosophy of the beautiful. Therefore the aesthetics of Pali literature means the beauty of Pali literature. What does the beauty of Pali literature consist in? Does it consist in the use of a special kind of language with similes, metaphors and parables by the Theras and there is to sensitively and clearly describe their feelings and emotions? Or does it consist in the delineation of Śanta rasa (the quietistic sentiment) which the ordained and the laity who follow the teachings of the Buddha come to experience, or does it consist in the exalted subject that this literature deals with or does it consist in a happy combination of all these? In order for a viable art to come into being what is most necessary is to effectively communicate our feelings, emotions and vision. Croce says that art comes into being when what we want to express is well expressed. If we fail to express it good art does not come into being. Croce was anticipated by a great Indian aesthetician, Bhattatauta by name, who says that real poetry comes into being when poets do not have only visions but they also have the linguistic ability to describe them in such a way that the readers feel the same experience as the poets have felt. Darsanad varnanadca. Pali literature, at least the canonical literature, has this quality.

Whereas other literature of the world has an element of imagination as is clear from what Shakespeare says in 'A Midsummer Night's Dream' (The poet in a fine frenzy . . . .) and what Coleridge says about imagination (See his Biographia literature, chapter xiv) as a synthesizing faculty which organises, harmonises and sees the true nature of things, Pali literature has grown out of the real experiences not only of the Buddha but also of all the Theras and Theris and other Upasakas and Upasikas. Each of them describes his or her experience. None of them, like a professional writer creates different characters and describes their experiences of pain and pleasure and other difficulties of life. There is no element of imitation or imagination here. From this point of view it stands apart from other literature of the world. There is one more aspect in which this literature is distinct from others. The protagonists whose utterances are found here are men and women who observed silā (precepts), practised samādhi (concentration) attained pañña (wisdom) themselves and expressed their joy of peace and bliss. This is not invariably the case with the artists and poets of other literature. Of course exceptions are there in so far as there have been some saint poets practically in all literature. But generally Imaginative literature is a matter of art and craft for professional writers. As far as Pali literature is concerned the Buddha and his disciples, both ordained and lay, describe their actual experiences that they had in their spiritual journey. Besides, they never feed and water human passions. No Plato therefore, can find fault with this kind of poetry and he can not dare expel the poets from his republic. They have described what they have seen and realised at the experiential level. Of the three types of knowledge the Buddha puts a premium on Bhavanamayi pañña i.e. wisdom that one attains by observing things at the experiential level. So when it is said here that there is no fire like craving (Natthi raga samo aggi), there is no metaphorical use of 'fire' here. As fire burns one, so do cravings burn the

Theras and Theris and other persons whose utterances and experiences form the warp and woof of this literature. They do not imagine that they are burning but they really experience that they are burning. When I underline this basic difference between Pali literature and other Imaginative literature I do not mean to detract and devalue the latter. It has its own value and the pleasure derived from reading it is like the twin brother of the highest spiritual pleasure (Brahmanandasahodara) as rightly said by Visvanatha. Imaginative literature goes a long way in ennobling human beings, chastening their feelings and educating them in such a way as they develop a taste for the good, the great and the beautiful. It also goes a long way in bringing about changes in society for the better and making people appreciate the higher human values. It also arouses people to take up arms against social injustice they suffer and brings out the best that is there in the so called wretched and the bad. The great works of literature like the plays and epics of Kalidasa, the great plays by Shakespeare, the Divina Comedia by Dante, Les Miserable by Victor Hugo, War and Peace by Tolstoy, the novels of Dickens and Dostoevsky, to name just a few, do have the elements of imitation and imagination but who would dare deny their great role in shaping human conduct and chastening and ennobling people's feelings and sentiments? Who would say that these works of art contain no element of truth? Poets and writers are very sensitive persons. They feel the pains and pleasures of the characters they create but are not attached to them as they effect a sort of empathy by de-individualizing all emotions, characters and situations and achieving what Edward Bullough calls 'psychic distance.' An emotion depicted in Imaginative literature loses all individuality as it is universalized.

But Pali literature stands apart and is a class by itself. It takes off from where other literature lands. It does not give to 'airy nothing, a local habitation and a name' and as it is based on wisdom gained at the experiential level it does not need to achieve the 'psychic distance' because there is nothing painful here. In Imaginative literature one needs to achieve 'psychic distance' because there are many painful and lachrymose emotions and situations in it. In Pali literature we have joy, light and liberation in place respectively of pain, darkness and bondage. The Theras and the Theris and others who follow the teachings of the Buddha and walk on the path shown by him overcome desire, tear asunder the darkness of ignorance, cut the fetters, destroy the asavas, obtain peace, become cool and quenched and come to the land of light and liberation.

Like all arts which draw their sustenance from life Pali literature also draws its sustenance from life and is not severed from it. But whereas other literature deals mostly with worldly experiences like pain and pleasure and delineates eight kinds of rasas like love, laughter, heroic, compassion etc. Pali literature deals mostly with spiritual experiences if I may call them so, different from worldly experiences. Even though they speak of worldly experiences they make them as sâcari bhavas (auxiliary sentiments) for the delineation of Santa rasa. These worldly experiences also lead them to quietude and tranquillity which constitute the permanent disposition of Santa rasa. The Buddha and other Theras and Theris experience this tranquillity and peace and attempt to delineate it. As we know, the summum bonum of life according to the Buddha is Nirvana which is a quiet state of desirelessness. Pali literature which is regarded as the literature preserving the words of the Buddha always keeps this high ideal in view and tries to depict the serenity and tranquillity which he realised under the Bodhi tree after extinguishing all his desires (tanha, trsna). The highest goal of life according to the Buddha is to achieve the state of desirelessness. Desires which keep on multiplying in life for various reasons and cause a man to be born again and again have to be annihilated so that a state of quietness and calmness is achieved.

How to achieve that state of desirelessness? When the Buddha propounded the philosophy of dukkha (suffering), he also propounded an action-plan to get rid of it. Suffering is a ubiquitous fact of life. It is not to be denied nor neglected. But as he transcended dukkha and crossed the ocean of four floods (the floods of sensuality, rebirth, speculation and ignorance) by walking on the eightfold path comprising sila, samadhi and pâa he prescribed this path to all who want to cross the ocean and come out of the wheel of life and death. If a man observes precepts, practices meditation and attains wisdom, he will understand the real nature of things, give up craving for them, develop nirveda (non-attachment) and attain nirvana. He will go beyond all burning and attain the peace which 'passeth understanding'. When the Buddha attained this state he came out with this solemn utterance.

> *Anekajati samsaram sandhavissamm anibbisam/*
> *Gahakarakam gavesanto dukkha jati punappunam//*
> *Gahakaraka ditthosi puna geham na kahasi/*
> *Sabba te phasuka bhagga gahakutam visankhitam/*
> *Visankharagatam cittam tanhmnam khayamajjhaga//*

> "Through many a birth I wandered in samsara, seeking, but not finding the builder of this house. Sorrowful is it to be born again and again. O house-builder, Thou art seen. Thou shalt build no house again. All thy rafters are broken. Thy ridge-pole is shattered. My mind has attained the unconditioned. Achieved is the end of craving." (*Dhammapada* 153 Tr. By Narada Thera)

On attaining enlightenment, it dawned upon him at the same time that craving of the builder of the house has ended and it has ended completely in all its diverse forms. This was the realisation of the Buddha at the experiential level. He achieved a state where there was no burning, no craving and no becoming. By practicing vipassana meditation he had known and seen at the experiential level that suffering is caused and multiplied by reacting to sensations, pleasant and unpleasant that arise because of the contact of sense organs with their respective objects and he had also known and seen that by remaining equanimous he could eliminate suffering. When he attained enlightenment it became all clear to him that there was no more clinging and aversion—the cause of suffering in him and he had achieved the unconditioned. That he ended all cravings completely is graphically described by 'broken rafters' and 'shattered ridge-pole.'

In his arduous spiritual journey the Buddha had realised the importance of pâa (intuitive wisdom) attained at the experiential level. Knowledge gained through learning and reflection cannot enable one to develop nirveda or non-attachment, because such knowledge is not perfect. Howsoever a person might know at the intellectual level that the objects they hanker after are impermanent, he cannot develop non-attachment but when he realises at the experiential level that all that come into being are bound to fade away and pass away he develops nirveda. This realisation is not intellectual or inferential but absolute knowledge based on truth (yathabhutâ ana) which enables him to develop nirveda (nirveda). This nirveda is the permanent disposition (sthayi bhava) of Santa rasa.

Through the gathas quoted above the Buddha successfully describes the peace that has followed the extinction of all his desires. They therefore delineate and embody Santa rasa.

Santa rasa is the supreme of all rasas. It represents the highest purusartha (moksa). Whereas all eight rasas like srngara (love), hasya (laughter), vira (heroic), karuna (compassion) etc. are worldly. Santa may be called supra-mundane. A great part of human psychology can be explained by eight sthayi bhavas which are inherent in us due to raga, dosa and moha but sama (calmness) trsnasksayasukhajnana (knowledge of the happiness that follows the destruction of desires)—the sthayi bhava (permanent disposition) of Santa rasa comes into being when all desires and the roots of akusala kammas (unwholesome actions) e.g. raga (craving), dosa (aversion) and moha (ignorance) are destroyed.

From a lot of discussions on the sthayi of Santa rasa it is clear that sama (calmness, equanimity) is really its sthayi bhava. It is a state of mind transcending duhkha and sukha, raga and dvesa and all desires. Namisadhu and Rudrata regard samayagjana (right knowledge) or tattvajana (knowledge of reality) as the sthayi bhava of Santa. According to Anandavardhana and Mammata trsnaksayasukhajnana(knowledge of the happiness that follows the destruction of desires) and nirveda (non-attachment) are respectively the sthayibhavas of Santa rasa. The tattvajana or the samyagjana or the trsnaksayasukhajnana of the Buddha and also the peace and freedom from burning that he experiences after annihilating all his desires are clear from the gathas quoted above. It is in this context that there is no fire like craving (Natthi ragasamo aggi) can be understood.

The Theras and Theris who were the disciples of the Buddha also attain this kind of tattvajana and enjoy peace and harmony after extirpating all their desires. Their verses also delineate Santa rasa. Thera Ratthapala seeing dangers in all sensual pleasures and seeing them burning left pleasure and pelf and became ordained out of faith in the Buddha. As sensual pleasures though variegated, sweet, and delightful with their various forms cannot satisfy, as no one can protect the mortal being, not even his friends, as he cannot take anything with him when he is dying, so seeing them on fire he became ordained. (See the gathas of Ratthpala Thera—Theragatha)

Kamehi lokamhi na hatthi titti, na miyamanassa bhavanti tana/
Ñati ca mitta athavā sahayā, nā miyamānassa dhanamanveti kiñci//
Kamahi citra madhura manorama, viruparupena mathenti cittam/
Adinavām kamagunesu disva . . . saddhayaham pabbajito//
(See verses 778 to 789)

He sees this body as a paited puppet, as a heap of sores, diseased, having no permanent stability, covered with skin and bones and resplendent with clothes enough to delude a fool but it can not delude one who is a seeker after the far shore (nibbana). This description of the body is very powerful and it does not fail to develop nirveda (non-attachment) in it. Thera Rakkhita who was a prince of Devadaha says that all his cravings, aversions and ignorance are destroyed and he is now cool and quenched. Eraka sees sensual pleasures as burning and frees himself from suffering by not craving for them. Thera Abhaya realises how asavas (cankers) increase when one is attracted towards the beautiful.

Rupam disvā sati mutthā, piyam nimittam manasikaroto/
Sārattacitto vedeti tañca ajjhosa titthati/
Tassa vaddhanti asāva, bhavamulopagamino//

(*Theragāthā*, 98)

Thera Radha purifies and develops his mind in such a way that aversions find no place there. This realisation that all his aversions are ended produces Santa rasa—the sentiment (rasa) of quietude.

His brother Suradha followed in his footsteps, took ordination, attained arahatship and came out with these utterances—my birth is ended and I have torn asunder the net of desire. Thera Nagasamala saw a beautiful woman as a snare spread by Death and obtained knowledge and freedom from the cycle of birth and death. Thera Mudita and Thera Mahapanthaka saw desire as an arrow and resolved not to sit idle even for a moment till it was taken out.

Tato me panidhi asim, cetaso abhipatthito/
Na niside muhuttam pi, tanhasalle anuhate//

(*Theragatha*, 514)

He sees desire as an arrow. This is a powerful visual imagery.

When an adorned and ornamented prostitute salutes Thera Sundarasamudda and invites him to enjoy the pleasures of senses with her and offers to give him wealth, right thought arises in his mind, he sees the dangers of sensual pleasures and develops nirveda (non-attachment) which is the sthayi bhava of Santa rasa. Thera Kappa utters in his verses the same thing that the Buddha has said about the asubha nimitta (sign of the unclean, impurity) that this body is and he does not develop any attachment to this. When he expresses this viraga Santa rasa is delineated.

Nanakulamalasampunno,mahaukkarasambhavo/
Candanikamva paripakkam, mahagando mahavano//
Pubbaruhirasampunno,guthakupena galhito/
Apopaggharano kayo, sada santati putikam//

(*Theragatha*, verses 567-68)

This body is full of different kinds of impurities, it is born of excrement. It is like a big mature abscess, a sore full of pus and blood which keep on dripping all the time. There are many Theras and Theris who find this body repulsive, smeared with flesh and blood, food for worms, vultures and other birds. They regard this body as foul, impure, smelling of urine, a frightful water bag of corpses, always flowing, full of impure things, some of them regard it as diseased and perishable. Those women who were infatuated with their own beauty like Khema and Nanda contemplate such bodies and develop nirveda. They are no longer attached to their bodies and instead of having attraction for them they develop repulsion. They cease to burn and become cool and quenched. Punna Theri's remark on human body is so graphic that it immediately produces revulsion and nirveda. If what is inside this body comes outside, we have to protect it with staff in our hands all the time from crows and dogs.

Sace imassa kayassa, anto bahirako siya/
Dandam nunam gahetvana, kake sone nivaraye//

Talaputa's longing for dwelling in the forest and practicing vipassana meditation after the poignant realization of impermanence is expressed in the following words:

> O, When shall I, who see and know that this
> My person, nest of dying and disease,
> Oppressed by age and disease,
> Is all impermanent
> Dwell free from fear lonely within the woods (See *Theragatha*, verse 1096)
> Yea, when shall these things be?

He admonishes his own self who had once inspired him to lead an ordained life lonely in the forest and who now drags him to live in the world and enjoy the pleasures of the senses by saying 'how come, you are cutting the roots of a tree which is about to give fruits'.

> *Ropetva rukkhāni yatha phalesi, mule tarum chhettu tameva icchasi/*
> *Thatupam cittamidam karosi, yam mam aniccamhi cale niyuñjasi//*
>
> (*Theragatha*, 1124)

A great conflict goes on in the mind of Talaputa. He has decided to live an ordained life but when he is tempted by his other self to come back to the world to enjoy the sensual pleasures the conflict becomes very sharp. As a result very powerful lyrical poetry comes into being. But Talaputa does not lose heart. He takes a strong resolve to cut off the creeper of desire with the sword of wisdom. This knowledge that he has extirpated all desires extinguishes all fires and he experiences peace and harmony.

Many Theris also have extinguished the fires of craving, aversion and ignorance and experienced peace. Therī Ūttarā says that she has rooted out all desires, attained nibbana and has become cool, free from all burning.

Samūlam tanhamabbuyha, sītibhūtāmhi nibbutā. (*Therīgātha*, 15)

Thera Sangha says almost the same thing. *Samūlam tanhamabbuyha, upāsantamhi nibbutā* (*ibid.*, 18)

How the experience of aniccatā (impermanence) leads to serenity, tranquillity and calmness can be seen in the utterances of Ambapali who is a unique example of how much she has learnt from the teachings of the Buddha. She was really very beautiful and was proud of it. But age has brought about tremendous changes in her. Her glossy and black curl now look like hempen, her hair once as fragrant as a casket of perfumes has the odour of hare's fur, her finely pencilled brows are seamed with overhanging wrinkles, her beauteous arms now hang feeble as withering branches, her two gem like blue eyes have become lustreless, her once pearl like teeth are broken, her once cuckoo like sweet voice has become harsh, her round, swelling, close together beautiful breasts now hang loose like the waterless water bags. (See gathas of Ambapali) in the Therigatha. The physical beauty of Ambapali has been so powerfully and glowingly described here that it compares with the description of beauty given by any great poet of any literature. Ambapali, though, expresses her tragic feelings of her 'wasted charms' very poignantly, does not feel disappointed and depressed. Instead she feels disillusioned and disenchanted. Her devastating realisation of the transitoriness of physical beauty reminds her of what the Buddha had said and realising it to be true she changes the course of her life and by practicing meditation she attains arahathood. There is no burning in her now. She has become cool and dispassionate. She has attained the real knowledge, developed nirveda and gives vent to her feelings in the gathas which delineate Santa rasa. Her knowledge of reality (vijja) and her extirpation of desire (acarana) are the permanent dispositions that evoke Santa rasa. The gathas describe her beauty from top to toe. This description of her beauty that might have evoked the sentiment of love (rasrngurasa) in her youth now delineates the sentiment of quietude (Santa rasa). Her conclusion is 'such was this body, now it is decrepit, the abode of many pains; an old house, with its plaster fallen off, not otherwise is the utterance of the speaker of truth.'

Ediso ahu ayam samussayo, jajjaro bahudukkhānamālayo/
Sopalepapatito jaragharo, saccavadivacanam anaññatha//
(*Theirgatha*, verse 270)

Theri Sumedha has realised with her wisdom that sensual pleasures are transitory. If they are indulged in they only lead to more suffering. Besides, the desire for sensual pleasures is not fulfilled howsoever much one indulges in them. This realisation (tattvajñana) on the part of Sumedha enables her to see sensual pleasures as they really are. They are like a butcher's knife and chopping block (asisunupāmā kamā), like the poised heads of snakes prepared to dart (sappāsiropāmā kamā), like blazing torches (ukkopamā), like heated iron ball (ayogulovā sāntatto), like cheating dreams (supinopama vâcaniyā), like javelins and spears (sattisulupamā kamā) like a pestilence (rogo), a boil (gando), like a pit of live coals (angārakāsu) and so on. She feels inspired by Dhamma and says "What will another do for me when his own head is burning? When old age and death are following closely one must strive for their destruction.

Kim mama paro karissati, attano sīsamhi dayhamānamhi/
Anubandhe jarāmarane, tassa ghatāya ghatitabbam//
(*ibid.*, 495)

She sees sensual pleasures like grass fire brands. They burn those who do not let them go. Realising all this she develops nirveda and all her utterances powerfully produce Santa rasa (the quietistic sentiment)

There are many apt and sublime similes in Pali canonical literature which powerfully help to describe the subject matter. Five hindrances (nivaraias) like kamacchanda (strong desire for sensual pleasures), vyapada (ill-will), thinamiddha (sloth and torpor), uddhaccakukucca (agitation of mind) and vicikiccha (doubt) are obstacles on the path of sadhana. Unless a man is free from them he can not concentrate his mind and attain insight wisdom.A man suffering from kamacchanda is like him who has contracted a loan, a man having vyapada is like a man diseased, a man having thinaiddha is like a prisoner, a man having uddhaccakukucca is like a slave and a man having vicikiccha is like a man who has lost his way. If he gets rid of them he is free from debt, from disease, from prison house, from slavery and from doubt. A man can be peaceful and calm and can feel joy only if he is free from these hindrances.

The joy that follows freedom from these hindrances forms the main theme of the four similes relating to the rupavacara jhanas. In the first jhana a yogavacara (who practises meditation) like a skilled bathman or his apprentice permeates his body within and without with joy. The second simile suggests that the joy he feels comes from within as water of a pool comes from beneath the ground. The third simile carries the idea of permeation further. The yogavacara fills himself more and more with joy just as lotus flowers are born in water, grow up in it and are pervaded, drenched, permeated and suffused with cool moisture thereof 'from their very tips down to their roots.' The fourth simile explains that not only is he filled with joy but also he is filled with a sense of purification, of translucence. Joy characterised by sublimity and purity forms the theme of the fourth jhana. There are other similes also which explain how his mind has become pure, serene and translucent. (See my Essay on Similes in the Samâaphala sutta)

The Tripitaka (Pali canonical literature) has many apt similes which go a long way in making the teachings of the Buddha clear. How to be born as a man is rare has been shown by the simile of a blind turtle in a deep wide and choppy ocean who comes on the surface every after hundred years and tries to put its neck in a one holed yoke which also is carried here and there by the mighty waves of the ocean. That so long as one indulges in sensual pleasures one cannot attain nibbana has been aptly shown by the two similes unheard of before in the Bodhirajakumara sutta. Howsoever much a sappy piece of stick thrown in water and a sappy and wet piece of stick away from water are rubbed with another dry stick, fire cannot be produced. Similarly nibbana is not possible so long as one indulges in sensual pleasures.

There are many such aesthetically gratifying, rich and suggestive similes which make the teachings of the Buddha clear. In conclusion it can be said that what the Buddha and his disciples wanted to communicate has been very clearly communicated with the help of similes metaphors and parables and they make us feel the same serenity and tranquillity which they have experienced through their utterances. Freedom from bondage, coming out of the cycle of birth and death, realising how sensual pleasures are dangerous, developing non-attachment to them and experiencing the quietist sentiment form the subject matter of Pali canonical literature and all these have been very well communicated. Even the description of Nature is done here in so sublime a manner that instead of arousing erotic sentiment it inspires Theras to meditate and get rid of all burning. They become cool and calm. (See my Essay on Nature in the Theragatha) Thus it is clear that the experiences of the Buddha and his disciples are very well conveyed by means of the language with similes and metaphors they use. They make us feel the nirveda they have developed and the peace and bliss they have attained. We enjoy the Santa rasa thus delineated here.

33

Buddhism: Modern Indian Society—A Perspective

Dr. Aravind Kumar

In the speeches and writings, Vivekananda occasionally speaks of the contributions made by Buddha & Buddhism towards Indian thought and society. The virtue of renunciation (sanyasa) is praised by him. According to him it is the basis of all ethics "Buddha was an embodiment of renunciation and perfect annihilation."[1] The Vedic religion with its stratification of society into fourfold caste system had degenerated into a pure materialism, with unnecessary rituals: In this critical juncture, there appeared the great master, Buddha—the teacher of equality, compassion and renunciation. Swamy Vivekananda says that "Buddha brought the Vedanta to light, gave it to the people, and saved India."[2]

In this paper an attempt is made to study the impact of Buddhism on Indian thought and society as an estimate of the relevance of Buddhist teaching to modern Indian society.

1. The Spirit of Renunciation

Buddhism made an impact on the spirit of renunciation and

ascetic life on the religion of India. Buddha repeatedly stressed the importance and ideal of renunciation. Since then Hinduism has absorbed into itself this Buddhist spirit of renunciation. The tradition of monastic ideas and of monastic abodes of Brahminical monks are traced to Buddhist religion. Though apparently Buddhism lost its importance in the land of its birth, in reality it can be seen as a reformed Hinduism. The ideal of renunciation still remains today the highest religious ideal. The great message of Buddha has melted into modern Hinduism and absorbed by Hinduism.

2. Modern Hinduism is post-Budhistic

According to Swamy Vivekananda modern Hinduism is largely Pauranika that is post Buddhistic in origin.[3] The worship of images, and building of temples, the doctrine of avatara, the reverence to cow, the prestige of vegetarian diet the emphasis on the principle of Ahimsa, the opposition to and almost disappearance of animal sacrifices, the idea of giving equality of opportunity in religion and devotional matters to sudras are the some of the features which are developed into Hinduism and post Buddhist.

3. Worship of Cow as Mother

On many instances and places we see that Buddha was criticising the sacrificial slaughter of animals including bulls, cows and calves. The notion of the cow as a mother (gomaata) was emphasised by Buddha. We find in the Buddhist canonical text the Suttanipaata,[4] that "like as our mother, father, brother, kin, cows are our greatest friends from whom balm comes," the Suttanipaata and Dhamapada gives details about the Buddhism setting forth the real virtues of true Brahmanas,which were lacking during his time. But they are the essential elements of Vedic Brahmanism.

4. Vegetarianism

Drinking of wine and eating of meat and fish have been greatly discouraged in India under the influence of Buddhism and Jainism. With the growth and popularity of Buddhist ethics and with the emergence of Vaishnavism, aversion to drinking wines, and interest in Vegetarian food became increasingly powerful. But the coming of Muslims in India again promoted the consumption of meat and wine on a large scale. The killing of animals for sacrifice however became, largely confined to a few royal families. Even today the followers of Sakta cult of Hinduism continue the sacrificial killing of animals. But modern Buddhists are all not vegetarians. But there are some Buddhists who are strict vegetarians.

5. Image Worship and Construction of Temple

The tradition of making images of the Buddha was inspired by the veneration of his followers or Buddha Bhakti which can be found in Tripitakas. A section of early Buddhists liked to adore the Chaityas or holy symbols such as the bodhi-tree, the wheel (chakar), and the lion seat (simhasana), the umbrella, the foot prints, and the begging bowl of the Buddha. Buddhists had started the veneration of chaityas and stupas as early as third century before Christ. Emperor Asoka is said have built a large number of stupas. The pali "Mahaparihibbana-sutta"[5] recommends the construction and adoration of stupas. The religious classic work of Buddhism "Saddarmpundarika sutta"[6] gives emphasis on the Buddha worship and Bhakti. The Buddhist art, architecture came into existence several centuries earlier to growth of Brahminical art and architecture. The some of the artistic elements of Buddhist art can be traced to the proto-historic art of Harappan period. The depictions of animal symbolism, human figures with religious affiliation were made during the Indus valley or Harappan period in historic times. We find that the anthropomorphic figures of Buddha and Jaina images were encountered first.

WAR AGAINST CASTEISM AND BROTHERHOOD OF MANKIND

Buddha was the first who attacked, caste system. In the opinion of Arnold J. Toynbee's remarks that Buddhism or Jainism had succeeded in captivating Indic world; caste might have been got rid of it, the equality of man or the universal brotherhood of mankind has been taught by several religions. But Buddha was the first to preach this great idea.

BUDDHA'S UNRIVALLED COMPASSION

Buddha was an embodiment of supreme compassion. This love and sympathy was unequalled. He had a great intellect and that heart which characterised his personality. The great virtues of Buddha have unparallel throughout the history of mankind. Buddha taught us how to sympathise with the wretched and poor living beings, sinner and the poor. He was the most unselfish man. He taught a religion of selflessness without any motive of selfishness. He preached in the language of the common man in order to reach the hearts of people. Buddha was a royal price, brought up in a luxurious life but renounced all comfort and royal throne to live an ordinary life among the poor and downtrodden. He preached good of all taught that a man has to be pure and holy and unselfish, he must find his life in others. Modern India needs the wonderful sympathy of Buddha, for the benefit of all humanity. He was ready to sacrifice his life for any one and everyone. All his life he ceaselessly worked for the good of all. He sought the ultimate good of all in thought, word and deed. He spread the message of love in all directions east-west-north and south above and below, until the whole universe was filled with this love, this is described in a verse in Mettasutta[8] discourse on loving kindness. "Just as a mother would protect her only child, even at the risk of her own life, even so let a man cultivate boundless heart towards all beings. Let his thoughts of infinite love pervade the whole universe. Above, below and across; without any obstruction without any hatred, without any enmity."

Today's world is full of strife, enmity and hatred among the people, the way to ultimate peace and bliss, which the Buddha had discovered constitutes the Buddhists medicine against all the ills of existence. Chadrakeerty the philosopher of 7th century calls him. "The Great king of doctors" the physician of the great decease of passion.[9] "Klesha-Mahaavyaadhi-chikitsakaa. Mahaavaidya-raajaa." In Suttanipata[10] Buddha was compared to a spiritual lamp the light emitted by him dispelled the darkness of mind. The Buddhists worship him as Teacher of men and Gods. Buddha-symbolically meant, light awakening, enlightenment, knowledge and wisdom. It also symbolises moral perfection and spiritual fulfillment Buddha recognised human freedom and equality of opportunity in social and religious life. Distinctions and discriminations based on race, colour caste and sex did not find place in his teachings, his teachings were truly universal. Selfishness, egoism, casteism and sex discrimination are curse of mankind. Buddha was the first to make a diagnosis of these terrible diseases of humanity. His way of universal liberation was open to all human beings.

He was the first-human being to give to the world a complete system of morality. Buddha preached the most tremendous truths. One of his great messages was the equality of man. Buddha was the first teacher who taught that one has to be self-reliant; who freed us not only from the bondages of our false selves but from dependence on the invisible being as beings called God or Gods. In Kalwasutta Buddha said that 'do not believe in what you have heard says the great Buddha, do not believe in doctrines because they have been handed down to you through generations, do not believe in anything because it is followed blindly by many do not believe because some old sage makes a statement, do not believe in truths to which you have become attached by habit, do not believe merely on the authority of your teacher and elders, gave a deliberation and analyse, and when the results agrees with reason and conduces to the good of one and all accept it and live up to it."[12]

A similar advice was given by the Buddha to Bhaddiya, "come now Bhaddiya, be not misled by proficiency in the books, nor by mere logic or inference, nor after considering reasons, nor after reflection on and approval of some theory, nor because it fit becoming, nor by the thought the recluse is revered by us.[13]

These passages show that the Buddha did not ask any one to accept. His teachings as a matter of authority or as out of respect for him. No other prophet in the religious history of humanity is known to have asked and taught in this spirit of rationalism. All the prophets appealed to divine guidance and faith in super human agency. The essence of Kalamasuttta is summed up by another Buddhist philosopher Shantarakshita in a beautiful Sanskrit verse. 'O Bhiksus, my words should be accepted by the wise not out of regard for me, but after due investigation, out as gold is accepted as true after heating cutting and rubbing.'[14] The emphasis in reason and experience is characteristic of Buddhism. In such a system of thought there is no room for any dogma or gospel as such. Buddha is an authority, no doubt, his authority rests on his enlightened—experience; which can be shared and verified by any one who makes the required efforts. Swamy Vivekananda has emphasized in his speeches and writings the following elements of the Buddha's teachings, renunciation, meditation unselfishness, universal brotherhood, and equality of mankind compassion towards all form of life, sympathy, for the poor and the miserable non-violence, or love practice of moral virtues rather than theoretical speculation, the spirit of critical enquiring and rational attitude; rather than submission to dogmas and traditional authority, fearlessness and uprightness in conduct, and constant effort to gain perfection. Respect for the faith of other men is a characteristic of the Buddhist teaching. Although a missionary religion, it was one of the teachings of Buddhism not to antagonise any other religion.[15]

The Buddha did not try to convert any one by conventional means such as claims to prophetic revelation, promise of salvation of threat of condemnations. He delivered his discourses and invited his audiences to examine them and know for themselves their desirability and truthfulness: Swami Vivekananda says that the unique element in Buddhism was its social element and Buddha was a social reformer.[16] As a result of spread of teachings of Buddha many social and religious evils, then current in India declined and in some cases disappeared. The Buddha taught the practice of mind control, meditation and emphasized the cultivation of social emotions. He lived the life of a liberated while active and alive.

KINDNESS AND CHARITY

One of the epithets of the Buddha is "the Great compassionate one" (Mahaa Kaarumika). Moved by supreme compassion (Maha Karuna) the Tathagata set in Motion the Wheel of Righteousness (dhrama-chakra). The Principles of Inoffensiveness (ahimsa), which is essential, is identical with friendliness (maitri) and compassion (Karuna) is placed at the head of the list of the Buddhist moral rules. Buddhism, says P.V. Bapat, is a religion of kindness, humanity and equality.[17] Aryadeva, a Buddhist philosopher of the second century A.D. tells us that the Buddha's dharma can be summed-up in two words ahimsa (in offensiveness) compassion (love) and Nirvana.[18]

According to Vivekananda, the spirit of compassion or kindness is the one out standing contribution of the Buddhist religion. Buddha taught kindness towards lower beings, since then there has not been a sect in India that has not taught the charity, to all beings even to animals this kindness, this mercy this charity, greater than any doctrine; are what Buddhism left to us.[19] Buddhism had taught the masses a moral way of living rendering Indian society so great.[20]

Notes and References

1. Completes Works of Swami Vivekananda Mayavati Memorial Edition, Calcutta, 1962-65, Vol. I, pp. 424-25, II, pp. 62-63.
2. *Complete Works*, Vol. II, pp. 62-63.
3. *Ibid.*, V. p. 229.
4. *Ibid.*
5. *Ibid.*
6. *Ibid.*
7. Arnold. J.Toynbee, A Study of History I. Abridged edn by D.C. Samvel New York, 1969, p. 350.
8. Suttnipatta ed. by J. Kashyap, Nalanda, 1989 trans. V. Fausboll SBEX. Delhi 1968. In the Kuddakanikaya I Nalanda 1959, p. 291.

9. *Jawaharlal Nehru: A Discovery of India*, London, 1956, p.121.
10. *Anguttaranikaya Nalanda*, edn. 1960, II, p.174.
11. *Ibid.*, II, p. 204. trans. by F.L. Woodward the Book of Gradual saying, II p. 200.
12. Tattvasangrah verse No. 3587—Pushbli. Dwarikadas Shastri. Varanasi 1958. p. 1115.
13. *Complete Works*, II, p. 497.
14. *Ibid.*, V, p. 309.
15. P.V. Bapat, *2500 Year of Buddhism*, pp. 1 and 415.
16. Chatushataks; XII.230 V. Bhatta Chaya, Calcutta, 1939.
17. *Complete Works*, VIII, p. 103.
18. *Ibid.*, I, p. 23.
19. *Ibid.*, III, p. 532.
20. *International Encyclopaedia of Buddhism*, Vol. 21 (India) ed. By Nagendra Krishna, Anmol Publication Pvt. Ltd., New Delhi, pp. 756-57.
21. Samyutta VII, p. 9.
22. Dhammapada (Nalanda ed. of the tripitakas), pp. 396-401, Max Muller, E.T.
23. Vinaya Pitaka II, 239.
24. *Op. cit.*, *Int. Eycl.* No. Nagendra Krishna, pp. 44B, Vol. 33.

34

Mind and its Phenomena and Purification of Mind as Taught by Buddha

B. Devendar

The word 'Philosophy' was etymologically derived from two Greek words 'Philein' meaning love and 'Sophia' meaning wisdom. So philosophy means 'To Love Wisdom'.

This etymological definition of philosophy is absolutely true in case of 'Buddhist Philosophy', because 'The Enlightened One' vigorously strove to make people acquire wisdom and then temper it with compassion for one's own benefit and for the benefit of many.

To acquire wisdom, mind has to be sharpened, controlled and purified. But before embarking upon this task, one has to known first what mind is and how it works. Among all the great men of the world who served mankind, it was Buddha who dealt elaborately with mind and matter and their functioning. He discovered many wonderful facts about them.

Buddha found that all our vocal and physical action are projections and manifestations of our mental actions, because everything starts first in mind and when the intensity increases, it is manifested in the form of vocal and physical actions.

For example, when a person sees a man who is his enemy or not in good terms with him, anger arises in his mind. When the anger increases, that person abuses the man and when the intensity of anger further increases, that person beats the man with his hand and if he has a weapon in his hand, he injures the man with the weapon or even kills him.

Similarly when a person sees a man who is his friend or in good terms with him, love arises in his mind. When the love increases, he expresses his love to that man by speaking a few words of kindness and when the intensity of love further increases, this person serves that man with his hands i.e., shakes hands with him warmly or presents him gifts or calls that person for a dinner etc.

It was found by Buddha that mind consists of three kinds of consciousness. They are, conscious mind, semi conscious mind and unconscious mind. Normally, only 5% of the mind of an ordinary man is conscious and the rest is made up of semi conscious and unconscious mind.

Conscious mind is superficial and is aware of only what is happening at the surface of the mind. Many thoughts come in to the mind in succession with great rapidity. The conscious mind feels them for a few moments and they pass on from the surface, i.e., from conscious mind. But after passing away from the conscious mind, these thoughts or mental objects go deep into the so called semi conscious mind or unconscious mind and go on reacting there, creating negativities and buildup so much tension that at the earliest opportunity, they come on to the surface of the mind and burst upon it, creating havoc. These thoughts that lie dormant in the semi conscious and unconscious minds are like sleeping volcanoes and at the opportune moments, they explode.

The unconscious mind is unconscious in the sense that the conscious mind is not aware of what is going on there, how Gordian knots are being made and tension is being built up.

When a man practices Insight Meditation taught by Buddha, the walls that divide the conscious mind, the semiconscious mind and unconscious mind get collapsed gradually and eventually result in a mind that is fully conscious and when all the secrets of nature get unfolded and the phenomena of the Universe are revealed, the mind becomes a super conscious mind.

Buddha mentioned the following facts also about mind:

> "The flickering, fickle mind is difficult to guard and control. The mind is hard to check, swift, flits wherever it list. The mind is hard to perceive and extremely subtle. A wise man straightens his mind as a fletcher, an arrow."
>
> "What ever a harm a foe may do to a foe, or a hater, to hater an ill-directed mind can do a person, a still greater harm."
>
> What benefit neither mother nor father, nor any other relative can do to a person, a well-directed mind does and elevates him."

Buddha explained the working of mind very lucidly. According to Him, the mind consists of four important factors, namely (1) consciousness, (2) Perception, (3) Feeling, and (4) Volition.

Consciousness

Consciousness is the recognition of an object at the six sense doors, namely at eyes, ears, nose, tongue, outer skin of the body and mind. Suppose a visible object is seen by the eyes, then the consciousness recognizes it as a sight and consciousness thus arisen is consciousness of sight. In the similar manner, when a sound is heard by the ears, consciousness of sound arises, when the nose recognizes a smell, consciousness smell arises, when the tongue recognizes a taste, consciousness of taste arises, when a tangible object comes in tough with outer skin of the body, consciousness of touch arises and when a mental object or thought is recognized by the mind, the consciousness of mind arises.

Perception

After the consciousness recognises a sensation, then perception cognizes and evaluates it as good or bad on the basis of previously accumulated information in the mind. For example, when the hear a word of praise, perception evaluates it as good and when the ears hear an abuse, then perception evaluates it as bad.

The previously stored up information in the mind is not necessarily be correct or reliable. This information is conditioned by so many factors, such as traditional beliefs, concepts, notions, ideas, impressions, opinions etc., which may not be genuine or based on actual facts. This accumulation of information in the mind of man starts right from his early childhood and goes on and on through out his life span.

Feeling

When once the perception evaluates a sensation as good or bad, then feeling arises based on that evaluation. When the sensation is evaluated as good, a biochemical reaction or an electro magnetic reaction takes place on some part of the body or on the entire body, resulting in a pleasant feeling.

Similarly when the perception evaluate a sensation as bad, then a different type of biochemical reaction or electromagnetic reaction takes place on a certain part of the body or on the entire body, resulting in an unpleasant feeling.

Volition

When a sensation is evaluated as good or bad, resulting in a pleasant feeling or unpleasant feeling, volition comes into picture. Out of all the four important factors of the mind, it is volition which is most important, because it is that part of the mind which reacts to sensations felt on the body and accumulates 'Sankhars', a Pali word meaning Karma Formations. 'Karma' means the 'Natural Law of Action and its Innate Result'. This Law is a self-governing law and does not require any external agency for its enforcement. To put it simply, it means that unwhole-some actions give unwholesome results and wholesome actions give wholesome results. It implies that as per the Law of Nature, we get in return what we give. Therefore, "If you want happiness, give happiness".

There are three kinds of Sankharas.

1. **Light Sankharas:** These are like lines drawn on water. These Sankharas cause very little Dukkha or Suffering.
2. **Medium Sankharas:** These are like lines drawn on wet mud. These Sankharas are deeper than light Sankharas and result in greater Dukkha or Suffering.
3. **Heavy Sankharas:** These are like lines drawn on hard rock with chisel and hammer. These Sakharas are the deepest and result in greatest Dukkha or Suffering. The Law is such that the deeper the Sankhara, the greater is Dukkha or Suffering.

When a pleasant feeling or sensation is experienced on the body due to the arising of a consciousness caused by any one of the six sense doors (eyes, ears, nose, tongue, outer skin of the body, mind) or more than one sense door in combination with the other sense door, volition reacts to that sensation by craving. That is that pleasant feeling is desired and sought after again and again.

Similarly when an unpleasant feeling is experienced, volition reacts to that sensation by aversion. That is that unpleasant feeling is hated and sought to be expelled out again and again.

When a neutral sensation or neither pleasant nor unpleasant sensation is experienced, volition reacts to that sensation by ignorance, that is that neither pleasant nor unpleasant feeling is ignored an results indifference again and again.

This is how the four parts of the mind work and volition by constantly reacting either with greed, hatred or ignorance, fills the entire psycho-somatic structure with tension, anxiety, fear etc. and the result is that, man experiences Dukkha (Suffering). This uneasy feeling disturbs the peace of mind and health of the body and both body and mind become ill.

This vicious circle of suffering rolls on and on making man's life miserable. The Enlightened one discovered a way to break this vicious circle, in the light of three characteristics of life. They are impermanence (Anitya), Suffering (Dukkha) and Essencelessness (Anatma).

Buddha found that everything in the word is constantly changing. As a matter of fact change is the property of life. Everything in the Universe Changes, but the 'Law of Change' does not change.

Buddha found that human body is nothing but the sum total of innumerable millions of Kalapas (Kalapa is the smallest particle conceivable), each about 1/466565th part of a particle of dust from the wheel of a chariot in summer.

Buddha found that matter changes at the rate of 10^{22} times per second and this is the final truth of matter. He also found that mind changes at the rate of 17×10^{22} times per second. This is the final truth of mind.

After realizing the final truth of matter and final truth of mind at the experiencial level in His mediation practice, Buddha transcended both the truths and realized 'The Ultimate Truth', became the Fully Enlightened one, obtained a Supra Mundane State, which is beyond mind and matter, beyond time and space and beyond the conditioned field or relativity.

Man has known for a long time that in dreams we can see and talk with someone who is deceased, but we say that it is in a dream and not in real life. Today, however, ESB, which stands for Electrical Stimulation of the Brain, reveals the startling fact that by stimulating certain brain cells by electrical impulses, one not only can see and hear without using one's physical eye or ear, but also one will be able to recall vividly events which occurred in the past. Further more, the brain cells can be activated in the parallel so that a number of events can be revealed at the same time, just as when number of electric lamps are connected in parallel, all the lamps light up when the circuit is on. This proves the fact that past, present and future can be revealed in one instant. Therefore, the 'Buddha-Nature', that is Enlightenment has no limitation in time. That is, it is beyond time. So, modern science has proved that a state of mind which is beyond time is possible.

The Enlightenment attained by Buddha is analogous to the realization of a fourth dimension by a person living in a three dimensional world, which an ordinary person cannot comprehend with his normal sense faculties.

Buddha found that if one is attached to the fleeting sensations experienced by him or dramatically described as the 'Passing Show', by labeling them as pleasant, unpleasant, good, bad etc, he is bound to experience suffering, because of the very transitory nature inherent in all things. And man cannot control these phenomena of eternal change. That is, it is beyond his capacity to contain things and keep them as they are. When analyzed, mind, matter and everything in the Universe are in a state of constant flux and turn out to be masses of tiny wavelets, always arising and passing away, with lightening rapidity. It implies the lack of self-enduring essence.

To sum up, the truth is , "that which changes every moment and which has no self enduring essence in it, can only be a source of misery and can not be a source of happiness."

Buddha found that the working of consciousness, perception and feeling is not harmful to man and not avoidable. But it is volition that is harming man by reacting to sensations. Buddha found that the vicious circle of suffering can be broken here. That is, if volition instead of generating reaction, generates wisdom in the light of the three characteristics of life, then instead of suffering, equanimity is realized and this calms down the mind and makes it peaceful, because Equanimity is purity.

Man is made up of body and mind. Both of them need food. Body requires food twice a thrice a day. But mind requires food every moment and the food for mind is greed, hatred and ignorance. An ordinary man feeds his mind with these three impurities. But, when once the man in his Insight meditation practice, that is in viapassana, builds up equanimity and dose not react to the sensations and dose not create new Sankharas, then the Law of Nature is such that, the mind feeds itself with the already stored up impurities of greed, hatred and ignorance, in the same manner that when a man is an fasting and dose not take any external food, the body sustains itself for sometime, with the excess food that is already stored up in the body in the form of fat etc.

When the mind feeds itself with the already stored up greed, hatred, ignorance etc then the corresponding sensations arise on the body, either pleasant, unpleasant or neutral. Being aware of the transitory nature of all these sensations, if the mediator remains equanimous without reacting to the sensations, then these stored up impurities in the mind get eradicated. Layers after layers of these impurities come on to the surface of mind, producing their corresponding sensations on the body and get eradicated, as the mediator is aware and equanimous and dose not react to them.

When once all these old mental defilements get eradicated and no new defilements are made, then such a person's insight develops into one's own reality by which it is possible to free the mind of negativities. This is a universal method. Observing the reality as it is, by observing the truth inside, is knowing oneself at the actual, experiential level. And as one makes progress in his practice, one keeps coming out of misery of defilements. From the gross, external, apparent truth, one penetrates to the ultimate truth of mind and matter. When one transcends into that and experiences a truth which is beyond mind and matter, beyond time and space, beyond the conditioned field of relativity, one realises the truth of total liberation from all defilements, all impurities all suffering. This is called Nirvana in Buddhism. But, what ever name one gives to this Ultimate truth, is irrelevant. It is the final goal of every one.

The mind of this liberated person is filled up involuntarily with "Four Divine Abodes" called "Brahma Vihara" in pali Language. They are Infinite Loving Kindness (Ananta Maitri), Infinite Compassion (Ananta Karuna), Infinite Sympathetic Joy (Ananta Mudita) and Infinite Euqanimity (Ananta Upeksha).

That is this liberated person radiates pure, passionless love towards all beings feels compassion for them for their suffering, feels happy by seeing them happy (This is called sympathetic joy) and. Always remains equanimous, not perturbed by the vicissitudes of life.

This liberated person spends all his energies in serving mankind, in removing their sufferings. He feels great joy in being of help to other in their efforts to reach perfection, because this person's perception is fully clarified and pure awareness is generated.

A fountain of pure love, that is love without a trace of passion, love out of compassion, love that is not conditional, love is spontaneous, love that does not expect anything in return, love that gives great joy to one who practices it and also to one who receives it and love that has became one's second nature, springs up from his heart, embracing the entire universe and filling it with thoughts of peace and happiness for all beings.

Whoever comes in contact with such a liberated person, feels immense happiness, experiences an undescribeable feeling of calm and peace, serenity and tranquility.

This technique of purifying the mind and getting liberated from all sufferings is the greatest gift bestowed upon mankind by Buddha and mankind is ever grateful to him. Perhaps the world will come to recognise Buddha as the greatest Scientist produced by mankind, who enunciated the truth about how mind and matter mutually work and how by the complete purification of mind, liberation is obtained. No other person in the world even up to this day did so much research about mind as Buddha did. Buddha anticipated Sigmund Freud by thousand of years, in the field of psychoanalysis.

Buddha enumerated fifty two kinds of properties of mind called 'Chetasikas' in pali language. They are: (1) Contact, (2) Feeling, (3) Perception, (4) Volition, (5) Concentration of Mind, (6) Psychic Life, (7) Attention, (8) Initial application, (9) Sustained application, (10) Effort, (11) Pleasurable interest, (12) Desire-to-do, (13) Deciding, (14) Greed, (15) Hate, (16) Dullness, (17) Error, (18) Conceit, (19) Envy, (20) Selfishness, (21) Worry, (22) Shamelessness, (23) Recklessness Distraction, (24) Amity, (25) Sloth, (26) Torpor, (27) Perplexity, (28) Disinterestedness, (29) Amity, (30) Reason, (31) Faith, (32) Mindfulness, (33) Modesty, (34) Discretion, (35) Balance of Mind, (36) Composure of Mental Qualities, (37) Composure of Mind, (38) Buoyancy of Mental Qualities, (39) Buoyancy of Mind, (40) Pliancy of Mental Qualities, (41) Pliancy of Mind, (42) Adaptability of Mental Qualities, (43) Adaptability of Mind, (44) Proficiency of Mental Qualities, (45) Proficiency of Mind, (46) Rectitude of Mental Qualities, (47) Rectitude of Mind, (48) Right Speech, (49) Right Action, (50) Right Livelihood, (51) Compassion, and (52) Sympathetic Joy.

Buddha disclosed many more facts about mind and its phenomena. But time and space do not permit me to mention them all. As a matter of fact, Buddha's Teachings are the largest spiritual literature in the world and eleven times the Bible. If Buddha's Teachings are compared to a 'Great Ocean of Nectar' then what I presented in my paper is like a small sweet candy from that great ocean of nectar. But the information given in this paper is sufficient to inspire a person to practice 'Vipassana Bhavana', that is, Insight Meditation, taught by Buddha and realise the ultimate truth.

Wise men say that the most effective way to express something in order to make others understand is to use the simplest language, because the more rigid the language, the less effective it is. I, therefore chose simple English in presenting this paper.

Out of the sacred text of the world, it is unique that only 'Dhammapada', the sacred text of Buddhists beings with mind and this shows the importance given to mind by Buddha and consequently the importance of mind in moulding man's destiny.

'Mano Pubbangama dhamma
manosettha manomaya;

manasache padutthena
bhasativa karotiva,
tatonam dukhamanveti
chakkamva vahato padam'.

'Mano Pubbangama dhamma
manosettha manomaya;
manasache pasannena
bhasativa karotiva
tatonam sukhamanveti
chaya va anapayini'.

These are the opening verses of 'Dhammapada' in pali language which give strong faith, great inspiration, self confidence, self reliance, self discipline and patience that are required to a person in his spiritual pursuit.

It is therefore proper for me to conclude my paper with the summary of these verses, as follows:

> "Mind is the fore-runner of all conditions. Mind is Chief and the mental concomitants are mind made. If one speaks or acts with an impure mind, then suffering (Dukkha) follows him even as the cart follows the Ox that pulls it.
>
> Mind is the forerunner of all conditions Mind is Chief and the mental concomitants are mind made. If one speaks or acts with a pure mind, then happiness (Sukha) follows him like his own shadow".

Bhavatu Sabba Mangalam
May all beings be happy.

35

Buddhist Precepts for Peaceful Co-existence

Dr. B.V.S. Bhanusree

The Problem of peaceful co-existence, not only at individual level but at national and International level, is not a new one in any society and any time. History of humanity witnesses it at every stage. Problems are multiplied in twentieth century viz., population explosion, threat of war, terrorism, thirst for power mishandling of technology, mistrust, petty jealousies and maladjustments among the individuals and nations are making human life miserable day by day. Moral values are badly challenged and fallen at stake. Human relations are wildly ridiculed. Harmonious and peaceful co-existence has become indiscernible and impossible.

Now, the question is, who is responsible for this disastrous conditions? While birds and animals are leading peaceful lives, why human being who comprises of intelligence and rationality is not able to make it? Man is considered as the highest product of evolution. Human life is highly valued by almost all philosophies. But man is denigrating his own self and life instead of making them richer.

The ordinary man, the common man or the average man is referred as "Puthujjana' in pali literature. According to Buddha they are uneducated and untrained average folk.[1] In Buddhist Nikayās we find the references about the ordinary man as he "is addicted to pleasure, and is at the mercy of his sources. He is enthralled by the eye with objects that charm, by the tongue with savours that charm, etc. He follows his natural desires, uncontrolled in the six fold sense sphere, and eats his fill with ravenous delight among the five sensual pleasures. He welcomes personal fame and praise but resents obscurity and blame. He is easily provoked to deeds of a morally unwholesome kind; he will murder his own father or his mother, inflict wounds or a saintly man, and cause dissension within the Buddhist sangtha. He is greedy and lustful. On the other hand, he resents any ill fortune; when afflicted with pain he is distressed and welcome with bewilderment about it; he finds that those things on which he sets his hopes frequently turnout to be a disappointment; he dislikes the sight of diseare, or old age or death; when old age comes upon him he mourns and pines and is tormented by sorrow, and finally he goes to purgatory. All this is become he is lacking in wisdom and in knowledge of the truth. Not only does he adhere to popular superstitions, but he knows not, he sees not things as they really are, the takes no account of those who are holy, those who are true, he does not comprehend which things should not be attended to; he knows nothing of the origination of compounded things and no is not set free from he power of ill; he fails to reflect adequately and to understand the experiences of life for what they really are."[2]

But, Buddha is optimistic in considering their present condition as not permanent or final. They have an important role[3] to play in the Buddhist scheme of things. In sigalovada Sutta of Digh Nikaya Buddha advised the householders/laity regarding domestic and social relationship, being asked by an young householder Sigala regarding his moral duties.[4] The sutta enumerated six sets of reciprocal role expectations or duties between parents and children; between pupils and teachers; husband

and with, friends and companions, masters and servants and finally householders and members of the Sangha for peaceful and harmonious co-existence.

Children are to support their parents, who once supported them; they are to perform the proper family duties, to maintain the family line; to uphold the family tradition; and they are to show themselves worthy of their heritage. Parents and to retrain their child from wrong doing to inspire him to virtue; to train him for a profession to contract a suitable marriage for him; and in due time to make over to him his inheritance.

Students are to serve their teachers by showing respect to them, by waiting upon them, by showing eagerness to learn, by supplying their needs, and by paying attention when they are being taught. Teachers in return are to give their pupils moral training, they are to inspire in them a love of learning, they are to instruct them in every subject are to speak well of their pupils and to protect them form any danger.

A husband is to cherish his wife by treating her with respect, by being kind to her, by being faithful, by allowing her proper due rights and by providing her with suitable ornaments. In return, a wife is to show her love for her husband by maintaining a well ordered household, by being hospitable to their relatives and friends by being faithful, by being thrifty, and by being diligent.

A man should recognize his obligations to his friends by making them gifts, by courtesy and benevolence towards them, by treating them as his equals, and by keeping his word to them, in return he may expect that they will take care of him or of his interests when he is unable to do so himself, they will provide him with refuge when he needs it, they will stand by him in times of trouble and will be kind to his family.

A good master is one who may be relied upon to show consideration towards his employees by allotting each one work suited to his capacity, by supplying them with good food and pay, by providing care for them when they once sick, by sharing with them any unusal delicacies which he receives, and by granting them regular time off from work. In return, employees or servants should show their affection for their master by being out of bed betimes and not going to bed until he has done so, by being contented with the fair treatment they receive, by doing their work cheerfully and thoroughly and by speaking well of their master to others.

Finally, the reciprocal duties of householders and members of the Sangha are setout. A good house holder ministers to the bhikkhus by showing affection for them in his actions in his speech and in his thoughts, by giving them warm welcome and ample hospitality and by providing generally for their material needs. In return, the members of the sangha are to show their affection for the householder by restraining him from evil courses of action, by exhorting him to do what is honourable by entertaining kindly feelings towards him, by imparting knowledge by dealing with his doubts, and by revealing to him the way to Nirvana.[5]

It is not irrelevant to quote the comment of T.W. Rhys Davids here, "We can realize how happy would have been the village or the clan on the banks of the Ganges, where the people were full of kindly spirit of fellow-feeling, the noble spirit of justice, which breathes through these nãve and simple sayings."[6]

For over a thousand years Buddhism was a living, dynamic and widespread religion in India and influenced its life in several ways. But due to the gradual and inevitable changes, its impact is diluted. Now, we are living in a time: "in which worldly power seems to be the only reality and in which brutal force is worshipped as the ultimate authority."[7] Present humanity is far from understanding the depths of the preaching of the Buddha. Man has become highly egoistic and self centered. Instead of inculcating friendship, love and compassion, he is creating a hostile atmosphere. His personality turned imbalanced and split. Instead of conquering he accepted his defeat at the feet of the world, ignorantly, slavishly and cowardly. How can such a person maintains peaceful co-existence in society?

Let us observe how the Buddhist thought, it attitude, and its ethics help the twentieth century man and his problems. The first and foremost thing is, the Buddha asked men to keep the doors of mind wide open to perceive the truth.[8] The problem and its solution lie within man only. It is for him how to deal with it. He advised men to develop an attitude of 'taking things as they are'. The world and its conditions constantly change. One must accept that the change is inevitable whether for better or worse. One is also expected to know that the world is not according to our whims and fancies.

So, Buddha propounded Middle path, avoiding both the extremes (self indulgence and self mortification) applied to both the practical and the spiritual life, gave birth with to a new thinking. As Anagarika B. Govinda opines "It would be the great remedy for the ills of the modern world in which the extremes in thoughts, in religion in politics and in life have torn humanity into pieces and have resulted in a hopeless struggle of all against all."[9] This Path constitutes Eight progressive steps[10] that culminates in suffering less and perfect state.

The Buddha instructed them not to follow blindly just because their master said, but follow them after testing carefully. One is expected to have right[11] view and understanding towards a particular problem. This will help to develop right mental attitude. Concern and selflessness will be inculcated, towards the fellow beings. That leads to Right speech. One must speak softly, kindly and truthful to others. This will develop good interpersonal relationships in a society. It leads to right action which constitutes a perfect harmony in thinking, speaking and acting. This also implies that one should not injure others either by speech or by action. One should not disturb others by interfering unnecessarily into their matters. So that his image will be heightened and he will be loved by to others.

This leads to right livelihood, which implies earning by right means, one should live by hard earned money, instead of by begging, borrowing or stealing. This develops a good and trustworthy relationships among men. This encourages right effort to overcome our weakness and to produce and cultivate the best within us. It leads to right mindfulness or contemplation of the body, the feelings, the mind and its phenomena. Then reaches the culmination—right concentration—the synthesis and internalization of all the previous steps in the intuitive state of mediation. At this stage his whole self will be expanded with love, compassion, joy and equanimity and extends his helping land to his neighbour, fellowmen countrymen and gradually to the whole humanity.

To conclude, mere profession of the unity of fundamentals of religion will be of no avail, if in our daily lives we create barriers between man and man. As Valisinha opined, "If our dealings with our fellow beings are dishonest, treacherous, arrogant, cruel and unsympathetic then all our prayers or worship in temples or the repetition of sacred words will not carry us one inch nearer to the goal of spiritual happiness."[12] It is our dealing with our fellow beings in the small acts of kindness or cruelty that we reflect the degree of our humanistic/spiritual growth.

Notes and References

1. Middle length sayings, Vol. I, p. 293 (Uninstructed ordinary man); gradual sayings, Vol. I, p. 25 (Uneducated many folk); Vol. IV, p. 108 (Common average folk) etc.
2. Trevor Ling, the Buddha: Buddhist Civilization in India and Ceylone Templesmith, London, 1973, pp. 134-5.
3. Between Leity and the Sangha there exists an important relationship not of reciprocity exactly, but of compensation, *ibid.*, p. 135.
4. Budha Ghosha opined that it was for the householder what the Vinaya or code of discipline, was for the members of the Sangha.
5. The last is the sixth duty. Every other class of citizen named has been given five duties but for the bhikku, there is this one extra, which thus stands by itself in a position of special emphasis.
6. T.W. Rhys Davinds: Buddhism, London, 1890 p. 148.
7. Buddhism in the Modern World: Anagarika B. Govinda, an article from an Anthology "The Religions of the World" published by Rama Krishna Mission, Calcutta, 1938, p. 366.
8. The first words of the Buddha after his enlightenment:
   "*Aparua tesam amatassa dvara*,
   "*Ye sotavanto, pamunchantu Saddham*"
   "Wide open are the gates of immortality"

"Ye that have ears to hear, release your faith!"
Ibid.

9. *Ibid.*, p. 368.
10. Ashtanga Magga: (1) Right understanding (Samma ditthi), (2) Right Aspiration (Samma samkappa), (3) Right speech (Samma Vacha), (4) Right Action (Samma Kammanta), (5) Right livelihood (Samma agieva), (6) Right effort (Samma Vayana), (7) Right mindfulness (Samma sati), (8) Right concentration (samma Samadhi).
11. To explain the modern mind, the Buddhsists have an excellent standard by which to judge what is what is wrong. As the removal of sufferiong is the main purpose of the Buddhist way of life energy thought, ward or action that would go to increase this saffeing would be wrong and every thought, ward or action which would help in removing it would be right.
12. Devapriya Vahisinha: The Buddhist way of life. An Anticle from the religions of the world, published by Rama Krishna Mission, Calcutta, 1938, p. 480.

References

Davids, T.W. Phys: Buddhism, London, 1890.

Nehru Jawaharlal: The Discovery of India, Meridian Books Ltd., London 1960.

Rahula, Walpola: Buddhist Studies in Honour of Walpole Rahule Gordon Fraser, London 1980.

The Religious of the World: The Rama Krishna Mission, Institute of Calcutta, 1938.

36

HISTORY OF ANDHRA BUDDHISM

DR. G. JAWAHARLAL

Andhra Pradesh is replete with the Buddhist monuments. In recent years, a number of Buddhist settlements, ranging from pre-Asokan times (4th-3rd century B.C.) to the Vishnukundins (5th-6th century A.D.) have been found due to untiring efforts of Archaelogists. Further, about 500 Buddhist inscriptions have been discovered so far. With the result, we are able to know that Buddhism in Andhra spread over a vast area extending Saripalle in the north to Nandalure in the south-west, Ghantasala and Kanuparthy on the east to Kotilingala and Kondapur on the north-west. Here an attempt is made to build-up the history of Andhra Buddhism relying mostly on epigraphical sources.

Hitherto, it is believed that the missionary zeal of the great Mauryan emperor, Asoka, Buddhism entered Andhra and grew into a state religion. Obviously, the reign of Asoka forms an important epoch in the history of Andhra Buddhism. His XIII Rock-Edict clearly states that the Andhra were living within Raja-Vishaya and following the Dharma. Afterwards, it became more popular from the Satavahanas. Further there is no reference to the Andhras in an early Buddhist chronicles though Assaka or Asmaka was reffered as one among the 16 Mahajanapadas. Non-mention of the Andhakas in the 1st Buddhist council, suggests that there was no Buddhist settlement in Andhra before Ashoka.

Contrary to this, the Suttānipāta narrates the story of Bāvari, a Brahmin teacher of Asmaka region in Dakshinapada who sent his disciples to meet the Buddha and learn from his teachings. The disciples met the Buddha and became arahats. One of them, Pingiya returned to Bhavari and spoke the essence of the teachings of the Buddha. Hearing it, Bhavari also attained arahathood.[2] The recent excavations at Kotilingala,[3] on the bank of the river Godavari in Karimnagar District, reveal the vestiges of ancient city, monastic and non-monastic dwellings, structures, a large quantity of ceramic wares, a good number of coins belonging to pre-Satavahana period namely Gobhada, Samagopa and silver punch-Marked coins. Relying on the antiques unearthed at Kotilingala, the excavators of the site are of the opinion that the Kotilangala was perhaps the place where the hermitage of the sage Bhavari stood, for it was situated in Kavitavana on the banks of the river Godavari. The existence of village named Velagatur in close vicinity to Kotilingala lends support to the above excavators view. Further, the recent excavations at Dhulikatta[4] (Karimnagar Dist.) Dantapuram[5] (Srikakulam Dist.) Gopalapatnam[6] (Viskhapatnam Dist.) Vaddamanu (Guntur Dist.) Where the occurrence of N.B.P. ware in association with the polished black knobbed ware reveal that these sites flourished as prosperous Buddhist centers and enjoyed trade contacts with the other Janapadas of Northeren India during pre-Christian times. Further, it is known from the accounts of Megasthanese[7] that there existed 30 fortified towns, equipped with elaborate military organization during 3rd century B.C. in Andhra. Thus Andhra possessed well established urban centers or Janapadas which patronised Buddhism at least a century or a couple of centuries before the visit of Megasthanese i.e. 5th-4th century B.C. like the Janapadas of Northern India.

Recent Archaeological findings have thrown fresh light on several aspects of Buddhism, especially its patronage by the local kings or chieftains before the propagation of Buddhism by Asoka. According to Kotthara Jathaka[8] Buddha travelled to Kosala, an adjoining region of Kalinga, to deliver a sermon to the Kottaharakas of Kosala. Later on, an Arama was built to commemorate the incident. Interestingly, excavations at Salihundam, encountered a pot with a Brahmi label inscription of 1st-2nd century A.D. characters from a Buddhist Chaitya. It reads Humkudo(de) yikarathavalakavochivanam-kottaharamo. Now scholars identified the Arama at Salihundam with Kottarama.

It appears that during the period of post- Asoka and pre-Satavahanas in the Deccan, Andhra was divided into several petty states or republics ruled by local chieftains or Rajas.

Among them, Rano Gobhada, Rano Narana and Rano Samagopa are known to have ruled over the tracts lying between the rivers, Godavari and Maneru in Northern Telengana region. Numerous coins of these kings along with punch marked coins were found in association with fine black and red ware, terracota figurines, iron objects, beads and bangles in the habitation area at Kotilingala. Besides, a Buddhist Monastery having apsidal chaityagriha and stupas belonging to the Theravada sect of the Buddhism of 3rd century B.C. was also found.[9] Almost similar structures within a fortified city have been noticed at Dhulikatta datable to 3rd century B.C., next comes the king Kuberaka who ruled over the tract along the south-east coast of Andhra with Bhattiprolu as its capital. It is known from the relic-casket inscription[10] that Raja Kuberaka was responsible for erecting the Maha-chaitya enshrining in it, the corporeal relics of the Buddha.

Of these local kings mentioned in the ephigraphs found at Vaddamanu[11] and Amaravathi[12] are Somaka and Raja Kumariyya respectively. Buddhist-vestiges along with a number of punch-marked coins and the Brahmi Label epigraphs datable to the period between 4th-3rd centuries B.C. to 1st-2nd centuries A.D. have been found. Another ruling family which had sway over the region between the rivers Godavari and Krishna was that of the Sadas known through their coins and Brahmi Label records found at

Guntupalli, a famous Buddhist site in West Godavari Dist.[13] Further, the discovery of a fragmentary Asokan- pillar edict in association with N.B.P. ware at Amaravathi,[14] suggests that the Buddhism was in prosperous stage since Asokan times in Andhra.

The Mauryan hegemony over the areas of the south western parts of Andhra was known from the discovery of minor rock edicts of Asoka at Jonnagiri or Erragudi[15] and Rajula Mandagiri in Kurnool Dist.[16] According to Mahavamsa, certain missionaries were sent to Mahisha Mandal during the Mauryan period. Perhaps, this might have taken place after the 3rd Buddhist council. This Mahishamandal corresponds with Krishna-Godavari regions with its capital at Masolia of Ptolemy (i.e. modern machilipatnam). A Brahmi inscription found at Salihundam[18] reads as "Dharama Rano Asoka sirino" which means of Dharamaraja Asoka siri. On paleographical grounds it is assigned to the 2nd century A.D. Here it is reasonable to presume that the Stupa and Vihara on the hill was built in the time of Asoka and that historical fact was inserted in the 2nd century A.D. at the time of its renovation. Thus during the time of Asoka, Andhra became a stronghold of Buddhism spreading from Salihunadam in the north to Bhattiprolu and Amaravathi in the south and Jonnagiri in the west.

After the decline of the Mauryan rule, the Satavahanas consolidated their empire, unifying all the petty chiefs and kings. In Andhra, the period of Satavahana rule (B.C. 200-200 A.D.) witnessed the growth and development of Buddhism and Buddhist art, besides maritime trade. Buddhism institutions received grants lavishly. Several caves and structures were built during this period. The king Gautamiputra Satakarni made a gift of land measuring 200 nivartanas to the monks. His mother presented a cave at Nasik. Pulumai II also donated a village to the monks. According to a traditional account Acharya Nagarjuna succeeded in converting Yajna-Sri to patronage Buddhism.[19] Then onwards, there was a change in the attitude of the Satavahanas towards Buddhism. The last Satavahana King Vijaya actualluy visited Sriparvata on Vaisakhapurnima. During the Satavahana rule, the Buddhist settlements at Amaravathi, Jaggayyapet, Ghantasala, Guntupalli, Bavikonda, Thotlakonda, Salihundam, etc., became renowned Buddhist piligrimage centers.

After the Satavahanas, Buddhism continued to receive the patronage by their successors who were originally staunch followers of Hinduism. The famous Buddhist centre at Vijayapuri i.e. modern Nagarjunakonda, became the cradle of Mahayana Buddhism under the Ikshvaku rulers and attracted the kings and missionaries from different far off regions like Ceylon, Kashmir, Gandhara, China, Tosali, Aparanta, Vanga, Vanavasi, Yavana, and Dravida as attested by the epigraphs found at the site.[20] The Mayidavolu plates of Pallava Sivaskandavarma (i.e.) A.D. 300[21] mentioned Dhanyakataka as the headquarters of Andhrapatha. Though there was no direct contribution to Buddhism by the Pallavas, the names of some of the kings like Buddhavarman, son of Sivaskandha, his successor Buddhyankara, another Buddhyanakara son of Kumaravishnu are enough to prove their learnings towards Buddhism.

The rule of Ikshvakus in Andhra (220-290 A.D.) marks a glorious epoch in the history of Andhra Buddhism after the Satavahanas. In the short period of their rule, Nagarjunakonda became one of the greatest Buddhist centers of India, and attracted the Buddhists of various sects like sthaviras, mahishkas, chetiyas, Aparaseliyas, Purvaseliyas and Bahusrutiyas.[22] Basically the Ikshvakus were Brahminical Hindus, while their queens, princesses, and other female members patronized Buddhism. Very recently a set of copper plates at Patagandigudem, hamlet of Kallachervu, Kamavarapukota mandal of West Godavari District was discovered. The discovery is of utmost significance as it provides for the first time a grant belonging to the Ikshvaku king Ehuvala Chantamula, as so far, no copper plate grant belonging to the Ikshvakus is reported. It registers some donation of land for the benefit of the monks in the city of Pithunda on the occasion of constructing a chatussala for the monstery.[23] It further states that the gift was meant for the enjoyment of the visitors, residents and monks. It consists of five plates engraved in Brahmi characters of 4th century

A.D. The language is Prakrit as we noticed in other Ikshvaku lithic records. They are also considered as the earliest copper plates found so far in Andhra or even in the whole of south India. Vijayapuri, presently Nagarjunakonda, reached its pinnacle as seat of Buddhist learning in a very short period. An inscription of Upasika Bhodisri[24] provides us a graphic account of the architectural activity that took place at Nagarjunakonda. Although the art of Nagarjunakonda was an offshoot of Amaravathi School, yet it had its own identity in the style of depicting elaborate Buddhist themes and also in carving human and animal figurines.

The end of the great Ikshvaku rule marked the beginning of decline in Andhra Buddhism. The successors of the Ikshvakus also played an important role in the spread of Buddhism during 4th-5th centuries A.D. The Salankayanas of Vengi (300-400 A.D.) made some liberal donations to the Buddhist monasteries though they were staunch followers of Brahmanism. It is known from a record found at Guntapalli[25] that the King Vijayanandivarman II made some gifts to the Mahavihara. Recent excavations at Peddavegi[26] brought to light remains of viharas, stupas, built by sects like Aparasaila and Aparamaha-vinayaseliyas. The Anandagotrins of Kandarapura (435-460 A.D.) paid some attention towards Buddhism. The Mattepadu grant of Damodaravarman describes him as a Buddhist.[27]

The Vishnukundins were the last powerful rulers after the Ikshvakus in Andhra. The extensive Buddhist site at Nelakondapalli in Khammam Dist. speaks for the meritorious services rendered by the Vishnukundins to Buddhism during 4th-5th century A.D. Here, excavations brought to light a number of huge free standing statues of Buddha carved in lime stone, a bronze image of standing Buddha, innumerable Vishnukundin coins, vihara, a Maha chaitya, votive stupas etc., which suggest the heyday of Buddhism under the Vishnukundins. The Chaitanyapuri inscription of Govindavarman (405-445 A.D.) fountd at Hyderabad records the constructions of a stone residential cell for the use of the persons attached to Govindaraja vihara. Further, it, assignable to the later half of the 4th century A.D. mentions the name of the King Govindavaraman who ruled in Telangana. With this discovery, the antiquity of modern Hyderabad goes back to the early centuries of Christian Era. The pair of copper plate sets were discovered in the village Tummalagudem[30] of Nalgonda Dist. The charters mention Vishnukundin kings, Govindavarman I and Vikramendravarman II who donated lands and gifts to the Buddhist monasteries of Indrapalangara which is identified with the area of Indrapalagutta, near Tummalagudem. Further, Patagandigudem plates of Vikramendravarma are engraved in early Telugu Kannada variety of 5th century A.D. and furnishes the names of 3 members of the Vishnukundin family-Govindavarman, his son Mahendravarma and grand son Vikramendravarma who is described as the lord of Trikalinga and Vengi territories. It registers a gift of land in favour of a mahavihara of Asanapura belonging to the Aryasangha, for the enjoyment of the monks and for the repairs of the Mahavihara, further, the grant contains the earliest reference to the territory of Trikalinga and the city of Aasanapura (modern Asinagudem in West Godavari Dist).[31]

Prithvi-Sri Mularaja (5th-6th century A.D.) who succeeded the Vishnukundins also patronised Buddhism. The 3 copper plate grants of Prithvi-Sri Mularaja from Kondaveedu,[32] records various gifts given to the Buddhist Sanghas. The first grant records the gifts to the Bhikshus of the Aryabhikshu Sangh, residing in the Mahavihara of Vaddaman (near Amaravathi) for their daily rituals. The second grant refers to the establishment of a Mahavihara in Tadikonda by the same kind. It also reveals the existence of various sects of Buddhist Sanghas like Sakya Bhikshu Sangha and Arya Bhikshu Sangha, the third grant refers to the monks of 18 fold Bhikshu sangha residing in the well known monastery established at Gunapasapura. The Kattachervu grant of King Harivarma, son of Prithvi-Sri Mularaja informs that the village, given by his father, was made free from all taxes by him for the benefit of the piligrims of the Arya Bhikshu Sangha.

After the Vishnukundins, Buddhism in Andhra lost its ground

and many settlements were deserted. This is confirmed by the accounts of foreign traveler Hieun-Tsang who visited Andhra during 6th-7th century A.D.[33] he informs that in Dhanyakataka which was once full of the Buddhist monasteries, only 20 were occupied by the monks of Mahasaghika School. Further, he also made a reference to the existence of one hundred deva temples worshipped by various sects. The subsequent rulers of Andhra were strong supporters of Brahmanical religion, Further, infiltration of Vajrayana Tantric-cult and Sakti-cult led to laxity in discipline and moral fervor. This resulted in the creation of a mystic sex symbolism and immoral practices. With the result most of the Buddhist institutions have lost their purity and importance.

Yet, some renowned Buddhist sites like Dhanyakataka, Salihundam, Guimmadidarru continued to the medieval times. The Bezawada epigraph of Somana Preggda (A.D. 1146) [34] of Vengidesa records some donations to pancharamas. The Kota chiefs of Dharanikota (A.D. 1182) [35] made donations to the Lord Buddha. The Bekkallu grant of Tribhuvanamalladeva (A.D. 1100)[36] refers to the construction of temples for Siva, Vishnu, Jina and Buddha. The epigraph of Kakatiya Prataparudradeva[37] (A.D. 1171) refers to the construction of a temple to lord Buddha at Naganur. The Korni plates of Anantavarmachodagangadeva[38] (12 century A.D.) describe the Buddhist site at Salihundam. The occurrence of clay tablets at Gummadidurru[39] (Krishna Dist.) in Nagari script, suggest the survival of Buddhism in Andhra for a quite longer period.

Thus the above analysis makes it clear that Buddhism in Andhra flourished for nearly 2000 years as on of the important religions right from 5th-4th century B.C. to 13th-14th century A.D. as confirmed by literary, epigraphical and archaeological sources. Buddhism, through Hinayana, Mahayana, and Vajrayana phases, flourished in Andhra for a longer period. Great teachers like Acharya Nagarjuna, Aryadeva, Dinnaga, Bhavaviveka, Buddhagosha etc who hailed from this region were largely responsible for the spread of Buddhism in Andhra.

Notes and References

1. Corpus of Inscriptions of Indicarum, Vol. 1, p. 66 ff.
2. Suttanipata, verse no. 1019 and also S. Datt, Buddhist Monks and Monasteries in India, 1960, p. 120.
3. Murthy, N.S.R., Excavations at Kotilingala (unpublished) and also his article on Kotilingala, in proceedings of A.P. History Congress held in 1992, pp. 33-34.
4. Krishna Sastry, Excavations at Dhulikatta, 1979 (unpublished)
5. Subrahmanyam, B., Excavations at Dantapuram, Srikakulam Dist., Annual Administrative Report of A and M, 1994.
6. Do: Excavations at Gopalapatnam, Annual Administrative Report of A and M, 1993.
7. Mc. Crindle, J.W., Anicient India as describe by Megasthenese and Arrian, pp. 140-141.
8. Fausball, V., The Jatakas, the Kattahara Jataka, No.7, Vol. 1, p. 113 ff
9. Sastry, D.L.N., Excavations at Pashigaon, Karimnagar Dist. 1988 (U.P.)
10. Epigraphia Indica, Vol. 2, p. 328.
11. Sastry, T.V.G., (ed.) Vaddamanu Exacavations and Explorations in Krishna Valley, BACRI, Hyderabad, 1983, pp. 4-5.
12. Annual Reports on South Indian Epigraphy, 1953-54, No. 57.
13. Sarma, I.K., Epigraphical Discoveries at Guntupalli, *Journal of Epigraphical Society*, Vol. 5, 1978, pp. 60-74.
14. Do: Some More Inscriptions from Amaravathi Excavations and Chronology of the Mahastupa, *Journal of Epigraphical Society*, Vol. 1, pp. 60-74.
15. Sircar, D.C., Select Inscriptions, 1965, pp. 50-52.
16. Epigraphia Indica, Vol. 35, pp. 211-218.
17. Geiger, W. (trans), *The Mahavamsha*, chapter XII, 1980, p. 82.
18. Gadre, A.S., Brahmi Inscriptions from Salihundam, E.I., Vol. 31, pp. 87-88.
19. Rama Rao, M., Buddhism and Buddhist Monuments in Andhra, Buddha Jayanthi Souvenir, 1956, p. 8.
20. *Epigraphia Indica*, Vol. 20, pp. 22-23.
21. *Epigraphia Indica*, Vol. 6, pp. 84-89.
22. *Epigraphia Indica*, Vol. 20, pp. 22-23.
23. *Buddhist Inscriptions of Andhra*, Secunderabad, 1998, p. 191.
24. *Epigraphia Indica*, Vol. 20, pp. 22-23.
25. *Indian Archaeology—A Review*, 1997-98.
26. *Epigraphia Indica*, Vol. 30, p. 201.
27. Gopalachari, K., *Early History of the Andhra Country*, 1976, p. 201 and see also E.I., Vol. 17, pp. 327-330.

28. Sastry, D.L.N., Annual Administrative Report of A & M, 1986, 1992-94.
29. *Buddhist Inscriptions of Andhra, Secunderabad* 1998, p. 196. And also see *JESI*, Vol. 1, Delhi, 2004, pp. 166-177.
30. Sastry, P.V.P., *Inscriptions of A.P.* (Nalgonda Dist.) Vol. 1, Hyd., 1992, p. 19.
31. Murthy, N.S.R., *Kevala-Bodhi*, Vol. 1, Delhi, 2004, pp. 166-177.
32. Krishna Sastry, V.V., Three Grants of Prithvi-Sri Mularaja from Kondavidu, 1992, pp. 2-3.
33. Waters, T., *On Yuan Chwang's Travels*, Vol. 2, p. 217.
34. Sastry, B.N., *Bezawada Durgamalleswardeva Sasanalu*, Hyderabad, 1989, p. 56
35. *Epigraphia Indica*, Vol. 6, p. 155.
36. *Inscriptions of A.P.* (Warangal Dist.), 1974, pp. 45-50.
37. *Inscriptions of A.P.* (Karimnagar Dist.), 1998, pp. 69.
38. *JAHARS*, Vol. 29 (Parts 3 & 4), p. 24.
39. *Annual Report of the Archaeology Department, ASI* (Southern Circle) 1926-27, pp. 155-56.

37

Ethical Values of the Buddhism—World Harmony and Peace

Dr. L. Vidyasagar Reddy

The concept of harmony in Buddhist thought incorporates aspects of human life, human relationship, the ethical standard and moral values, Dhamma and his teachings etc. Buddhism and its ethical values have a greater relevance in the modern context of National and International harmony. Today, the whole humanity is struggling with conflicts generated by several problems in the field of Political, Economical and Social etc. And we find there is not a single country in the world free from tense situation, disharmony, disorder and disputes. In this turbulent situation Buddhism has given a serious thought to the problems of world harmony and peace.

In this paper I attempted to focus on significant ethical values of Buddhism, like observance of the code of discipline, inculcating the spirit of selfless service to the humanity, compassion, tolerance.

The 6th Century B.C. was the age of religious unrest, a time of intense intellectual activities in many parts of the world. This period saw many eminent religious thinkers who radically changed the course of History by providing new ethical ideas. History had witnessed socio-religious changes from India to China in the east to as far as Greece and Rome in the West.

ETHICAL VALUES

The Buddha was primarily a moral teacher similar to Mahavira. Both repudiated the idea of Supreme God, and laid stress on moral progress without being dependent on any Creator of Universe. As Dr. B.M. Baru, says, "The Buddhist holds that the hypothesis of a personal god is inconsistent with the law of Karma. The Jains, like Buddhists, also admit the efficacy of individual actions in determining fate. He too does not find any urge to postulate God as the dispenser of reward and retribution—It is Karma alone which determines the course of an individual through different births."

As a stepping stone to the path of spiritual progress, the Buddha asked his followers to practice constantly the five precepts (Panca Sila):

> The Buddha held that life is constantly changing and all conditioned things are transient. Whatever is transient is painful, and where change and sorrow prevail, the question of permanent immortal does not arise. The Buddha in particular criticized the theory of permanent soul as a selfish system from the ethical point of view, as it meant the solitary pursuit by the soul of its own release. He did not accept that there was an immortal entity which survived the death of the body and was born in other forms through a series of incarnations Nevertheless, the principle of sansara wandering (rebirth) was accepted by the Buddha.

The essence of Buddhism lies in the four Noble truths: suffering; its cause; its cessation; and path leading to the cessation of suffering. The ways to Nibbana' (Means the cessation, of greed (raga) aversion (dvesa) and delusion (Moha) these are three factors which Buddhism identifies as the rules of all that is morally un wholesome). Emancipation in Buddhism or the path that leads to cessation of suffering, higher wisdom and peace of mind is known as the Nobel-Eight fold path or the middle path of the eight factors of this path, the first two are grouped under the heading of wisdom; the following three the under morality, and the last three under concentration.

The Buddhist ethical code of discipline for the monks and nuns contains as many as 227 rules which an aspirant for the attainment of Nibbanna is expected to observe. A similar strict, rather more rigid, code of discipline has been prescribed for the Jaina monks and nuns, Ethics are similar. But rules of discipline are sometimes extreme and impractical.

The Buddha said, "Be ye lamps unto your selves, work your own salvation with diligence," thus in both cases, emphasis is on self-help, self discipline. But there is a fundamental difference in approach. The Buddha holds that 'mind' is the Nerve center of every human activity. The very first verse of the Dhammapada says, "all mental states have mind as their fore-runner; mind is their chief, and they are mind-made. If with a pure mind, one speaks or acts, happiness follows him close like his never-departing shadow". *Vipassana*, mind training is more important than the various abstinences which border upon asceticism.

Alexander Cunningham; a famous archaeologist made the following observation:

> "Buddhists propagated the religion by the persuasive voice of the missionary, many others by the merciless edge of the sword. The peaceful progress of Buddhism was illuminated by the cheerful faces of the sick in Monastic Hospitals, by the happy smiles of travelers reposing in rest houses by the road side."

In respect of true love developed in humanity, under the influence of Buddhism, Sir Edwin Arnold, in his classic "The Light of Asia" remarked that Buddhism had made Asia mild.

Buddha advised Buddhist monks and nuns and all His followers to work diligently for "Bahujana Hitaya, Bahujana Sukhaya." Meaning "for the welfare of many, for the happiness of many." The History of Buddhism is rich with the life stories of many great men and great women who made great sacrifices, and traveled to distant lands. In this context let us take Asoka's contribution in spreading Buddhism in India and abroad. Ashoka made all endeavors to spread the lords teaching through out his domain by carrying out series of humanitarian services. He started sending missionaries to other countries. His son Mahindra and daughter Sangamitra introduced Budhism in Sri Lanka where it flourishes even today, almost retaining purity. In *Mahavamsha*, Mahindra is designated, as "The great Mahindra the converter of the island." From Sri Lanka Buddhism spread to Burma and Siam, modern Thailand and then to China and Annam. Describing entry of Buddhjsm in China Sir Charles Eliot remarks, "In China, Budhism entered by more than one road. It came first by land from central Asia. . . . Introduction by this route in 62 A.D. (probably Kanishaka's effort in propagating Mahayana Buddhism is referred here). Secondly when Buddhism was established, there arose a desire for accurate knowledge of the true Indian doctrine. Chinese pilgrims went to India and Indian pilgrims came to China. . . . It was then that Bodhi Dharma landed on Canton in 520 A.D. A Third stream of Buddhism namely *Lamaism*, came to China from Tibet under the Mongol dynasty (1280 A.D.)." Buddhism aided by unceasing missionary zeal by Ashoka and Kanishka spread to other countries like—Hellenistic Kingdom of Asia, Africa and Europe to Syria, Afghanistan and Egypt, Cyrene, Macedonia and Epirns to Bactria and China, thus Buddhism did not Confine to the boundaries of India rather it expanded beyond and went on to become a world religion. Dr. B.R. Ambedkar strongly felt that only Buddhism can bring true love and interpreted Buddhism as a world-transforming religion and it is amenable to every common man.

Under the impact of Buddhism, human activity was greatly reflected. Rabindra Nath Tagore wrote the following remarks "in no other times India reached such a high peak of prosperity in art, science, commerce, and sovereign-power, as was achieved with the advent of Buddhism and in later ages under the direct influence of the Buddhist civilization."

Albert Einstein, who is considered as the greatest scientist of the twentieth century, gave the following statement:

> "The religion of the future will be a cosmic religion. It should transcend a personal God and avoid dogmas and theology. Covering both the natural and spiritual . . . into meaningful unity. Buddhism answers this description. If there is any religion that could cope with modern scientific needs, it would be Buddhism."

Buddhism is religion; philosophy, psychology, science and way of life. It is not concerned with god, soul, sin theories but with morality and nature. It preaches that the world is not created by supernatural being but evolving continuously as per the law of cause and effect. However, it tells us that there are divine beings in the Universe.

Today Buddhism remains as a great civilizing force in the modern world. Buddhism awakens the self-respect and feeling self-responsibility of countless people and stirs up the energy of many a nation. Buddhism has satisfied the spiritual needs of many.

WORLD HARMONY AND PEACE

The world Harmony means concord, unity, peace amity, friendship, consistency, consonance, conformity etc. The concept of Harmony in Buddhist thought incorporates two aspects of human life, personal life and social life. Buddhism covers not only about the whole humanity but also about all living beings.

His Holiness The Dalai Lama pointing out the fundamental similarities among world religions. With this perspective efforts are being made in various parts of world for better understanding among religions. The need for this is particularly urgent now.

There are certain tasks facing religious practitioners concerned to world peace. Under the present conditions, there is definitely a growing need for human understanding and a sense of universal responsibility.

The main message of Buddhism is compassion, love, forgiveness, tolerance, contentment, self discipline and concepts of brotherhood. In the present Global unrest; Buddhism is the only remedy for achieving world social harmony, peace, happiness, and prosperity. At this juncture I would like to mention the first sermon preached by Lord Buddha, while revolving wheel of Dhamma at Saranath.

"Wander, O Monks, for the gain of the many, for the welfare of the many, for showering forth compassion on the world; for the good, for the gain; for the welfare of the gods and man."

According to Ven Dr. R. Nandiswara Nayaka Thera, "Buddhism in world history is one epoch making campaign totally revolutionizing the norm of thought, manner of speech, way of life, trend of civilization, development of mental culture highlighting and aspiring for a soaring height of spiritual attainment, transcending the mind from the mundane to the super-mundane state."

References

Dr. B.R. Ambedkar, *The Buddha and his Dharma*, Buddha Bhoomi Publications, Nagapur, 1997

Gail Omvedt, *Buddhism in India*, Sage Publications, New Delhi, 2003.

Goyal, S.R., *A History of Indian Buddhism*, Kusumanjali Prakasham, Meerut, 1987.

Narada Maha Thera, *The Buddha and his Teachings*, Published by Singapur Buddhist Mediation Center.

Chopra, P.N., *Contribution of Buddhism to World Civilization*, S. Chand & Co. Ltd., Delhi, 1983.

Sutta Nipata.

Majjhima Nikya, Ashvalayan Sutta No. 93 etc.

Soma Thera, B.P.S., *The Contribution of Buddhism to World Culture.*

Sircar, D.C., *Inscriptions of Asoka*, New Delhi, Ministry of I and B., 1975.

Barua, Dipak Kumar, *Role of Buddhism in National Integration*, Homage Bhikku Jadadish Kashyap, Nava Nalanda Mhavihara, 1986.

Laxmi Narasu, P., *The Essence of Buddhism* [Ananada Buddha Vihara] Hyderabad.

Dhammanada, Ven, Gems of Wisdom.

Ven, Piyadassi, *Spectrum of Buddhism.*

Dr. Lella Karun Yakara, *Modernization of Buddhism*, Gyan Publishing House, New Delhi, 2002.

Journals

1. Salarjung Museum B1—*Annual Research Journal*, Vol. XXXVII, XXXVIII, 2000-01.
2. *Suhrullekha*—April, June 2003.
3. *Suhrullekha—Quarterly Journal*, October, December, 2001.
4. *Suhrullekha—Quarterly Journal*, April, June, 1999.
5. *Suhrullekha—Quarterly Journal*, October, December, 2003.

38

Problems and Prospects for the Development of Tourism Potential of Buddhist Heritage Sites in Andhra Pradesh

Dr. T. Dayakar Rao and Dr. P. Sadanandam

INTRODUCTION

Andhra Pradesh State is rich in Buddhist cultural heritage with numerous Buddhist sites including stupas, Viharas, Chaityagrihas with distinct features of art and architecture. Antiquating of some of the Buddhist sites goes back to pre-Ashokan times. It reached its zenith during the Satavahana and Ikshvāku periods i.e., 300 B.C. to A.D. 300. It was the hay day in the cultural history of Buddhism in Andhradesa. The two schools, Theravada and Mahasanghika, and also their sub-sects flourished during this period. The style of art and architecture in Andhra Pradesh is named as Amaravati School.

LOCATION OF A.P.

Andhra Pradesh 12°14: - 19°54 north latitude 78°50 - 84°45 east longitude is one the states of Indian Republic and came into existence in November 1956. The location of Area has great significance. It is a melting pot of many cultures South and North. It has been a theatre of rich heritage of culture, art and architecture. It constitutes a vital tourist region in its urban and rural landscape. It is blessed with beautiful countryside, watered by thirty-four rivurlets and major rivers include Godavari, Krishna, Tungabhadra. Pennar and Vamsadhara are navigable to certain point. Andhra Pradesh commands a coastline of nearly 1000 km. The land is with rocks, forests, hills, and lush green fields. Water falls and lakes, rimmed with a crescent of golden beaches washed by blue sea. The landscape was found congenial for Buddhists to set up their viharas and stupas.

OBJECTIVES

The paper intends to focus the Buddhist sites as resourceful attractions for promotion of tourism. In the light of the revival trend of Buddhist religion in India, the development of Buddhist circuit Tourism is most welcome.

ATTRACTIONS

Buddhist Monuments and Remains

Nearly 100 above sites are explored and some of them excavated by Archaeological department. These are some of the important sites; Vaddamanu, Bhattirpolu, Gudivada, Jaggayyapeta, Alluru, Ghantasala, Pedaganjam, Pedavengi, Gummadidurru, Chandavaram, Dhupadu, Goli, Sankaram, Bavikonda, Ramtirtham, Salihundum, Dhulikatta, Kotilingala, Pashigaon, Sthambhampalli, Kondapur, Tirumalagiri, Phanigiri, Gajulabanda, Vijayawada, Vardhamanakota, Yeleswaram, Nelakondapalli, Mudigonda, Karukonda, Govindaraja Vihara, Indrapalanagara (Thummalagudem).

Amaravati (Lat. 16°34'N: Long. 80°21'E) is a small town situated on the bank of the river Krishna about 35 kms. to the north of Guntur town. The Buddhist site locally known as Dipaladinne (Hill of lamps) is to the south of the town. Having its origins during Pre-Asokan times, received rich additions during the Satavahana, Ikshvaku and Pallava periods to become the most magnificent of the Buddhist monuments in the contemporary world. It is an important Buddhist site lies near the ancient Satavahana capital Dhyankata, now called Amaravati located 50 kms. from Vijayawada. Amaravati was one of the four important places of Buddhist worship in the country. Over two thousands years ago, on the south banks of the river krishna at this point stood the Mahastupa, the largest stupa in the country, 36.5 m. across and girdled by a 4.2 m circumambulatory path. Built of Kiln-burnt bricks and faced with marble slabs. The Mahastupa is richly adorned with carvings portraying scenes from the life of Buddha along its dome and the outer and inner sides of railing. Amaravati is considered sacred pilgrim centre for Buddhists in south India.

Nagarjunakonda (Lat. 16°31'N: Long. 79°14'E) is situated on the right bank of the river Krishna in Palnadu taluk of Guntur district. It is about 166 kms. to the south east of Hyderabad and about 147 kms. from Guntur town. The nearest railway station is Macherla, about 32 kms. from the site. The hill got its name after the famous sunyavada Buddhist teacher Nagarjuna who probably stayed at the site during the last years of his life. The township has grown up namely Vijayapuri the ancient capital of Ikshvaku kings was situated in the valley on the right bank of the river Krishna. This site is a land mark in the cultural history of the Andhras have thrown wonderful light on the different aspects of Andhra history and culture especially on the history of religion and art. There is a famous reservoir, in that an island museum was constructed on the hill to preserve all important antiquities. Nagarjunasagar called also Vijayapuri and Nagarjunakonda. The relics of Buddhist civilization dating back to the third century A.D. that were excavated here and carefully preserved in island museum. Nagarjunasagar is a man-made lake. There is Mahachaitya and many stupas. An inscription in Brahmi characters states that the sacred relics of lord Buddha lie within the Mahachaitya. The most remarkable antiquities has brought to light, the remains of a ancient Budhist university. Vihara and monasteries and an Aswamedha sacrificial altar, standing Buddha of 4 meters (13 ft.) high, sculptural reliefs having episodes from life of Buddha are illustrated on carved lime stone as well as prehistoric finds in the from of tools from paleolithic and neolithic times. 11 Kms. down stream from the dam are the Ethipothala water falls, set in a beautiful valley. The Chandravanka stream here plunges from a height of 21.3 meters (70 ft.) into a lagoon and flows on through a green valley much frequented by tourists. There is an airstrip on Nagarjunasagar's right bank where charters can operate as there is no regular air service. Bus services to Nagarjunasagar are run by the A.P.S.R.T.C. from several towns including Hyderabad. The Indian Tourism Development Corporation (ITDC) runs a luxury site seeing day tour every Sunday from Hyderabad. Comfortable accommodation is available at well appointed State Government Rest houses at the dam which provides Indian and Western cuisine. Accommodation: Vijaya Vihar Guest House, Project House, MIG Rest House, Archaeological Guest House, Ethipothala Guest House, Rest House of Public Relations and Trunk Telephone Calls including other miscellaneous information services like guide and motor boat at Island Museum available.

Tirumalagiri, Phanigiri and Gajulabanda Villages are situated at about 40, 65, 70 kms. from Jangaon towards Suryapet road in Nalgonda district. The antiquities are preserved in Victoria Museum, Vijayawada and State Archaeological Museum, Hyderabad. There are stupas and viharas.

Nelakondapalli is situated 30 kms. away from Khammam town nearer to Jaggayyapeta a famous Buddhist centre in Krishna district. There is one of the big stupas in South India. Stone and metal images preserved in different museums of A.P.

REVIVAL OF BUDDHISM IN INDIA

About a hundred years ago Buddhism in India started to rejuvenate itself. After receiving ordination Mahavira Swami settled in Kushinagar, in the year 1891. Anagarika Dharmapa (Sri Lanka) founded the Maha Bodhi society of India in our country. The Government of India recognized the social importance of Buddhism. According to Bhikshu Sangharakshita Buddhism said to have revived in India with Ashoka Chakra Inscribed on national flag in 1947. The relics of Arhat Sariputra and Mauglayan taken back to India from Victoria and Albert Museums in Europe at the instance of Mahabodh Society of India. In the year 1956-57, the 2500 anniversary of Buddha's Parinirvana was organized on nation-wide. In 1959, the Dalai Lama along with 8,50,000 Tibetans reached our country, refuses and settled in Dharmashala, North India.

Andhra Pradesh has truly been called the "Cradle of Buddhism." At present all major Buddhist sites are under the care of Archaeological Survey of India (A.S.I.) and the remaining sites are looked after by the Estate department of Archaeology and Museums to improve the amenities at Buddhist sites to develop the basic infrastructural facilities like roads and accommodation facilities. These Buddhist areas are totally of rural back ground and do not have the minimal infrastructure facilities except Nagarjunakonda and Amaravati.

So far, Department of Tourism of A.P. Government and are trying to improve the tourist amenities at few-selected Buddhist sites such as Nagarjunakonda and Amaravati by taking up projects of conservation and renovation of sites.

The Buddhist circuits should be identified where multiple chain of destinations and sites offered to tourists which cater similar needs circuits offer benefits to the tourists then individual tourist destinations.

CONSERVATION OF MONUMENTS

The monuments should be protected with conservation by

giving structural stability and good presentation. The monument has to be designed and developed by landscape and other attractions. We have to protect the monument from the decay from the climate and environmental effects i.e., solar radiation, (thermal movement) rainy water and drainage. The following aspects are important while conservation work is in cooperation. Prevention of deterioration, preservation of the existing state. Consolidation of the fabric. Restoration, rehabilitation, reproduction and reconstruction. The technicians should have the knowledge of understanding the construction technology of old historic buildings and able to preserve artistic and historic value of structures and able to record objects and structures. Cautions about any alternation or removal of the material.

To promote and develop the Buddhist sites, we have to take the assistance of the various departments like archaeological department, non-governmental agencies, universities, co-operative societies, INTACH, UNESCO and ICROM. Local community centers, consultants, tourism travel and leisure organisation, forest and wild life department of environment, retired personnel, other social organisation and development forums, transport departments, tourism and hospitality organizations, public work departments, electricity and irrigation departments, public and private sector hotel chains, resort companies, Buddhist missions and housing board, etc.

CONCLUSION

There is a big scope of Buddhist tourism promotion in A.P. State. These Buddhist resources make the state as potential in tourist market. The Buddhist heritage relocates the culture and ethos of bygone day's i.e., gospel of truth and non-Viennese which is more relevant than ever in the present context of violence and nuclear holocaust. Though the historic remains are being conserved by the ASI there Seems big crisis of tourism amenities needs to visitors. The Government of A.P. is maintaining a few tourism information centers but owing to lack of organizational management it remained failed to motivate affluent clientele. Special scheme is needed to mobilize funds so as to create infrastructure and amenities. Government aid and intervention could be used to create and stimulate initiatives by small scale and family enterprises. The creation and development of small business would also make it possible to employ more local man power. These business are more likely to purchase on the local market, thereby increasing the value of multiplier effect in the job creation field, as well as activating and speeding up the revival of local activities, including handicrafts, transport, the provision of basic food stuffs, catering services and other type of assistance for travelers. We have to use the world's communication media. Internet. T.V., Radio, Press, Publications, to create a greater awareness among the potential tourists and thus stimulate them to travel abroad and see for themselves what is happening. The appropriate media and for effective publicity including news papers, brochures, folders and maps etc., should be produced and distributed. Close co-ordination with heritage tour operators. Planners and distributors should be maintained. High quality literature should be used in the language of inbound tourists. We have to give incentives, bonus to the staff personnels and travel writers.

References

Annual Reports of Archaeology and Museums Government of A.P., Hyderabad.

Baneerjee, A.C., 1973, *Buddhism in India and Abroad*, The World Press (Pvt.) Ltd., Calcutta.

Buddhist Pilgrimages and Tours in India, Trishul Publication, Noida.

Brown, Percy, 1976, *Indian Architecture*, (Buddhist and Hindu Periods), Bombay.

Bapat, P.V., *2500 Years of Buddihism.*

Bhatia, A.K., *Principles and Pracatices of Tourism.*

Bhatra, G.S. and Chawla, A.S., *Tourism Management—A Global Perspective.*

Brochures of Dept. of Tourism, Government of A.P., Hyderabad.

Cunningham, A.R., 1924, *Ancient Government of A.P.*, Hyderabad.

Surendra Nath, Mjumdar Sastri, Calcutta.

Diwkar, R.R., 1980, *Bhagawan Buddha*, Bharatiya Vidya Bhavan, Bombay.

Gupta, S.P. and Lal Krishna, 1974, *Tourism, Museum and Monuments of India*, Oriental Publishers, Delhi.

Jagmohan, Negi, *Development of Tourism.*

Jitendar Das, D., *Buddhist Arhitecture in Andhra Pradesh.*

Mitra, Debala, 1971, *Buddhist Monuments*, Sahitya Samsad, Calcutta.

Pant, Sushila, 1976, *The Origin and Development of Stupa Architecture of India*, Varansasi.

Proceedings of Andhra Pradesh History Congress. 1994, 1995 and 1996.

Proceedings of Oriental Congress. Guntur, 1986.

P.R. Ramachandra Rao, Amaravati, Youth advancement Tourism and Culture Dept., Government of A.P., Hyderabad.

P.R. Ramachandra Rao, Amaravati, The Art of Nagarjunakonda, Published by Dept. of Tourism, Government of A.P., Hyderbad.

Special Volume on Buddhism, Published by Salarjung Museum 2000-01, Vol. No. XXXVI-XXXVIII.

INDEX